INTERNATIONAL THEMES AND ISSUES

VOLUME
5

CONTESTED FIELDS

INTERNATIONAL THEMES AND ISSUES
A joint series of the Canadian Historical Association
and the University of Toronto Press

SERIES EDITOR | Pierre-Yves Saunier

Canadian
Historical Association

Société historique
du Canada

UNIVERSITY OF TORONTO PRESS

INTERNATIONAL THEMES AND ISSUES
A joint series of the Canadian Historical Association
and the University of Toronto Press

SERIES EDITOR | Pierre-Yves Saunier

CONTESTED FIELDS

A Global History of Modern Football

ALAN MCDOUGALL

UNIVERSITY OF TORONTO PRESS
Toronto Buffalo London

© University of Toronto Press 2020
Toronto Buffalo London
utorontopress.com
Printed in Canada

ISBN 978-1-4875-9457-2 (cloth)   ISBN 978-1-4875-9458-9 (EPUB)
ISBN 978-1-4875-9456-5 (paper)   ISBN 978-1-4875-9459-6 (PDF)

Library and Archives Canada Cataloguing in Publication

Title: Contested fields : a global history of modern football / Alan McDougall.
Names: McDougall, Alan (Alan James), author.
Series: International themes and issues (Toronto, Ont.) ; v. 5.
Description: Series statement: International themes and issues ; volume 5 |
    Includes bibliographical references and index.
Identifiers: Canadiana (print) 20190214031 | Canadiana (ebook) 2019021404X |
    ISBN 9781487594572 (cloth) | ISBN 9781487594565 (paper) | ISBN 9781487594596 (PDF) |
    ISBN 9781487594589 (EPUB)
Subjects: LCSH: Soccer—Social aspects. | LCSH: Soccer—Political aspects. |
    LCSH: Soccer—History. | LCSH: Sports and globalization—History.
Classification: LCC GV943.9.S64 M34 2020 | DDC 796.334—dc23

We welcome comments and suggestions regarding any aspect of our publications—please feel
free to contact us at news@utorontopress.com or visit us at utorontopress.com.

Every effort has been made to contact copyright holders; in the event of an error or omission,
please notify the publisher.

University of Toronto Press acknowledges the financial assistance to its publishing program of
the Canada Council for the Arts and the Ontario Arts Council, an agency of the Government of
Ontario.

Canada Council   Conseil des Arts
for the Arts   du Canada

ONTARIO ARTS COUNCIL
CONSEIL DES ARTS DE L'ONTARIO

an Ontario government agency
un organisme du gouvernement de l'Ontario

Funded by the   Financé par le
Government   gouvernement
of Canada   du Canada

Canadä

FSC
www.fsc.org

MIX
Paper from
responsible sources
FSC® C016245

Contents

Illustrations

Acknowledgements

This book would not have been possible without the generosity, humour, and intelligence of Pierre-Yves Saunier, editorial board chair for the CHA/UTP International Themes and Issues series. I thank the editorial board members for their support, as well as the anonymous readers who commented so thoughtfully on my manuscript. I am grateful to Natalie Fingerhut, Janice Evans, and the UTP editorial, marketing, and production teams for helping to turn the manuscript into a book. A similar debt of gratitude is owed to Karen Taylor for her meticulous copy-editing.

Contested Fields is a work of synthesis. It stands on the shoulders of the many scholars who have made sport a rich international field of research. Reading this research has given me new insights into football's status as "the global game." Any errors of comprehension or interpretation in what follows are mine alone.

For providing material on Soviet and Hungarian football, respectively, I would like to thank Mathieu Boivin-Chouinard and Johanna Mellis. For bouncing around early ideas, my thanks go to the gents of the Predictions League. Leon Quinn read the manuscript with his unfailing instincts for storytelling and academic decluttering. This one's for Alex Alves, *Kumpel!*

I am forever grateful to Mum and Dad, for sharing their love of sport and imparting the values that shape how I think and write about the world. My wife Erika read the manuscript twice with kindness, patience, and a brilliant eye for detail. Her belief in the book and its author was unwavering. My daughters, Sophie and Lotte, have happily indulged Daddy's football obsession. They shine the brightest light in my life, one that not even Liverpool's six European Cups can match. To my football family: love, thanks, and YNWA.

Abbreviations

AFC	Asian Football Confederation
ALFC	Asian Ladies Football Confederation
BFC	Berliner FC Dynamo
CAF	Confederation of African Football (Confédération Africaine de Football)
CONCACAF	Confederation of North, Central America and Caribbean Association Football
CONMEBOL	South American Football Confederation (Confederación Sudamericana de Fútbol)
DBU	Danish Football Association (Dansk Boldspil-Union)
DFB	German Football Association (Deutscher Fußball-Bund)
EPL	English Premier League
FA	Football Association
FASA	Football Association of Southern Africa
FC	Football Club
FFP	financial fair play
FIFA	Fédération Internationale de Football Association
FLN	National Liberation Front (Front de libération nationale)
GDR	German Democratic Republic
IGLFA	International Gay and Lesbian Football Association
MLS	Major League Soccer
PNF	National Fascist Party (Partito Nazionale Fascista)

SASF   South African Soccer Federation
SASL   South African Soccer League
UEFA   Union of European Football Associations
WPL   Women's Professional League
WUSA   Women's United Soccer Association

Modern Football: A Timeline

1848 First rules of modern football, written at Cambridge University.
1863 Founding of English football's governing body, the Football Association.
1871 First FA Cup, the world's oldest knockout cup competition.
1872 First international men's match, between England and Scotland.
1881 First international women's match, between England and Scotland.
1885 English FA legalizes professionalism.
1888 Founding of English Football League, the world's first national league.
1893 Founding of Argentine Football Association, South America's first national association.
1895 Founding of British Ladies' Football club, the world's first women's football club.
1900 Football debuts at the Olympic Games in Paris.
1902 Twenty-five people are killed at a Scotland-England match at Ibrox Park, Glasgow; first international match outside Britain, between Austria and Hungary in Vienna.
1904 Founding of FIFA.
1916 First transcontinental competition between national teams, the South American Football Championship; founding of CONMEBOL.
1920 First intercontinental international match, between Egypt and Italy at the Antwerp Olympics.

1921   English FA bans women's football.

1924   Introduction of professional league in Austria, the first outside Britain; Uruguay wins the football tournament at the Paris Olympics.

1927   Founding of Mitropa Cup, the first major European club competition.

1930   First FIFA World Cup in Uruguay.

1931   Introduction of professional league in Argentina, the first outside Europe.

1933   Expulsion of Jews from German football.

1937   Basque team tours Europe during the Spanish Civil War.

1941   Women's football is banned in Brazil.

1942   "Death match" in German-occupied Kiev.

1950   World record audience of 200,000 people at the Maracanã Stadium in Rio de Janeiro sees Uruguay defeat Brazil to win the World Cup.

1953   "Match of the century," Hungary's 6-3 victory over England at Wembley.

1954   Founding of the AFC; founding of UEFA.

1955   First floodlit international match, between England and Spain at Wembley.

1956   Real Madrid wins the first European Cup.

1957   Founding of CAF; first Africa Cup of Nations tournament in Sudan, won by Egypt.

1958   FLN team begins international tour to support Algerian independence.

1960   First European Championship, won by the Soviet Union; first Copa Libertadores, won by Peñarol from Uruguay; first Intercontinental Cup, won by Real Madrid.

1961   Founding of CONCACAF; abolition of maximum wage in England.

1963   First CONCACAF Championship, won by El Salvador.

1964   Football's worst stadium disaster occurs at a match between Peru and Argentina in Lima, where 328 people are killed; first African Champions Cup, won by Cameroonian club Oryx Douala.

1966   Political prisoners on Robben Island, South Africa, form Makana Football Association; CAF boycotts the World Cup in England.

1967   First Asian Club Championship, won by Israeli club Hapoel Tel Aviv.

1969   "Football War" between El Salvador and Honduras.

1970 First unofficial women's World Cup in Italy.
1971 Sixty-six people are killed at a Rangers-Celtic game at Ibrox; English FA lifts ban on women's football.
1974 João Havelange replaces Stanley Rous as FIFA president.
1976 Apartheid South Africa is suspended from FIFA.
1979 Ban on women's football in Brazil is overturned.
1982 Sixty-six people are killed at Moscow's Lenin Stadium during a UEFA Cup match between Spartak Moscow and Haarlem; Corinthian Democracy movement begins in Brazil.
1984 Football debuts at the Paralympics in New York.
1985 Fifty-six people are killed in a fire at Bradford City's stadium in northern England; thirty-nine people are killed when Liverpool supporters charge Juventus supporters before the European Cup final at the Heysel Stadium, Brussels.
1988 Ninety-three people are killed at the Dasarath Rangasala Stadium in Kathmandu, Nepal.
1989 Ninety-six people are killed in the Hillsborough disaster in Sheffield, England.
1991 First FIFA Women's World Cup in China; forty-one people are killed at a match between Kaizer Chiefs and Orlando Pirates in Soweto, South Africa.
1992 Creation of English Premier League; UEFA rebrands the European Cup as the Champions League.
1994 England introduces all-seater stadiums.
1995 Bosman ruling allows the free movement of out-of-contract footballers in the European Union and abolishes foreign quotas on EU nationals.
1998 Sepp Blatter replaces João Havelange as FIFA president.
1999 Breakthrough third Women's World Cup in the United States.
2001 Founding of UEFA Women's Cup; forty-three people are killed at a match between Kaizer Chiefs and Orlando Pirates at Ellis Park, Johannesburg; 127 people are killed at a match between Hearts of Oak and Asante Kotoko in Accra, Ghana.
2002 First World Cup in Asia, cohosted by Japan and South Korea.
2003 First Homeless World Cup, in Graz, Austria.
2006 *Calciopoli* scandal in Italy.
2009 UEFA Women's Cup is rebranded as the Women's Champions League; nineteen people are killed at the Ivory Coast-Malawi match at the Stade Félix Houphouët-Boigny, Abidjan.

2010   First World Cup in Africa, hosted by South Africa; UEFA introduces financial fair play.

2011   Al-Ahly and Zamalek ultras play a leading role in the Egyptian Revolution.

2012   Seventy-four Al-Ahly supporters are killed in the Port Said Stadium riot.

2015   Sepp Blatter resigns as FIFA president; Islamic State terrorist attacks on Paris target a France-Germany football match.

2018   Video Assistant Referee system debuts at the World Cup in Russia; FIFA awards the forty-eight-team 2026 World Cup to Canada, Mexico, and the United States.

1 | Introduction

One Sunday in the spring of 1944, there was a football match near the Polish town of Oświęcim. The writer Tadeusz Borowski kept goal for one of the teams. When the ball went out of play behind him, Borowski saw people pouring out of railway cars and on to a loading ramp. The women wore summer dresses, the men white shirts. They sat on the grass and gazed through a fence toward the football field. Borowski collected the ball and returned to the game. A few minutes later, the ball again went out of play. This time, he saw with astonishment that "out of the whole colourful summer procession, not one person remained." Between these two moments in a football game, "right behind my back, three thousand people had been put to death."[1] Borowski was a prisoner and hospital orderly at Auschwitz-Birkenau, the largest Nazi concentration and extermination camp. Here, 1.1 million people, mostly Jews, died during the Second World War. The loading ramp behind the football pitch led to the crematoria. The people from the railway cars had been walked to their deaths in gas chambers.

A year later, another football match took place in another Polish town, Katowice, to mark the end of the Second World War in Europe. On 8 May 1945, a team of Poles played a team of Italian death camp survivors that included the chemist and writer Primo Levi. In front of a large crowd, the match dragged on for over two hours, thanks to the antics of the referee, a secret police captain from the occupying Soviet military forces. Blasting his whistle like a train, the captain took "a crazy and inexhaustible pleasure from his misinterpreted duties as director of the game."[2] By the time the game ended, rain was falling heavily. The Italians returned on foot to their distant transit camp. Levi got a lung infection, but recovered. After a circuitous journey, he arrived home in Italy in October 1945.

The football stories of these two Holocaust survivors—one quietly horrific, one quietly hopeful—place the world's most popular sport at the dark heart of modern history. Amid the genocidal violence of the Second World War, football was ubiquitous, an international cultural practice played at any time and in any place. Stadium historian Simon Inglis has called the markings of the football pitch one of "the signs and symbols of the twentieth century."[3] The recollections of Tadeusz Borowski and Primo Levi suggest that he has a point. The football pitch that Borowski helped to build gladdened Hungarian Jews when they arrived at Auschwitz in 1944: "Green turf, the requisite white goal posts, the chalked lines of the field of play—it was all there, inviting, fresh, pristine, in perfect working order."[4]

A source of escape, a propaganda tool, and a joyous but fleeting means of free expression: as its presence in the Holocaust revealed, football was a sport embedded in the international history of the modern world. During the late nineteenth century, football emerged as a major legacy of Britain's formal and informal empires. It spread quickly across Europe, South America, and Africa. More hesitantly, it made inroads in North America and Australasia. Today football is arguably the world's most popular pastime, an activity played and watched by millions of people—and the focus of a rich body of research. How did football influence the history of the modern world? And how have historians dealt with the rise of the global game?

Football's Origins and Internationalization

"Football is as old as the world," claimed the president of the sport's international governing body (FIFA), Sepp Blatter, in 2004.[5] In fact, no evidence suggests that humans manufactured, let alone played with, a spherical object before 2000 BCE. Later premodern societies played ball games that emphasized kicking rather than handling. Chinese writer Li Yu (50–130 CE) recounted a pastime in which "A round ball and a square goal / Suggest the shape of the Yin and Yang / The ball is like the full moon / And the two teams stand opposed."[6] This is probably a reference to *cuju* (kick-ball), a sport played under the Han Dynasty (206 BCE–221 CE), using a stitched leather ball filled with fur or feathers.

Other premodern civilizations had equivalents to *cuju*. Chinese imperial influence encouraged ball games elsewhere in Asia, such as *sepak raga*, a cross between football and volleyball played with a rattan ball in the Malay Peninsula, and the courtly ball game of the medieval Japanese elites, *kemari*. Among the Indigenous peoples of Central America, ball games were central planks of social and cultural life. Archaeological evidence from Belize, Guatemala, Honduras, and Mexico reveals that ball courts, early variants of the stadium, were widespread in the Aztec and Mayan civilizations. What the Aztecs called *Tchatali* was played by nobles and commoners, and even had its own deity.

Ball games have a shorter history in Europe. In the gladiatorial contests and chariot races in ancient Rome, or in the original Olympic Games in ancient Greece, barely a ball was kicked in anger. Ball games did not appear widely across the continent until the medieval period. *Egil's Saga*, an Icelandic saga written between 1220 and 1240, suggests that Icelanders played team-based ball contests in front of spectators from as early as the tenth century. In England various forms of "folk football" were recorded from the thirteenth century onwards. More than crude displays of force, they often evolved complex rules and strategies. At the same time, in the public squares of the Italian city of Florence, men of all social backgrounds began to play a brutal but structured courtyard ball game known as *calcio*.

None of these ball-kicking and ball-handling games was more than a distant cousin of association football as it was refined and codified by the English Football Association (FA) in the 1860s and 1870s: an eleven-a-side game on a demarcated pitch, in which only the goalkeeper handled the ball and the ten outfield players tried to kick a round leather ball into the opposition's goal. But the modern game undoubtedly had roots in ball-playing pastimes that predated the Industrial Revolution. In Italy the term *calcio* still means football, even if the Florentine and FA versions of the game appear to have little in common.

In *The Sports and Pastimes of the People of England* (1801), Joseph Strutt described football as "formerly much in vogue among the common people of England, though of late years it seems to have fallen into disrepute, and is but little practised."[7] Football, Strutt noted, was banned by Edward III in 1349, by Richard II in 1389, and again by Henry VIII and Elizabeth I in the sixteenth century. His account anticipated narratives that distanced the rule-bound game of the Victorian era from its allegedly unruly forebears. Yet popular tradition and regulated competition were not easily separable. The rough physicality of football or football-like games at nineteenth-century public (i.e., private) schools such as Eton was not so different from the organized mayhem of the Shrove Tuesday football games played across England from the sixteenth century onwards. The real difference was class. The history of pre-industrial and early industrial football was often a history of attempts to suppress it. Political, religious, and business elites, like the town council in Derby in the 1840s, viewed the Shrove Tuesday match as "the assembly of a lawless rabble ... creating terror and alarm to the timid and the peaceable."[8] It was a different story when the sporting "rabble" featured Britain's future leaders in the privileged confines of the public school system.

The mid- to late nineteenth century saw the global spread of organized sport. Governing bodies were formed, rules formalized, and league and cup competitions established, not only in football but in other sports including ice hockey, rugby union, tennis, and other codes of football (American and Australian). Why did the British version of football, effectively pronounced dead by Strutt in 1801, undergo such a transformation? And why did it, rather than another sport, become the world game?

Many factors shaped football's leap into modernity. More than other sports, it benefitted from the sustained economic growth of the nineteenth century, underpinned in Britain, and then elsewhere, by industrialization and urbanization. The Industrial Revolution pulled farm workers to rapidly growing cities, where time and space were closely regulated. Football was simple to play and far shorter in duration than, for example, a cricket match. In the age of the factory, the railway, and the newspaper, it became the quintessential urban sport—and a vital expression of new forms of community.

This transition only happened in the final quarter of the nineteenth century. The bridge between premodern folk football and the modern game of association football was, paradoxically, provided by the English public schools. Previously archaic places that served the aristocracy, schools such as Eton, Rugby, and Winchester developed during the nineteenth century into education and play spaces for the sons of Britain's industrial bourgeoisie. Organized, team-based sport was central to the revitalized system. The Victorians emphasized "muscular Christianity." Sport should cultivate the manly values of self-control, loyalty, and physical strength. These elements, rather than intellectual prowess, displayed a gentleman's character.

From the 1840s onwards, the talking point was not whether public schools should play team sports but which sport it should be. Divisions emerged between advocates of a catch-and-run game (which became rugby) and those, such as J.C. Thring, who preferred a dribbling and kicking game. Thring wrote ten rules for what he called "the Simplest Game" in 1862, while working as a teacher at Uppingham School. A year later, the clubs that founded the FA in London effectively adopted this set of rules as the "Laws of the Game." Though public schools became better known for rugby—the split between the kicking and handling games was confirmed in 1863—their role in football's modern revival was vital. Football quickly outgrew its (partly) elitist origins. It was not debates about rules in pubs and gentlemen's clubs in Cambridge, London, Nottingham, or Sheffield that popularized the sport but the radical changes wrought by industrialization. By the 1870s, football was established in working-class communities. Work-free Saturday afternoons, rising wages, and the decline of cruel sports such as bearbaiting and cockfighting opened a space for cheap, simple forms of recreation. Churches, factories, and schools provided fertile grounds for new teams. A dense railway network and rising literacy rates helped to turn a series of local contests into something bigger. With the introduction of a nationwide cup competition (the FA Cup, 1871) and a professional national league (1888), football became a paying spectacle, as well as a game played in parks and back alleys. The result was a remarkable social change. Football, a minority pastime three decades earlier, was now Britain's most popular sport.

Narratives about football's globalization tend, understandably enough, toward Anglocentrism. The opening of John Foot's history of Italian football is typical: "In the beginning there were the English."[9] In Brazil the mythical "year zero" was 1894, when the Anglo-Brazilian Charles Miller returned from England with two leather footballs, one under each arm. Football has usually been regarded as a cultural offshoot of Britain's trading empire: a strange, alluring game that arrived on the feet of sailors and was unloaded at the docks alongside other imperial commodities.

The stock image underplays the complexity of football's path(s) to global pre-eminence. Historian Matthew Brown argued in 2014 that many English-language works on football's origins in Latin America examined only the three powerhouses, Argentina, Brazil, and Uruguay. They featured little or no research in Portuguese or Spanish. They replicated outdated "great men" theories of history in their emphasis on the role of "founding fathers" such as Miller in Brazil and the Scot Alexander Watson Hutton in Argentina. Brown suggested that "mutual influence," the interplay between imperial stimulus and local agency, better explained football's rise. People of Hispanic descent founded Bolivia's first football club, Oruro. Only two of the twenty-five founder members of the Concepción club in southern Chile were British.

This polygenetic approach works elsewhere too. Football in Bulgaria was once assumed to have arrived with British sailors via the Black Sea ports at the turn of the twentieth century. Recent research suggests that the game was played inland earlier, especially around the capital city, Sofia. The prime movers were not the British but the Swiss and the Turks. Switzerland's role in proselytizing football, largely through a network of Anglophone but international private schools, suggests the transnationalism of the game's early history. Cosmopolitan, Swiss-educated figures included the founder of FC Barcelona, Hans Gamper, and the Italian national team coach, Vittorio Pozzo.

For the urban elites of Europe and South America, football's appeal had less to do with "Englishness" than with modernity. Like tourism, photography, or cinema, the game broke with customs of the past and epitomized a forward-looking, liberal worldview. The relationship between modernity and football was not always straightforward. The sport's early success in Poland, for example, came not in the industrialized centres of Łódź or Warsaw but in the predominantly rural region of Galicia, where it found favour not only in cities such as Kraków and Lviv but among smaller communities of orthodox (Hasidic) Jews and Ukrainian peasants.

Institutional history likewise complicates the idea that football was Britain's gift to the world. The Dutch FA proposed an international governing body in 1902, but attempts to interest the English FA went nowhere. The Fédération Internationale de Football Association (FIFA), founded in Paris in 1904, adopted an Anglo-Gallic name, but it was a continental European project. Founder members came from Belgium, Denmark, France, the Netherlands, Spain, Sweden, and Switzerland (see the appendix for a list of association members). The English FA joined FIFA in 1905, left in 1920, rejoined in 1924, and left again in 1928. Only after the FA rejoined FIFA in 1946 did English officials commit to helping to administer the world game.

What was true of organizations was true of competitions. Europe's first club competition, the Mitropa Cup (1927), focused on the central European nations of Austria, Czechoslovakia, and Hungary. South America pioneered international competition between national teams. A continental federation (CONMEBOL) was founded in 1916, thirty-eight years before Europe took the same step. Earlier that year, Argentina hosted the inaugural South American Football Championship, known today as the Copa América. Uruguay, winners of the 1916 and 1917 tournaments, played a pivotal role in globalizing football. The Uruguayans won the Olympic football tournaments of 1924 and 1928. They hosted and won FIFA's inaugural World Cup in 1930. French journalist Gabriel Hanot eulogized the "beautiful football ... varied, rapid, powerful, effective" of the Uruguayan players, "who are to the English professionals like Arab thoroughbreds next to farm horses."[10]

Around the world, as in Uruguay, football was gradually "creolized" (i.e., localized or nationalized). On the African islands of Zanzibar, British workers from the Eastern Telegraph Company introduced the game in the 1870s. By the 1920s, it was hugely popular among Zanzibari males. Football provided an autonomous social and political space. Clubhouses offered extensions of relaxed *bara̧za* (doorstep) conversations with neighbours. Matches gave teams from poor, working-class, and former slave communities the chance to defeat social superiors. Anglophile influence on Argentinean football, exemplified by the dominant Alumni team of the early twentieth century, gradually succumbed to home-grown authority. In 1913, Racing Club of Buenos Aires became the first team with no players of British origin to win the national championship.

As Argentina's institutions and clubs were nationalized, narratives about a "national" style of play emerged. Sports newspaper *El Gráfico* proselytized *criollo* (creole) football in the 1920s and 1930s, describing it as a skilled, streetwise approach distinct from the physical play of the country's British pioneers. Argentina's *criollo* style borrowed from neighbouring Uruguay, just as the short-passing "Danubian School" crossed borders, spreading from Vienna, Budapest, and Prague to Poland, where clubs such as Cracovia rechristened it "the Kraków style." This central European model was itself shaped by Scottish influences, as the game there departed from the more direct play common in late-nineteenth-century England. Stereotypes about England's "kick and rush" tactics remain, as does football's hoariest style cliché: Brazil's reputation as purveyors of the "beautiful game" (*o jogo bonito*). Sociologist Gilberto Freyre observed in 1938 that the cleverness, speed, and spontaneity of Brazil's players at that year's World Cup "reminds one of dancing and *capoeira*, making the Brazilian way of playing football a trademark, which sophisticates and often sweetens the game invented by the English."[11] The trademark has since become an enduring symbol of Brazilian football and, indeed, Brazilian nationhood.

As the Danubian and Argentinean examples suggest, "national" styles of play often resulted from an international cross-pollination of players, coaches, and ideas. A history of football tactics might locate major shifts in how the game was played in one country: the "WM" formation invented by Arsenal's Herbert Chapman in England (which added a defender to counter the new offside law of 1925); the hyper-defensive *catenaccio* (door-bolt) system perfected by Italian sides in the 1960s; the fluid positional interplay of "total football" associated with the great Dutch teams of the 1970s; or the short-passing *tiki-taka* style of Barcelona and Spain's national team in the early twenty-first century. But these were all international stories. Dutch "total football," for example, built on the tactical intelligence and attacking versatility displayed by the great Hungarian side of the 1950s. Ways of playing were not beholden to national borders, whatever the stereotypes to the contrary.

Globalization had its blind spots. Paradoxically, football was exported more successfully to, and indeed beyond, Britain's informal empire than it was to British colonies. Why football took deeper root in Austria than Australia is not a simple question to answer. Factors include climate (which made hockey a more suitable national game in Canada); politics (the Irish nationalist rejection of English sports); class (rugby union's elite promotion as a nationalist vehicle in New Zealand); and race, which shaped white distaste for football in South Africa and in Australia, where it was narrow-mindedly dismissed as "wogball." In the White Dominions of Australia, New Zealand, and South Africa, as in India, elite-dominated, amateur pursuits (rugby or cricket) embodied the imperial ethos of duty and sacrifice. Football, with its commercial and working-class associations, was the poor cousin.

There are many theories about American "soccer exceptionalism." Cultural and political ties between Britain and its former colony remained strong in the late nineteenth century, but football's journey across the pond was a difficult one. When association football arrived in the 1890s, the sporting landscape in the United States was already crowded. Elite colleges and universities, led by Harvard, had created their own, handling-based version of football (gridiron) two decades earlier. Baseball was the established summer sport and the sport of the masses. Moreover, in the 1890s, a game that was almost as cheap and easy to play as football appeared on the scene: basketball. Rather than entering mainstream culture, as it did in many other countries, football initially became the sport of immigrants and outsiders. It did not disappear. Thriving soccer cultures developed in places such as Philadelphia and St. Louis. By the late twentieth century, in contrast to its profile elsewhere in the world, the American game's core appeal was as a safe, middle-class alternative to lucrative professional sports, especially among women and the young.

Football was popular in British India. Particularly in Calcutta, inter-caste and British-Indian competitions gave the sport a political edge. The nationalist Mohun Bagan club, founded in 1889, challenged British stereotypes about the effeminate educated Bengali and his incompatibility with imperial ideals of masculinity. In 1911, in front of a crowd of 80,000 people, Mohun Bagan defeated the East Yorkshire Regiment 2–1 to win Calcutta's leading tournament, the IFA Shield. The triumph was grudgingly praised in the British press and gloriously celebrated in local newspapers: "It fills every Indian with joy and pride to know that rice-eating, malaria-ridden, barefooted Bengalis have got the better of beef-eating, Herculean, booted John Bull in [this] peculiarly English sport."[12] Yet cricket and, to a lesser degree, field hockey became India's national sports, not football. India won Olympic field hockey gold in 1928, 1932, and 1936. Cricket, as elsewhere in the British Empire, was the sport of the elites. It reflected better than football the caste-based divisions in Indian society and, importantly, offered a spectacle in which an Indian team could challenge the imperial motherland. As in the United States, football survived in India, but lived in the shadow of other sports.

Football was not all-conquering, but no sport could match its international reach by the early twentieth century. One medical student recalled the "fury" football unleashed in French Indochina before 1914, as locals rushed to create teams in Hanoi, Saigon, and elsewhere. Eighty-eight Vietnamese clubs existed by 1939. Why did football, rather than baseball, cricket, cycling, or rugby, have the widest appeal?

Unlike baseball or cricket, football is cheap and simple to play. The rules are easy to follow. It requires little equipment and can be played on almost any solid surface with almost any spherical object. Khamis Fereji recalled his youthful playing days in Zanzibar in the 1920s: "For a football we would buy a tennis ball, they were cheap in those days ... And then we would run off and play anywhere there was a little space. We played with each other in the narrow streets ... or we would go over near the port."[13] His experience was replicated across the globe, from the *favelas* of Brazil to the back alleys of industrial northern England. Football's cheapness and simplicity made it accessible to the working class—and to everyone else.

This accessibility, importantly, was collective. Football appealed as a team sport and community activity. "Good government in Italy," noted American political scientist Robert Putnam in 1993, "is a by-product of singing groups and soccer clubs, not prayer."[14] Civic-minded inclusivity gave football a prominence that even popular individual sports such as boxing struggled to match in the long run. Whether in the form of monumental stadiums, ramshackle neighbourhood grounds, or simple, lined grass or asphalt surfaces, football spaces became ubiquitous parts of the landscape. Such is football's topographical influence on the 174 small, kin-based communities that line the Napo River in Amazonian Peru that they are designed and organized around the local football field.

Communal visibility is matched by the game's versatility. Traditionally contested by two teams of eleven players, football can accommodate greater and smaller numbers. More than any other sport, it is a mass participatory *and* spectator sport. Football can be a political statement, a means of exercise, an opportunity to socialize, and a form of belonging—whether to a local, national, or international community. It is an escape from everyday concerns and an integral part of daily life. In his 1977 poem, "Football at Slack," Ted Hughes captured the sport's ability to provide joy amid a grim industrial setting and the aftermath of two world wars: "But the wingers leapt, they bicycled in air / And the goalie flew horizontal / And once again a golden holocaust / Lifted the cloud's edge, to watch them."[15]

For all of its versatility, football is rooted in custom. It follows a fixed calendar of dates, which builds rituals and routines that serve as markers of historical time, segmenting and ordering people's lives. Other sports such as golf and tennis are almost year-round activities, but no sport is regularly played and watched in so many places by so many people as football. The sense of continuity is true of elite-level competition, but it also applies to recreational football. The Norwegian writer Karl Ove Knausgård recalled this aspect of his childhood simply: "Autumn in the rain, winter in the snow, spring in the mud, summer in the heat: football, football, football."[16]

Finally, football's appeal is tied to its unpredictability. This applies to all sports to some degree. But the fact that goals are so rare in football—no other sport has such a miserly scoring system—always makes it possible that the underdog can upset the favourite. It makes the moment of scoring more consistently meaningful, for players and spectators, than in other sports, where points or goals are scored more freely. One goal in a football game, to use a commentator's cliché, can change everything.

Historians and Football

"An astonishing void: official history ignores football. Contemporary history texts fail to mention it, even in passing, in countries where it has been and continues to be a primordial symbol of collective identity."[17] Writing in 1998, Uruguayan novelist Eduardo Galeano was not the first or last person to make such a lament. Football's relationship with the academic discipline of history has rarely been close. When historian James Walvin first published his book on British football, *The People's Game*, in 1975, he was struck by his colleagues' indifference to sport. The Trinidadian Marxist and historian C.L.R. James noted something similar in *Beyond a Boundary* (1963), his memoir about cricket and politics in the West Indies. How, James asked, could histories of Victorian England be written without discussing the era's most famous Englishman, the cricketer W.G. Grace? James, whose brother Eric was a leading figure in West Indian football, well understood the significance of cricket and football to the rise and fall of the British Empire.

When James and Walvin were writing, few academics placed sport at the centre of the story of modern Britain. There was a similar aversion elsewhere. Italian filmmaker Pier Paolo Pasolini wrote extensively about the game before he was beaten to death next to a football pitch outside Rome in 1975. Yet his analyses aroused no academic interest. It would be many years before football became a respectable research topic. Antonio Papa and Guido Panico's social history of *calcio* was published in 1993. Seminal works on English football (by Tony Mason) and French football (by Alfred Wahl and Pierre Lanfranchi) appeared in 1980 and 1995, respectively.

Sport, then, climbed only slowly into the ivory towers of academia. Other forms of mass entertainment, from fashion and film to pop music and print culture, attracted more attention from historians. As late as 2010, the editors of a volume on South African football despaired that "many conservative and progressive scholars find football (and sports) research superficial and banal; the former dismiss it as the embodiment of 'low culture,' while the latter denigrate it as an 'opium of the masses,' a distraction from engaging with truly pressing concerns such as poverty and class struggle, environmental degradation, gender inequality, unemployment, homelessness, the HIV/AIDS pandemic, crime, corruption and so on."[18]

Academy snobbery, though, was not universal. And if historians often did not take football history seriously, the same was true of the game's practitioners. Much of the football industry—players, coaches, supporters, and media—understands history to mean memories of great games and star players, rather than political, economic, or sociocultural analysis. In most countries, football history presents itself in closed, repetitive, and nostalgic ways, as if, in David Goldblatt's words, its authors "would prefer us not to bring the big bad world into the game at all."[19]

In the preface to the second edition of *The People's Game* (1994), James Walvin welcomed the abundance of football scholarship in the twenty years since his book first appeared. A number of factors had raised the sport's academic profile. Shifts toward social and cultural history, and the subsequent broadening of acceptable subjects for research, helped to bring sport in from the cold. So did the greater willingness of historians to undertake interdisciplinary work. This turned a perceived weakness of sports studies, its lack of an academic "home," into a strength, as the subject was tackled not only by historians but by sociologists, anthropologists, economists, and kinesiologists.

Changes in the field were matched by changes on the field. The threat of hooliganism in the 1970s and 1980s created scholarly networks that examined and theorized the causes and consequences of football violence. Football's retreat from hooliganism in the 1990s then opened wider avenues of research. In Britain, this shift had various landmarks: the 1989 Hillsborough disaster, which led to the introduction of all-seater stadiums; England's semi-final appearance at the 1990 World Cup in Italy, accompanied by the tears of star midfielder Paul Gascoigne and a rare, credible football song, New Order's "World in Motion"; the start of the Premier League, bankrolled by Rupert Murdoch's cable television company, BSkyB, in 1992; and, published in the same year, Nick Hornby's *Fever Pitch*, an influential account of the author's obsession with Arsenal FC. By the mid-1990s, football—a pariah sport just a decade earlier—had become a success story. Academics, like politicians, could hardly fail to take notice.

In the foundational decades of sport history, the 1970s and 1980s, there was a clear road ahead for scholars such as James Riordan (writing about the Soviet Union), Richard Holt (France and Britain), Allen Guttmann (the United States), and Hans Joachim Teichler (Germany). Weaving sport into the tapestry of national history, their accounts emphasized how a sport was founded and developed, how it was played and otherwise consumed. Many key figures were not historians. Anthropologists and sociologists produced the most sophisticated analyses and the most extensive fieldwork, from Clifford Geertz's essay on Balinese cockfighting to John Hargreaves's *Sport, Power and Culture* (1986), a reading of sport's role in British life influenced by the Italian Marxist Antonio Gramsci. The relationship between theory-driven sociologists and evidence-based historians was often uneasy, as Richard Holt recognized in *Sport and the British* (1989), in which he devoted a separate essay to the subject.

In the second, developmental phase (beginning in the 1990s), sports history widened its approaches. With a click of the button, it is now possible to read an array of football research. The study of the sport has become more institutionalized. In 1996, De Montfort University in Leicester opened its International Centre for Sports History and Culture, where football plays a prominent role in research and teaching. In 2000, *Soccer & Society* became the first English-language journal devoted to football. Academic conferences on sport take place regularly throughout the world. Kay Schiller and

Chris Young argued in 2009 that the status anxiety of sports historians was no longer justified. Others disagree. Historians still play second fiddle to sociologists in the field. Most sports historians can recount attending large conferences where sport was absent from the program. Nonetheless, there can be no doubt that historians take football more seriously than they did thirty or forty years ago.

Reflecting the sport's protean place in popular culture, the history of football opens many doors. Football can shed light on local rivalries and ethnic identities, and interrogate national myths. It can function as a tool of class and gender analysis, as well as a means of understanding the relationship between work and play. Football, more than other sports, can be understood as a substitute for, or echo of, religion. A Buddhist monk once justified bringing a gold statue of English player David Beckham to his Bangkok temple with the argument that "football has become a religion and we have to share the feelings of millions who admire [him]."[20] Football can be used to illuminate political history (particularly, though not only, under dictatorships), socio-economic history, and cultural history.

Finally, football can look beyond local and national concerns to international viewpoints. The relatively young field of transnational history is ideally suited to football, an international sport that has crossed national (and other) borders for more than 150 years. The aims of transnational history—historicizing contacts between societies; acknowledging foreign contributions to domestic polities and communities; and examining organizations and individuals that have lived in between and across societies—can help us to understand and explain football's enduring appeal. What FIFA and others have long called "the world's game" is now beginning to get the transnational scholarship that it deserves.

About *Contested Fields*

Contested Fields introduces readers to key aspects of the global game, synthesizing research on football's international role in reflecting and shaping political, economic, and sociocultural developments over the past 150 years. Interrogating the costs and benefits of the game's path to success, the book shows how and why football matters in the modern world, as a flexible and resilient part of the social fabric and as a site of political power and resistance.

Each chapter analyzes one element of football's international story. Chapter 2 uses the migration of players and coaches to examine football's role in "intercultural exchange." Chapter 3 examines the relationship between money and football, from early tensions between amateurs and professionals to the game's arrival as poster child for twenty-first-century capitalism. Chapter 4 focuses on competitions, most notably the quadrennial World Cup, as exemplars of football's lucrative but controversial international appeal. The following two chapters study football's role in empowering, and marginalizing, social groups often excluded from power. Chapter 5 tackles the issue of gender. It presents an alternative history of the global game, with women's football as the focal point, and examines evolving notions of masculinity. Chapter 6 examines race as a source of inclusion and exclusion, from the Nazi persecution of Jewish footballers to the colonial and post-colonial assertion of black African identities through the game. Chapter 7 explores the stadium as a contested political and social space and, on occasion, as a site of tragedy. Chapter 8 examines the history of spectatorship, whether live in draughty, industrial-era grounds or on television screens as part of a post-national audience in a bar in modern-day Abuja or New York. Finally, Chapter 9 considers the precarious balance between power and resistance in examples of football confrontation: how the politics of the game has been shaped by war, dictatorship, and activism.

Notes

1 Tadeusz Borowski, *This Way for the Gas, Ladies and Gentlemen*, trans. Barbara Vedder (London: Penguin, 1976), 83–84.
2 Primo Levi, *The Truce*, trans. Stuart Woolf (London: Abacus, 2002), 266.
3 Simon Inglis, *Sightlines: A Stadium Odyssey* (London: Yellow Jersey, 2000), 23.
4 Imre Kertész, *Fatelessness*, trans. Tim Wilkinson (New York: Vintage, 2004), 89.
5 Quoted in David Goldblatt, *The Ball Is Round* (London: Penguin, 2006), 3.
6 Quoted in James Walvin, *The People's Game: The History of Football Revisited* (Edinburgh: Mainstream, 1994), 11.
7 Joseph Strutt, *The Sports and Pastimes of the People of England* (London: Methuen, 1903), 93–94.
8 Quoted in Richard Holt, *Sport and the British: A Modern History* (Oxford: Oxford University Press, 1989), 37–38.
9 John Foot, *Calcio: A History of Italian Football* (London: Harper Perennial, 2007), 1.
10 Quoted in Goldblatt, *The Ball Is Round*, 245.
11 Quoted in Tiago Maranhão, "Apollonians and Dionysians: The Role of Football in Gilberto Freyre's Vision of Brazilian People," *Soccer & Society* 8, no. 4 (2007): 514.
12 Quoted in Paul Dimeo, "Football and Politics in Bengal: Colonialism, Nationalism, Communalism," *Soccer & Society* 2, no. 2 (2001): 68.
13 Quoted in Laura Fair, "'Kickin' It: Leisure, Politics and Football in Colonial Zanzibar, 1900s–1950s," *Africa* 76, no. 2 (1997): 226.
14 Robert D. Putnam, *Making Democracy Work: Civic Traditions in Modern Italy* (Princeton, NJ: Princeton University Press, 1993), 176.

15 Ted Hughes, "Football at Slack" (1977), *The Times Literary Supplement*, April 8, 2014, http://www.the-tls.co.uk/articles/public/football-at-slack/ (accessed 13 July 2017).

16 Karl Ove Knausgård and Fredrik Ekelund, *Home and Away: Writing the Beautiful Game*, trans. Don Bartlett and Séan Kinsella (Toronto: Knopf Canada, 2017), 12.

17 Eduardo Galeano, *Soccer in Sun and Shadow*, trans. Mark Fried (London: Verso, 2009), 209.

18 Peter Alegi and Chris Bolsmann, eds., *South Africa and the Global Game: Football, Apartheid and Beyond* (London: Routledge, 2010), 4.

19 Goldblatt, *The Ball Is Round*, xiii.

20 Quoted in Ross McKibbin, "Sports History: Status, Definitions and Meanings," *Sport in History* 31, no. 2 (2011): 172.

2 | Migrations

Born in Buenos Aires in 1926, Alfredo Di Stéfano began his football career at one of Argentina's leading clubs, River Plate, in 1947. A players' strike in 1949 led him to Colombia, along with a multinational cast of footballers from Latin America and Europe. Di Stéfano played for Bogotá's Millonarios FC until 1952, enjoying a lavish lifestyle and the free-flowing football of what the club's many admirers called the *ballet azul* (blue ballet). After joining Spanish side Real Madrid in 1953, he became a superstar. Di Stéfano brought international credibility to the dictatorship of General Francisco Franco, a Real Madrid supporter and Di Stéfano admirer. During his eleven years at the club, Real Madrid won the European Cup five times and earned countless domestic honours. When he retired in 1966, Di Stéfano had played international football for three countries (Argentina, Colombia, and Spain), been twice named European Footballer of the Year, and was once kidnapped by an armed revolutionary group in Venezuela. His coaching career took him home to Argentina, briefly to Portugal, and then back to Spain, where he lived until his death in 2014.

Di Stéfano's contemporary, Bernhard ("Bert") Trautmann, was born in the German port city of Bremen in 1923. Trautmann joined the Nazi youth organization, the Hitler Youth, shortly after Hitler came to power in 1933. He served on the Eastern Front during the Second World War. Transferred to the Western Front in 1944, after winning five medals including the prestigious Iron Cross (First Class), Trautmann was captured and imprisoned in a POW camp in northern England. Released in 1948, Trautmann refused repatriation, married a local girl, and played football for amateur team St. Helens Town. A year later, despite loud anti-German protests, he signed as a goalkeeper for First Division club Manchester City. Trautmann's long and successful career there, and his public transformation from bad to good German, was defined by his performance in the 1956 FA Cup final. After suffering a serious injury early in the game (later diagnosed as a broken neck), he stayed on the field to help Manchester City to a 3–1 win over Birmingham City. After retiring in 1964, Trautmann began a coaching career that took him back to Germany and then to Burma, Tanzania, Liberia, and Pakistan. Like Di Stéfano, he settled in Spain, where he died in 2013.

As the biographies of Di Stéfano and Trautmann illustrate, the global movement of players and coaches was a fundamental feature of modern football. The game often blurred concepts of nationality: the Argentine who became a Colombian hero and Spanish icon and the German who became an (honorary) Englishman. The dizzying number of countries involved in these two stories testifies to football's role in "cultural transfer," a term for professional expertise and knowledge circulation that crosses borders and showcases the dynamic role of foreign influences on "national" cultures. The stories also speak to the intersection of personal, economic, and political factors in the lives of migratory footballers. The peripatetic journeys of Trautmann and Di Stéfano were shaped by the mid-twentieth-century experiences of war and dictatorship, as they were shaped by quintessential concerns about marriage, family, and career.

In the past thirty years, migration has become one of the best-developed areas of football scholarship. The sport has been studied using various models of international political economy. Modernization theory emphasizes the universal, progressive transition from premodern to modern societies. Dependency theory and Immanuel Wallerstein's world systems theory both reject this optimistic evolutionary path, showing how resources flow from the impoverished periphery to the dominant core, thereby perpetuating inequality. Whether highlighting the freedoms or chains of labour mobility, much of this work agrees that football migration reflects the asymmetries of globalization, while maintaining distinctive features of its own.

Conditioned by alterations to government immigration policies, by war and political upheaval, and by changes in the regulations of FIFA and continental and national federations, football migration can take many forms. It has not always matched global flows, as the stop-start history of player movement to the United States shows. Migratory routes for elite women footballers have often differed from those of their male counterparts. Migration can be transcontinental. It can take place within countries—for example, the well-beaten path from northern and central Ghana to the country's football heartland between Kumasi and Accra—and within continents. Most of Uruguay's 625 overseas footballers between 1958 and 1983 played in Brazil or Argentina, not Europe. Football migration, finally, is not just about professionals. The sport's informal networks have shaped migrant routes and experiences, from post-apartheid South Africa to reunified Germany.

Within these migration stories (some short-lived and some lifelong), there are more failures than successes. For every Di Stéfano and Trautmann, there are thousands like the Cameroonian player Samuel Ojong. After two years at professional clubs in France and Switzerland, Ojong was left in 2003 with no contract and no obvious place to go: "When you come back from Europe, people ask you what you have been up to. You can't stay here for two years and come back empty-handed. Even if you don't have a contract anymore, it's better to stay."[1]

Chapter 2 showcases a multilayered approach to football migration. It examines the early overseas experiences of British players and coaches; the subsequent internationalization of migration networks; the politics of football migration, especially in colonial and post-colonial states; the global migratory upsurge since the 1990s; and alternative patterns of migration in the women's and amateur games. The chapter shows how football was a part of, and apart from, labour movement in the modern world, reinforcing the sport's importance to transnational histories of economic and cultural exchange.

Insular Missionaries? Early British Migrants

Early British attitudes to football mixed insularity and worldliness. Many Englishmen and Scotsmen spread the gospel, but these well-travelled, open-minded individuals lacked institutional support. FA officials were uninterested in football beyond British shores, as the organization's frosty relations with FIFA attested. FA Councillor Charles Sutcliffe stated bluntly in 1928, "I don't care a brass farthing about the improvement of the game in France, Belgium, Austria or Germany. The FIFA does not appeal to me. An organization where such football associations as those of Uruguay and Paraguay, Brazil and Egypt, Bohemia and Pan Russia, are co-equal with England, Scotland, Wales and Ireland seems to me to be a case of magnifying the midgets."[2]

From the arrival of professionalism in 1885, the movement of players and coaches complicated Sutcliffe's closed-shop idyll. Migration made English football dynamic. Scottish footballers strongly influenced the game south of the border. When Liverpool FC was formed in 1892, the owners looked to Scotland for the nucleus of their new team. In the 1892/93 season, Liverpool's "Team of the Macs" consisted exclusively of Scots. Leading English clubs, like the Preston team that won the 1888/89 league title without defeat, often had more Scottish than English players. This reflected a wider Scottish influence on the English game that ranged from tactics (the switch from a dribbling to a passing game) to stadium design. Though a professional league began in Scotland in 1890, talented players looked to the wealthier English competition for opportunities. In 1910, Scots accounted for 168 (19.3 per cent) of the English Football League's 870 footballers.

British footballers have often been typecast as reluctant travellers. Given the strength of competitions in England and Scotland, and widely held beliefs about the global supremacy of British football, this was hardly surprising. Yet British professionals were found in unlikely places. The majority of players in the American Soccer League (1921–31) were English, Scottish, or Irish. Seven English professionals played alongside Alfredo Di Stéfano in Colombia during the early 1950s. In the late 1950s and early 1960s, there was a short-lived exodus of stars to the Italian league, led by Welsh striker John Charles, who played with distinction for Juventus. Less well known was the healthy presence of British players in the newly professionalized French league of the early 1930s. At the peak of traffic across the English Channel in 1932/33, forty-three Britons (11.9 per cent of total players) played in France.

Wealthy overseas competitors never posed an existential threat. This was due partly to the robustness of the British game and partly to the inability of British players to settle abroad. The much-quoted (though seemingly apocryphal) remark of Liverpool striker Ian Rush about his single, unhappy season at Juventus in 1986/87—"it was like playing in a foreign country"—was shorthand for the difficulties that footballers faced in adjusting to new cultures, languages, and playing styles. It echoed the comment of a French journalist, after he encountered the post-1932 imports at clubs such as Marseille and Nîmes: "The English are so sure of their superiority that they will not think of adapting to our rules and traditions."[3]

British coaches and administrators were more influential than British players. In many countries, the game's much-mythologized founding fathers were British: the Scot Alexander Watson Hutton (Argentina);

the Anglo-Brazilian Charles Miller; the Charnock brothers (Russia); the English doctor James Richardson Spensley (Italy); and the English teacher William Leslie Poole (Uruguay). Even if local agency played a more significant role than most "great men" accounts concede, such expatriates founded clubs and associations, drew up rules, and created competitions. For most of the twentieth century, Britain was an international byword for football expertise. Between 1910 and 1940, at least 101 British coaches worked in continental Europe. Destinations tended to be close to home: France, the Netherlands, Switzerland, and northern Spain between the two world wars and Scandinavia after 1945. British coaches were found in further-flung places too: English-speaking countries such as Australia, South Africa, and the United States; post-colonial African and Asian states; Mediterranean countries such as Greece and Turkey; and South America.

Of the many early-twentieth-century British coaches who made their reputations abroad, the most famous was Jimmy Hogan. Born in 1882 in Lancashire, the heartland of English football, Hogan had a modest playing career. He began coaching shortly before the First World War. Over the next three decades, which included stops in Austria, England, France, Germany, Hungary, the Netherlands, and Switzerland, Hogan became one of Europe's leading coaches. In Austria, his partnership with national team coach Hugo Meisl (see Chapter 6) pioneered the quick-passing style that helped the *Wunderteam* (wonder team) to dominate European football in the early 1930s. As MTK Budapest coach (1914–21 and 1925–27), Hogan modernized Hungarian football along similar lines. The process culminated in Hungary's 6–3 victory over England at Wembley Stadium in 1953. After that game, the Hungarian coach Gusztáv Sebes claimed, "We played football as Jimmy Hogan taught us. When our football history is told, his name should be written in gold letters."[4] Though Hogan never enjoyed the success in Britain that he did abroad, he worked as an FA instructor and coached three English clubs, Brentford, Aston Villa, and Fulham, as well as Scottish giants Celtic. His career personified football's fluidity, and its consequent importance as a vehicle for cultural transfer.

Europeanizing and Globalizing Migration Networks

From the beginning, moving with the ball was not confined to British merchants, sailors, teachers, and missionaries. Continental Europeans often played an equally important role. Switzerland ("little England") served as a conduit between Britain and southern Europe, helping to spread football to such places as Bulgaria and Italy. Though the Charnock brothers introduced football to textile workers in Moscow, it was a Russian-born Frenchman, Georges Duperron, who translated the rules of the game into Russian. In St. Petersburg, Duperron organized Russia's first team (1896) and first league competition (1901). He managed the Russian team at the 1912 Stockholm Olympics and cofounded the All-Russian Football Union in the same year. A key figure in Paraguay was Dutch physical education teacher William Paats, who introduced football to pupils at his school in Asunción in 1899. If the soft power of sport turned football into the global game, this was a European, not just a British, undertaking.

Founded in 1904, the European-dominated international governing body, FIFA, intervened only patchily in the question of player movement. In certain cases—the American Soccer League of the 1920s or the Colombian league of the late 1940s—renegade competitions operated outside FIFA jurisdiction, attracting overseas players with the promise of better salaries and lifestyles. In others, FIFA stayed out of disputes between national associations, having no legal recourse, and no desire, to challenge citizenship laws. FIFA's global ambitions did not always square with the authority of its members. Even as it became international, football was nationalized.

Despite war, dictatorship, and economic crises, the international traffic in players and coaches rarely let up. On the eve of the First World War, as Anglo-German relations collapsed, German FA (DFB) officials came to Liverpool to interview twenty British candidates for the position of national team coach, including Jimmy Hogan and the chosen candidate Fred Pentland. Amid the ruins of the former Habsburg Empire after 1918, tensions between the new nation-states of Austria, Czechoslovakia, and Hungary were high. Yet Czech clubs continued to sign Viennese players. Viennese clubs paid generous salaries to bring Hungarian footballers, whose country was briefly a communist republic, to the Austrian capital. These migratory paths fostered the distinctive short-passing style of central European football in the interwar period.

Migratory networks expanded between the two world wars, helped by the proliferation of international matches and competitions, and football's increased popularity. These networks were increasingly Europeanized. Jimmy Hogan noted in 1933 that, outside the Netherlands, British coaches were in less demand than their Austrian, German, and Hungarian counterparts. In Italy, home to forty-five Hungarian coaches, William Garbutt was the sole British representative. Britain's intermittent absences from FIFA, coupled with cutting-edge tactical innovations in Central Europe, shifted the balance from island to continent.

Players' movements followed wider paths. The Italy squad that claimed the World Cup on home soil in 1934 contained five players born and raised in Argentina or Brazil. Alongside Englishmen, there were Yugoslavs, Algerians, and Moroccans in the French league in the 1930s. Larbi Ben Barek joined Marseille in 1938, having worked as a cleaner for a gas company in his Moroccan hometown of Casablanca. He became one of France's most celebrated players. Ben Barek appeared seventeen times for the national team and was, in 1948, the first French player to sign for a major European club, Spain's Atlético Madrid.

The exemplary figure in the Europeanization of migratory networks was the Hungarian player and coach Béla Guttmann. During his career, Guttmann played for eight teams, coached twenty-one teams, and lived in fourteen countries. His experiences were inseparable from the European Jewish experience in the twentieth century. Guttmann was born in 1899 in Budapest, the second city in the multinational Habsburg Empire, and home to 170,000 Jews (a quarter of the city's population). During Guttmann's formative years, football became popular in Hungary. He soon caught the eye of Jimmy Hogan's MTK, one of Budapest's leading clubs, associated (not entirely accurately) with assimilated middle-class Jews.

After twice winning the league with MTK, Guttmann left Hungary in 1922. He had little choice, given the violent anti-Semitism that accompanied the collapse of Hungary's short-lived Soviet republic in 1919 (led by the Jewish Bolshevik Béla Kun) and the subsequent "White Terror" under Admiral Miklós Horthy. Arriving in Vienna, Guttmann joined SC Hakoah, a Zionist sports club and safe haven from anti-Semitism. At Hakoah, Guttmann, a stylish centre back, starred in the team that won the Austrian league title in 1925. Following a successful tour to the United States a year later—a total of 224,000 people attended Hakoah's ten games—Guttmann, like most of his teammates, stayed behind to play in the American Soccer League. He played for various New York clubs, including the Brooklyn Wanderers and New York Hakoah. To supplement his income, Guttmann taught dance to dock workers and opened a bar. He lost most of his savings after the 1929 Wall Street crash.

Guttmann returned to Europe in 1932. He had already coached successfully in Austria, the Netherlands, and Hungary when the Second World War began. Long shrouded in mystery, how Guttmann survived the Holocaust—and the mass deportation of Hungary's Jewish population to Auschwitz in 1944—has only recently come to light. After hiding in a Budapest attic for several months, he and another prominent coach, Ernő Egri Erbstein, escaped from a labour camp and narrowly avoided genocide. His father and sister were murdered at Auschwitz.

Guttmann's coaching career after 1945 was as triumphant as it was international. It included stops at Ciocanul in Romania (1946); AC Milan in Italy (1953–55); São Paulo in Brazil (1957–58); Peñarol in Uruguay (1962); Servette in Switzerland (1966–67); and Panathinaikos in Greece (1967). Guttmann never stayed long anywhere. Historical circumstances and individual temperament shaped a story of restless cultural transfer. Guttmann's longest spell at a club was his most successful. In three years at Portuguese club Benfica (1959–62), Guttmann won the European Cup, the continent's premier competition, twice. He resigned after being refused a pay rise. Guttmann prophesied that the club would not be European champions in the next 100 years. The "Guttmann curse" is alive and well. In eight European finals since 1962, Benfica have lost each time.

Béla Guttmann's career reflected an internationalization of football's migratory networks, particularly after the Second World War. A number of factors were at play here: the global economic boom of the 1950s and 1960s; peace and (relative) international stability; the uneven spread of professionalism; the collapse of Europe's empires; and affordable international travel, especially by air. In a mobile and affluent age, athletes crossed borders with ever-greater regularity. Between 1945 and 1962, 117 North African footballers migrated to France. Two-thirds of them came from Algeria, then waging a violent struggle for independence from France. Before liberal economic reforms gave the green light to mass migration in 1965, fifty players left communist Yugoslavia for Western Europe. By 1971, the figure had jumped to 300. Croatian club Hajduk Split was effectively an export company, developing young players and then selling them abroad after the age of twenty-eight, chiefly to clubs in Belgium, France, and West Germany.

Migration led not only to Western Europe. Good but not elite players looked further afield to semi-peripheral football markets. The Yugoslav diaspora flourished in Australia, Canada, and the United States. Clubs were founded on ethnic identities previously submerged beneath the Tito regime's socialist ideology. Violence frequently marred matches between Croat and Serb teams in Australia. In Rhodesia (today Zimbabwe) during the minority rule of the 1960s and 1970s, a Scottish football diaspora formed part of a white labour hierarchy. Tommy Burns, who spent the summer of 1975 on loan at the all-white team Salisbury Callies, recounted in his autobiography a "race riot" that followed a testy encounter with a black team, Chibuku. In Zimbabwe, as in South Africa, "old boy" émigré networks ensured white-minority dominance in the sporting as in the political field.

A sense of solidarity in migrant communities broke down some (though rarely all) of the barriers to assimilation. When one Hungarian migrant, newly arrived in Sydney in 1961, sought transport, he was told to seek advice at a football match involving the St. George-Budapest team. A week later, an earlier migrant found him a new car at a decent price. From such small acts, migrants put down roots in a new country. Research on the migration of African footballers to Portugal between 1949 and 1975 (chiefly from its colonies Angola and Mozambique) reveals similar patterns. Newcomers took guidance from more experienced migrants. They undertook "secondary migration" from one Portuguese club to another. With few exceptions, they kept an outward distance from Africa's liberation movements, focusing on the kind of apolitical assimilation into colonial spaces expressed by the most famous of the cohort, Benfica's star forward Eusébio: "I don't get involved in politics. I don't like politics. My only politics is football."[5]

The Politics of Migration

Not everyone shared Eusébio's opinion or experiences. Major movements in twentieth-century history—communism, fascism, and decolonization—often politicized football migration. In the Spanish Civil War (1936–39), football divided along political lines. There were rival associations, one loyal to the democratic Spanish Republic, the other to Franco's nationalist forces. Even before nationalists occupied the Basque region of northern Spain in the summer of 1937, Basque athletes rallied to the Republican cause. The president of the Basque Republic, José Antonio Aguirre, was formerly a centre forward at Athletic Bilbao, pre–civil war Spain's leading team (under English coach Fred Pentland) and a rallying point for Basque autonomy. Aguirre created a Basque national team (El Euzkadi), which began an international tour in April 1937, playing exhibition matches to raise awareness of, and funds for, the Republican cause. El Euzkadi visited Czechoslovakia, France, Norway, Poland, and the Soviet Union.

The visit to the socialist motherland was especially important, given the contentious nature of Soviet support for the Spanish Republic. Amid the terror of Stalin's Great Purges, which fed on suspicion of foreigners and fifth columnists, the Basque representatives offered a rare encounter with the outside world. Welcome banners proclaimed that "communism will sweep away all borders." There were 2 million ticket requests for the Basque team's games in Moscow. Ninety thousand people watched the visitors defeat Dynamo Moscow 2–1, one of six wins in seven games on Soviet soil. Success on the pitch was not matched by success on the battlefield. The Basque players began the 1937 tour as ambassadors for the Spanish Republic but ended it as stateless refugees. Only two of thirty touring players returned to Franco's Spain. The rest built new careers and lives in Argentina, Chile, and Mexico.

Football politics in Spain drove players into exile. The reverse happened in another fascist country, Italy. Mussolini's desire to nationalize sport led to the 1926 Viareggio Charter, which legalized professional football and created a national league. Foreign players, around eighty of whom played in Italy during the 1925/26 season, were banned. A loophole in the charter, though, allowed each team to field two players of Italian extraction. These players were known as *rimpatriati* (returnees), Italian-born emigrants, or sons of Italian-born emigrants, who now came "home."

Between 1929 and 1943, 118 South American *rimpatriati* (60 Argentineans, 32 Uruguayans, and 26 Brazilians) migrated to Italy. The most famous of them was Raimundo Orsi, who starred for Argentina at the 1928 Olympics. When Orsi signed for Juventus shortly after the tournament, he received a monthly salary of 8,000 lire (eight times what a doctor or lawyer earned), a FIAT 509 car, and an apartment. His transfer triggered fierce debates about citizenship and identity in Argentina and Italy. Was Orsi an Argentinean of Spanish descent (*criollo*), an Italian, or both?

Orsi enjoyed a glittering career in Italy. He helped Juventus to win five league titles. He scored Italy's opening goal in the 1934 World Cup final win over Czechoslovakia. The identity question, though, never went away. None of the three *rimpatriati* in Italy's 1934 World Cup squad received the prestigious decoration for sporting merit from Mussolini. The honour went to less ethnically ambiguous squad members such as Giuseppe Meazza, who did his military service and spoke keenly about serving fascism. In contrast to Meazza, three leading *rimpatriati* at AS Roma returned to South America on the eve of the 1935/36 season to avoid being called up to fight in the Second Italo-Ethiopian War. Orsi too was by then back in Argentina. The fascist press railed against the unpatriotic Roma trio, but the *rimpatriati* contribution to Italian football was vital. While some players, especially homesick Brazilians, returned quickly to South America, many others— such as the Uruguayan contingent at Bologna—settled in Italy. The politics of migration was multidirectional. Hybridity and fluidity mattered more than definitions of citizenship theoretically grounded in *jus sanguinis* (right of blood).

When Soviet tanks invaded Hungary in November 1956 to crush an uprising against communist rule, the national football team was the country's most successful export. Olympic champions in 1952, the *Aranycsapat* (golden team) built around Ferenc Puskás, Sándor Kocsis, and Nándor Hidegkuti lost once in fifty matches between 1950 and 1956. The loss came against West Germany in the 1954 World Cup final. Popular dismay at the unexpected defeat shaded into anti-communist demonstrations that, some argue, foreshadowed the 1956 uprising. Players from Budapest's two leading clubs, Honvéd and MTK, were abroad when Soviet forces invaded. They were playing on European tours, hastily organized by then Honvéd coach Béla Guttmann to keep them out of trouble back home.

Communist rule was reimposed, but Hungarian football never recovered. Two hundred and forty footballers left the country, including the entire Hungarian youth team and players from every first and second division club. This was part of an exodus that numbered 200,000 people, or 2 per cent of the population. Among the most prominent departees was Ferenc Puskás. Puskás immigrated to Spain, where he starred alongside Alfredo Di Stéfano in the great Real Madrid team of the late 1950s and early 1960s.

If Hungary's refugees were players first and political figures second, the opposite was true of their Algerian contemporaries. Algeria's struggle for independence from France gave radical expression to the politics of football migration. Frantz Fanon wrote in *The Wretched of the Earth* (1961) that "decolonization is always a violent event." It involved, he argued, fundamental changes in social relations, whether in "individual encounters, a change of name of a sports club, the guest list at a cocktail party, members of a police force, or the board of directors of a state or private bank."[6] Sport, and football in particular, was integral to this transformation in Algeria, albeit in more contested ways than Fanon suggested.

Between 1945 and 1962, 76 Muslim (as opposed to European) Algerians played professional football in France. Eight represented the national team. The open-door policy, like the inclusion of Algerian teams in the French Cup after 1956, reflected Algeria's status as an overseas French *département* (province) and France's desire to retain one of its oldest colonies. Algerian nationalists in the FLN (National Liberation Front) had different ideas. FLN leaders, including later Algerian president Ahmed Ben Bella and Yacef Saadi, star of Gillo Pontecorvo's iconic anti-colonial film *The Battle of*

Algiers (1966), were keen footballers. They understood the sport's power in the liberation struggle. The uprising against French rule that began in 1954 was planned when FLN representatives met under the cover of the World Cup in Switzerland that summer. A key moment in escalating the Algerian War occurred in 1957, when an FLN operative assassinated the president of the pro-French Algerian assembly at the French Cup final.

Algerian migrant footballers were pulled in different directions. Some settled in France, marrying local women and doing military service. Others were drawn to the anti-colonial struggle, especially when the FLN created a national team in 1958. Like El Euzkadi during the Spanish Civil War, it spent the next four years touring the world, playing matches and advocating independence. The "revolutionary eleven" included nine professionals with contracts at French clubs. FLN leader Ferhat Abbas claimed that their defections "advanced the cause of Algerian independence by ten years." "These stars of French football have become *fellaghas* [armed revolutionaries]," lamented the magazine *Paris-Match*.[7] The departed included two stars of France's squad for the forthcoming World Cup in Sweden. Mustapha Zitouni initially asked if he could leave after the tournament, before crossing the border to join the FLN squad in Italy. Saint-Étienne striker Rachid Mekloufi was one of France's best players. He had played for the national team since 1956 and led the French army team to the world military championship in 1957. By joining the FLN team, Mekloufi gave up more than the opportunity to play in Sweden. He became a deserter.

The FLN depicted the departed players as revolutionaries. FIFA regarded them as outlaws. The organization refused to recognize the FLN team, as Algeria remained a French colony, and unsuccessfully attempted to prevent the newly independent nations of Morocco and Tunisia from playing the revolutionary eleven. From a political perspective, as Abbas had predicted, the FLN tour of Africa, Eastern Europe, the Middle East, China, and North Vietnam worked. The team played to large crowds, raised awareness of the cause, and helped to create the political climate that led Algeria to achieve independence from France in 1962.

Political migration was not without ambiguities. Several FLN players, such as the former Angers midfielder Amar Rouaï, disliked being depicted as simply "anti-French" or the victims of French racism. After the Algerian War, many of the team, including Rouaï and Rachid Mekloufi, returned to France, part of a wave of post-independence migration from North Africa that reshaped France's urban landscapes. When he captained Saint-Étienne to the French Cup in 1968, Mekloufi received the trophy from French president Charles de Gaulle, who told him, *"La France, c'est vous"* ("You are France"). In the 1970s and 1980s, Mekloufi had three spells coaching Algeria's national team. He was briefly, in 1988, president of the Algerian FA. Mekloufi's migrations defied easy categorization. Like Raimundo Orsi or Ferenc Puskás, he exemplified the hybrid identities of football's transnational elite.

Football Mobility since the 1990s

Modern footballers have always crossed borders. Beginning in the 1990s, however, there was a global upsurge in player movement. Changes in regulations in many European leagues allowed more overseas players to join clubs. Federations relaxed previously strict rules about the number of overseas-based players eligible to represent national teams. These shifts reflected the economic orthodoxy of the late twentieth century. Neo-liberalism, associated with Ronald Reagan in the United States and Margaret Thatcher in Britain, emphasized open markets and deregulation. Three developments aided football's (at times arrhythmic) dance to the neo-liberal tune: the collapse of communism in Eastern Europe and the Soviet Union (1989–91), which opened new markets for migrant players; the lucrative spread of televised football; and the 1995 Bosman ruling, which banned restrictions on European Union foreign players in EU member states.

The changes revolutionized migration. When the English Premier League (EPL) began in 1992, it featured 177 English players (73.1 per cent of total players). At the start of the 2013/14 season, this figure had dropped to 75 (34.1 per cent of the total). In Italy's Serie A during the 1994/95 season, the final year before the Bosman ruling, 63 overseas players took to the field. By the 1999/2000 season, the figure had increased almost fourfold to 228. Across top-flight clubs in eleven European countries, including England and Italy, the number of foreign recruits more than doubled between the 1995/96 and 2004/05 seasons, from 882 to 1,803—or from an average of 4.8 to 9.8 overseas players per club. The upsurge drew mostly from Europe, Africa, and South America, but few countries were untouched. Japan exported four players in the 1995/96 season. Two years later, following its debut at the World Cup, twenty-eight players went overseas, including the country's biggest star, Hidetoshi Nakata, who joined Italian club Perugia. By the 2012/13 season, sixty-eight Japanese players could be found abroad, in elite competitions in England and Germany; in smaller leagues in Estonia, Latvia, and Montenegro; and in emerging destinations such as Australia and the United States.

The vast increase in player movement changed football's global landscape—at both ends of the migratory chain. In Europe, the ideal (or idealized) destination for most migrant footballers, foreigners became commonplace even in lower-profile domestic competitions. In 2009, I took a group of Canadian students to a football match in the Polish Ekstraklasa (first division) between Cracovia and Zagłębie Lublin. The standout performer was Lublin's Senegalese striker Mouhamadou Traoré, one of three overseas players in Lublin's squad that day (the others came from Portugal and Zimbabwe). Traoré equalized for the visitors in the sixty-fifth minute, ensuring a 1–1 draw. It was one of twelve goals in 81 Ekstraklasa appearances. This was only part of a peripatetic career in his adopted homeland. Between 2008 and 2018, Traoré played for eight clubs at every level of the football pyramid, from Lublin in the Ekstraklasa to Pogoń Wronin in Klasa A, the seventh tier of Polish football.

Mouhamadou Traoré's story is one of thousands, largely unknown, that underpin the contemporary history of African football migration (see Figure 2.1). There were 350 African players in Europe in 1996. In 2000, there were 1,000. By 2006, one-fifth of player transfers *between* European clubs involved Africans. Amid the avalanche of growth statistics, two trends stood out. Traoré represented one trend—the shift from North to West Africa as Europe's primary source of players—but not the other. Born in 1982, Traoré was in his mid-twenties when he moved in 2008 from CSS Richard-Toll in northern Senegal to Glinik Gorlice in southern Poland. Most African players in Europe were by then far younger. In the 2002/03 season, the average age of African footballers in the Union of European Football Associations' (UEFA's) top eight leagues was 19.2 years, more than five years younger than the average age of European football migrants. Even taking into account the fact that many African players lacked birth certificates and that agents could more easily sell youthful talent to buyers, this was a disturbing gap.

The youthfulness of this migrant labour, and its vulnerability to exploitation by unscrupulous clubs, raised alarm bells. The UN Commission on Human Rights warned in 1999 of a modern-day "slave trade" in African footballers. In 2003 FIFA President Sepp Blatter attacked "neo-colonialist" European clubs who "engage in social and economic rape by robbing the developing world of its best players."[8] Two years earlier, FIFA introduced regulations aimed at protecting minors (defined as players under the age of eighteen) from clubs and agents on the hunt for cheap overseas talent.

FIGURE 2.1 Transfers of Footballers from Africa's Top Four Exporting Countries to the Rest of the World, 1997–2013

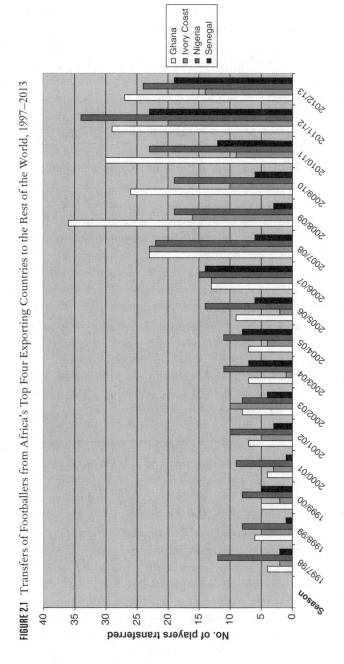

Source: Adapted from Mac Bryla's interactive map of football transfers, 1900–2013. Map available from the data blog of *The Guardian*: https://www.theguardian.com/football/datablog/interactive/2013/nov/14/113-years-of-international-football-player-transfers.

These measures, though, were often circumvented, in particular through a target of Blatter's ire, academies.

Since the 1990s, academies have been integral to the networks linking African football labour to labour markets in Europe and elsewhere. Often seen as symbolic of the privatization of African football and of the unequal partnership between European clubs and indigenous feeder organizations, academies take four main forms. The first are Afro-European ventures. European clubs quickly recognized the possibilities for developing offshore talent. In Ghana, one of Africa's leading exporters, academy investors since 1999 include Feyenoord, Ajax, and FC Utrecht (the Netherlands), Red Bull Salzburg (Austria), and FC Midtjylland (Denmark).

The second category of football academies is African: schools run by local clubs or associations. Founded in 1994, the MimoSifcom academy at ASEC Mimosas Abidjan became the continental leader, developing many of the Ivory Coast's best-known players. The Touré brothers, Kolo and Yaya, went from MimoSifcom to the ASEC first team before embarking on successful careers in England and Spain. In Ghana, where youth development programs dated back to the early years of independence, the football association runs a centre of excellence on the outskirts of the capital, Accra. Most leading clubs have academies too. Operations were not always clean. A 1999 judicial inquiry into the overseas transfers of 150 Ghanaian players found numerous cases of corruption involving high-level officials.

The third group is composed of academies operated by private organizations. The Red Bull Academy in Sogakope in the Volta region of Ghana opened in 2008 and closed its doors just six years later. Though nominally an Afro-European venture, tied to the energy drink company's Austrian club, Red Bull Salzburg, the Red Bull Academy bore many of the trademarks of older European business models in Africa. Fieldwork revealed that the academy's European managers showed little understanding of local tribal structures; permitted an "apartheid" system of employment, in which black workers were called "monkeys" and "baboons"; and failed to honour promises to provide education and drinking water.

Not all private academies met Red Bull Ghana's unhappy fate. Doubts, though, remain about local benefits. This is especially true in the fourth and final category, the ad hoc academies that form part of an African "shadow economy" in which individuals and organizations focus less on coaching and education than on financial gain. By the mid-2000s, there were 160 unofficial academies in Senegal and 500 illegal football centres in Accra. Varied in size, structure, quality, and ambition, they tended to have no affiliations with local clubs or national associations. They served as crude talent filters for agents and other interested parties looking to sell young players to Europe.

At their worst, Africa's football academies have perpetuated a form of neo-colonial exploitation in which raw materials (in this case athletic ability rather than cash crops such as sugar) are sourced, refined, and exported for overseas consumption. Academies could be sites of upward mobility. Reflecting on his time at the Centre Aldo Gentina, an academy in the Senegalese capital, Dakar, goalkeeper Tony Sylva spoke of how it changed his life: "Being in the academy you immediately felt privileged." Sylva enjoyed a successful career in France's Ligue 1 and played for Senegal at the 2002 World Cup. His was not a typical story. As the Chadian journalist Emmanuel Maradas observed in 2001, for every future academy star, "there are thousands of others investing millions of hours of practice ... without even reaching the first hurdle. Only a handful out of each year's intake will ever make a living from football."[9]

Even among the successful minority, the migrant experience was often difficult. Nigerian footballers Edward Anyamkyegh and Samson Godwin signed for Ukrainian club Karpaty Lviv in 2001. Bankrolled by oligarch Petro Dyminskyy, the club represented the Eastern European edges of football's post-communist globalization. Anyamkyegh's route to a city in Western Ukraine typified the circuitous migratory paths of late capitalism: the long-held dream of becoming a star in Europe; a trial at the French club Bordeaux in 1998, which ended in the hands of an unscrupulous agent; a return home to injury and obscurity; and a second return to Europe, this time at Sheriff in Tiraspol, capital city of the former Soviet republic of Moldova. Anyamkyegh did well at Sheriff. The club cashed in. He was sold to Karpaty, a club flush with money from Dyminskyy's buying and selling of Western Ukraine's gas, oil, and coal reserves in the 1990s.

Like most Nigerian players who came to Ukraine in the early 2000s, Anyamkyegh did not fare well. The attacker scored only three goals in forty-eight appearances. He was sold to the Finnish club KuPS in 2004, the first of five stops in Finland before his retirement in 2011. Anyamkyegh struggled with the cold Ukrainian winters, as he did with communication in a polyglot dressing room. Racism manifested itself less in open hostility than in a sense of otherness. There were fifty Africans among Lviv's population of 850,000. In the neighbourhood McDonald's, children stared in astonishment at Anyamkyegh. Local-born players, under threat for their jobs, internalized the idea that Anyamkyegh and Godwin were lazy and stopped passing to them. There is no archetypal African migrant footballer's experience, but Anyamkyegh's story—with its tropes of the corrupt agent, limited labour rights, nomadic European outposts, cultural dislocation, and racial prejudice—is more representative than most. Hostility was hard to displace. As Senegalese player Souleyman Sané stated in 1993, "For the four years I have played in the [German] *Bundesliga*, I have often heard 'Blacks go home!' and I never managed to get used to it."[10]

The world's biggest exporter of footballers remains the country most closely identified with the global game, Brazil. A 2015 report on the origins of 18,660 foreign footballers at more than 6,000 clubs around the world had Brazil far out in front, exporting 1,784 players. Its closest rival, Argentina, exported 929 players. Brazil ranked first in Asia (437 players, with Nigeria a distant second with 127 players), first in Europe (with 1,134 players, almost twice as many as second-placed France), and first (by a smaller margin) in North America's Major League Soccer (MLS). Brazilian players, in other words, were everywhere.

Alex Bellos's 2002 history of Brazilian football opens not in the cathedral of the national game, Rio de Janeiro's Maracanã Stadium, or among beach footballers in the same city, but in the fishing village of Toftir in the Faroe Islands. In 1999, ambitious local team B98 signed four Brazilian footballers. One quickly returned home. The other three—Marcelo Marcolino, Messias Pereira, and Marlon Jorge—stayed. They helped B98 to finish third in the league in 2000 and thereby qualify for European competition. Bellos's interviews with the trio reveal the complexities of the migrant experience. The best of the exports, striker Marcelo, spends much of his time, like Edward Anyamkyegh in Lviv, watching satellite TV. He veers between criticism of Faroese culture ("Here people don't have lives ... parties here are more like ... death-watches") and gratitude for the opportunities that B98 has provided. Messias, who reads the Bible to combat loneliness, displays a similar ambivalence: "I consider myself lucky to be here. But I also consider myself unlucky that I am not playing somewhere better." Marlon, the most integrated of the trio, contemplates becoming a naturalized Faroese, as a means of playing international football. He views the upcoming game with the Belgian side Lokeren as a shop window: "The idea is to play really well and then leave for another team that pays more money."[11]

Many of the players discussed in this section—Mouhamadou Traoré, Edward Anyamkyegh, and the Brazilian trio at B98—had little impact on the grand narratives of European football. Their modest careers played out in obscure and shifting locations. Among them, only Anyamkyegh has more than a skeletal Wikipedia entry—and it is in Finnish. Yet their stories and experiences form part of a history of intercultural transfer that, perhaps more than anything else, characterizes football's contribution to the modern world.

Alternative Routes

On his visit to the Faroe Islands, Alex Bellos met another Brazilian, Robson, who in 1999 signed for Gí, a club in the village of Gøta. Unlike his countrymen at B98, Robson never made it in the Faroe Islands. Signed because of the cultural capital that surrounds the words "Brazilian footballer," rather than because of his talent, Robson appeared just once for Gí. He then got a job at the fish factory, met a local girl, and became a father. With mixed feelings—loneliness, but also pride in his family and material wealth—his life was now rooted in a village far from his home in northern Brazil.

Football was integral to the identity of many migrants, even if they lacked the skill to play professionally. Historians and sociologists have begun to examine how amateur football has shaped migratory patterns and behaviour. This poses a different set of questions. In professional football, integration into the host society can be fast-tracked by success and money. Lower down the pyramid, tensions between assimilation and isolation can be harder to resolve.

In the early 1970s, Antonio and Linda Demoura emigrated with their three children from Portugal to France. They settled in the small town of Saint-Marcellin in the Rhône-Alpes region. At first, theirs was a classic migrant success story. Initial hardships led, via hard work, to acceptance and assimilation. Football was central to this transition. A talented youth player, Antonio Demoura found friends at the local football club. He coached, helped to build a new clubhouse, and billeted visiting players from Toulouse. In 1985, his wife had a stroke. Five years later, he lost his toes in a lawnmower accident. The model immigrants had the rug swept from under their feet. Antonio lost his job as a foreman in a repair shop and was limited to low-paid, unskilled jobs. His wife was denied unemployment insurance. Debts mounted, and the couple's oldest daughter was forced to leave university. Most hurtfully of all, the doors of the local football club were slammed shut. Antonio, in his words, was "completely dropped": "19 years of service to the club, and never a thing for me, I always delivered; as a coach, I was the one who got the most championship titles, I was the one who put together the best team and now I'm just a nobody." When the mayor rewarded club members for their achievements, Demoura received nothing. "If my name was Dupont or Durand," he concluded in 1992, "I'd have my medal. But my name is Demoura."[12]

In the mining region of Nord-Pas-de-Calais in northern France, football was viewed, for much of the twentieth century, as an integrative force. It contributed to an assimilated French identity that erased class, racial, and national differences. Among the Poles who settled in the region after the First World War, the exemplar of this narrative was Raymond Kopa (born Kopaszewski), the greatest French footballer of the 1950s. Kopa won three European Cups with Real Madrid and starred for the national team at the 1958 World Cup.

Isolated from French society, Polish newcomers to Nord-Pas-de-Calais in the 1920s and 1930s initially saw football clubs and other cultural associations as autonomous spaces. They soon chafed against the limitations of a closed system. Particularly after the Second World War and the nationalization of the coalmining industry in 1948, Polish footballers joined amateur clubs whose identities were rooted in working-class communities that brought together migrants and French citizens. Football's integrative power was also reflected in the many Poles at the local professional team, Racing Club de Lens.

The second wave of migrants to the coalfields found football to be a less inviting means of assimilation. White, Catholic *Polaks* used the sport to become "our boys" (or "good" migrants). Muslim migrants from North Africa could rarely follow the same path. Racing's star Algerian player, Ahmed Oudjani, was an isolated figure. For amateur players of Algerian or Moroccan descent, faced with racial exclusion and the decline of the coalmining industry, football did not typically offer the upward mobility open to Oudjani, or to Kopa before him.

In Nord-Pas-de-Calais, football did not automatically mean integration or exclusion. Research on Germany's largest migrant group, the 2.5 million people of Turkish descent, likewise suggests that acculturation was not necessarily at the expense of Turkish identities. Between 1985 and 1997, there were significant increases in "single-ethnicity" football teams in the cities of Münster, Duisburg, and Wuppertal. This "ethnification" subsequently slowed down, more because it reached saturation point than because of a shift toward more "German" identities among second- and third-generation Turkish immigrants. A 2001 survey of people of Turkish descent from the same region found that that 80 per cent of respondents supported Turkish rather than German professional clubs. As with the previously mentioned French examples or with Asian cricketers in Britain, there were rarely either-or cases of integration versus separation in German amateur football. Numerous factors shaped intercultural contact, including perceptions of discrimination at multi-ethnic clubs and the desire for cultural affiliation with people of one's own ethnicity, but also playing standards.

Amateur football fosters what sociologist Pierre Bourdieu calls "social capital," the series of networks that allows migrants to gain footholds in host societies and work for a common purpose. In post-apartheid South Africa, patterns of migration from the poor, rural settlement of Nomhala to Cape Town (almost 1,000 kilometres to the west) were influenced by the village's (and the nation's) favourite game. There was a strong correlation between the *imiɀi* (homesteads) close to the football pitch in Nomhala's west end and the *imiɀi* set up at Site 5, the settlement in the Cape Town metropolitan area where many migrants from Nomhala resided. More than 80 per cent of migration to Site 5 was traced to a young villager who moved to Cape Town in 1989 and encouraged football-playing friends to follow him. Nomhala's football networks were thus "translocalized" to the migrant settlement in Cape Town. In 2010, there were twenty teams in the Site 5 league, including Nomhala's own Mighty Doves, founded in 1998. The team's function extended beyond the football field. The Mighty Doves offered a support network that could, for example, provide access to jobs for unemployed fellow villagers. It had ramifications back home. Nomhala's village team named itself the Mighty Doves in 2000. Migration thus served a dual purpose, reinforcing football's role in village life and drawing the next generation of villagers to Site 5, where they played in a proper league, wearing full kits and good football boots, on pitches with chalk markings and nets.

Migratory patterns in women's football differ from those in the men's game. A number of factors shape this alternative history. They include the later development of the women's game; the prominence of destination countries such as Japan, Norway, and the United States (none of which was a powerhouse in men's football); players' limited earning potential; and the small number of professional or semi-professional leagues available to them. A 2016 study suggested that women could make a living from football in only 22 of 147 FIFA-affiliated countries. Even more than for their male counterparts, mobility has been, and remains, imperative to the careers of talented female players.

When the women's game gained international traction in the 1970s, emigrants came largely from Scandinavia. An estimated twenty-eight players left Denmark, Norway, and Sweden to play abroad between 1971 and 1999. Of their three main destinations—Italy, Japan, and the United

States—only Italy was a force in men's football. It was also in the vanguard of attempts to professionalize women's football. Sif Kalvø, in 1971 the first Norwegian to go abroad, played for three Italian clubs. Her salary was equivalent to that of a Norwegian school teacher. Kalvø was part of a small but cosmopolitan group of players that included England's Sue Lopez, who spent a year at Roma in 1971, and Maria Scevikova from communist Czechoslovakia.

Hardly prime destinations for male footballers, Japan and the United States were central to increased labour mobility in the women's game. Japan introduced a professional league in 1995. It became a magnet for international footballers, including a clutch of Scandinavians at the short-lived Nikko Securities Dream Ladies. The United States was attractive for a different reason. The University College Soccer Program, begun in the late 1980s, offered overseas players scholarships. This allowed them to play amateur football at a high level and receive a free education.

The 1999 World Cup in the United States, the largest women's sports event in history, led to a marked increase in the global movement of players. Founded in 2000, the Women's United Soccer Association (WUSA) was the world's first fully professional women's league. Though WUSA folded in 2003, the United States emerged as the lead attraction for elite footballers. It was home to 30 per cent of all migrant players in 2009, including half of the national squads of Canada and Trinidad and Tobago and one-third of Brazil's squad. Top European leagues were the next most popular destinations, accounting for 19 per cent of migrants. Despite the financial crisis then gripping Europe, ninety-five overseas footballers played in the Danish, Norwegian, and Swedish leagues. Most of the imports were from elsewhere in Scandinavia (52 per cent of the total), but there were substantial numbers from North America (15 per cent), elsewhere in Europe (12 per cent), and Africa (11 per cent). In the twenty-first century, the term "the global game" applied to women's football just as much as it did to men's.

The reverse of the equation told a similar story of increased, and increasingly diverse, transnational exchange. In 2013, the top three exporters of women players were Canada (88.9 per cent of its players), Mexico (77.9 per cent), and Wales (75 per cent). A more familiar face, Brazil, was high on the list, with players in twenty-two receiving countries. Brazilians played at all levels, from elite competitions in the United States, Japan, and Sweden to cash-strapped leagues in Cyprus, Poland, and Serbia. Brazilian defender Rosana dos Santos Augusto exemplified modern football as a mobility project. Between 1997 and 2007, she played for five clubs in Brazil, three in the United States, two in France, and one apiece in Norway and Austria. Like her male counterparts, Rosana (as she was commonly known) was part of a restless transnational elite: multilingual, experienced, and comfortable at home and in host societies.

Drawing contrasts with men's football, some migration scholars have highlighted "love of the game" as the primary reason for women playing abroad. This was rarely the whole story. As in the men's game, skilled foreigners could be rapidly naturalized to boost the quality of football in countries with big ambitions but poor infrastructure and small domestic pools of players. Since Equatorial Guinea started playing international football in 2002, fifteen "mobile players"—from Cameroon, Nigeria, Burkina Faso, and Brazil—have represented its national team. As in the men's game, economic factors encouraged players to move. Pioneers such as Sif Kalvø and Pia Sundhage, who left Scandinavia for Italy in the 1970s and 1980s, noted that love for the game and love for the money that it offered often went hand in hand. Financial motives became more apparent after 1999. When WUSA's successor, the Women's Professional League (WPL), was launched in the United States in 2009, it attracted some of the world's best players. Brazil's Marta Vieira da Silva, universally known as Marta, earned an annual salary of US$500,000 at FC Gold Pride in Santa Clara, California.

Yet motivations were different in the women's game, where huge salaries and wealthy leagues remain uncommon. In the WPL, which lasted from 2009 to 2012, Marta's earnings were atypical. The average league salary in 2010 was US$27,000; in the same year, the MLS's top earner, David Beckham of the LA Galaxy, made US$6.5 million. In Germany's Frauen-Bundesliga, often regarded as the world's best women's competition, only three players earned more than 100,000 Euros (US$118,000) in 2012. Even for very good players, football rarely provides a sole, steady means of income. It even more rarely provides the post-career financial security taken for granted at the top of men's football. Women players bear comparison with migrant blue-collar workers (in the ceiling on what they can earn) and young, skilled professionals, for whom work abroad is often short term and experiential.

In this situation, it is unsurprising that non-economic factors—the desire to travel, a sense of cultural or linguistic affiliation, a love of playing football—play a larger role in the migration of elite female than elite male footballers. Whether there will be a convergence of experiences remains open to debate. The modern history of football migration—multidirectional, multilayered, and subject to constant evolution—suggests that this form of transnational cultural exchange is unlikely to stand still for long.

Notes

1 Quoted in Raffaele Poli, "Migrations and Trade of African Football Players: Historic, Geographical and Cultural Aspects," *Africa Spectrum* 41, no. 3 (2006): 411.

2 Quoted in Pierre Lanfranchi and Matthew Taylor, *Moving with the Ball: The Migration of Professional Footballers* (Oxford: Berg, 2001), 46.

3 Quoted in Lanfranchi and Taylor, *Moving with the Ball*, 56.

4 Quoted in Norman Fox, *Prophet or Traitor? The Jimmy Hogan Story* (Manchester: Parrs Wood, 2003), 11.

5 Quoted in Todd Cleveland, "Following the Ball: African Soccer Players, Labor Strategies and Emigration across the Portuguese Colonial Empire, 1949–1975," *Cadernos de Estudos Africanos* 26 (2013): 37.

6 Frantz Fanon, *The Wretched of the Earth*, trans. Richard Philcox (1961; New York: Grove Press, 2004), 1.

7 Quoted in Laurent Dubois, *Soccer Empire: The World Cup and the Future of France* (Berkeley, CA: University of California Press, 2010), 193, 196.

8 Quoted in Paul Darby, "Gains versus Drains: Football Academies and the Export of Highly Skilled Football Labour," *The Brown Journal of World Affairs* 18, no. 2 (2012): 266.

9 Sylva and Maradas quoted in Peter Alegi, *African Soccerscapes: How a Continent Changed the World's Game* (Athens, OH: Ohio University Press, 2010), 116, 119.

10 Quoted in Lanfranchi and Taylor, *Moving with the Ball*, 188.

11 Marcelo, Messias, and Marlon quoted in Alex Bellos, *Futebol: The Brazilian Way of Life* (London: Bloomsbury, 2002), 7, 12, 14.

12 Quoted in Pierre Bourdieu et al., *The Weight of the World: Social Suffering in Contemporary Society*, trans. Priscilla Parkhurst Ferguson (Stanford, CA: Stanford University Press, 1999), 363–64.

3 | Money

The 1974 World Cup in West Germany is not remembered fondly. Amid a global economic crisis, and in the shadow of the Palestinian terrorist attack on Israeli athletes at the 1972 Munich Olympics, the tournament was underwhelming. The bright spot was the fluent interplay and technical brilliance of the Dutch team, which reached the final with its *totaalvoetbal* (total football). Games, though, were generally low-scoring and defensive. The Netherlands lost the final to West Germany. It was not a victory that captured the imagination, either at home or abroad.

Yet the 1974 World Cup was very important in football's global history. Shortly before the tournament, João Havelange replaced Sir Stanley Rous as FIFA president. Rous had held office since 1961. A former schoolteacher and referee, the Englishman epitomized the patrician, Eurocentric governance of world football that had been FIFA's modus operandi since 1904. For Rous, sport and politics were to be kept as far apart as possible. Money was a necessary evil. Twenty years younger than Rous, Havelange, a sports entrepreneur and ex-Olympian, had no qualms about politicking for votes, or about spending money to get them. He pledged to de-Europeanize FIFA, develop the game in Africa and Asia, and maximize football's commercial potential.

June 1974 was a watershed, the moment when FIFA began its global transformation from administration-focused sports institution into dynamic, profit-driven enterprise. Havelange was true to his election promises. FIFA gave more World Cup places to teams from Africa and Asia. Corporate sponsors such as Adidas and Coca-Cola invested in FIFA development programs. The sale of television and marketing rights to the World Cup skyrocketed, orchestrated by a Swiss-based firm with close ties to FIFA, International Sport and Leisure. The 1974 tournament made profits of 50 million DM (US$12.9 million). The 2010 World Cup in South Africa earned FIFA US$4.2 billion.

Commercialized on an unprecedented scale since 1974, football is today often called "big business." Economists recognize that, by all measurable standards, this is not an accurate description. The world's richest football club, Real Madrid, had revenues of US$475 million in 2009. This was roughly one-thousandth the revenues earned in 2008 by oil giant Exxon, the largest company on the S&P 500. Even the smallest company on the American stock market index, titanium producer TIMET, had revenues more than double the size of Real Madrid's. Economic value cannot be assessed on club revenue alone. Football creates substantial profits for (to name a few examples) the advertising, gambling, telecommunications, and transport industries. But it is not a mainstay of the global economy.

Football is not big business, and it is rarely good business. Most football clubs, like most states, operate at a loss. The biggest clubs often make the biggest losses. Of the sixteen English clubs floated on the stock exchange in the mid-1990s, only six increased their revenues and paid out dividends to shareholders. Most ran at a loss. But twelve of the sixteen improved their average league position after flotation. For serious investors, football clubs are not sensible propositions. Yet play and profit have been closely bound together since the beginnings of modern football, both in the popular imagination and in the administration of the game.

Chapter 3 examines the international history of the business of football from economic, political, and sociocultural perspectives. It first surveys the game's economic history, from late-nineteenth-century business connections to expansion in the globalized markets of the twenty-first century. Attention then turns to the evolving economic status of players, from the first, fierce debates about professionalism to the rise of transnational celebrities such as David Beckham and Cristiano Ronaldo. The chapter next focuses on corruption, from early cases of match-fixing to recent scandals in Italian football and at FIFA. Finally, the chapter examines football's relationships with its chief stakeholders: club owners, sponsors, and broadcasters.

Football: A Short Economic History

Football emerged in the golden age of industrial capitalism. A confluence of factors—industrialization, urbanization, improved public transport, increased literacy, rising wages, increased leisure time, and professionalization—made football the sport of the working class in England and Scotland. It was also the sport of Britain's industrial elite. Local businessmen funded the stadiums built in working-class neighbourhoods from the 1890s onwards. The founder of the English Football League, Scottish draper William McGregor, described football as a big business as early as 1905. The men who ran the game, though, were hardly ruthless profiteers. In the 1908/09 season, only six of sixty-two English clubs paid their shareholders dividends. As limited liability companies, English clubs took the business of football seriously, but profit was often subordinate to sporting concerns, from player purchases to the development of facilities.

When the English Football League started in 1888, Germany was fifteen years from its first nationwide competition and seventy-five years from its first professional league. The sport there initially attracted white-collar workers. Clerks and shop employees, the social strata between the working class and the *Bildungsbürgertum* (educated middle class), were the chief exponents of this fluid, sociable amateur pastime. The German FA (DFB), founded in 1900, scorned professionalism, but it was an astute financial operator. Through membership fees, match ticket sales, and tax breaks, the organization was turning a healthy profit by 1914.

Outside Europe, the relationship between football and commerce was far removed from the British model. In the French colony of Congo, the game was a contested social and political space, not a field for economic activity. For black teams in the Poto-Poto and Bacongo neighbourhoods of the capital city, Brazzaville, European funds provided equipment and facilities such as balls, nets, and shirts—but not at the cost of autonomy. The French authorities, in predictable contrast, disbursed materials as a means of control and sought to limit black autonomy via the European-controlled Native Sports Federation. The showpiece Marchand Stadium got new tennis courts and changing rooms. Black football teams played in torn or second-hand kits. When African footballers left the Native Sports Federation in 1937, the spark was the federation's attempt in the previous year to ban local players from playing in boots. This was less about safety or saving money than it was about returning African players to their barefooted, "primitive" street football origins. The boots ban symbolized the limited economic means of black players and a colonial discourse focused on control and discrimination.

Football's first phase of globalization—the international diffusion of the game from the 1870s onwards—ended after the First World War. In the second phase, which lasted from the 1920s until (arguably) the 1960s, football became a more standardized and more interconnected commercial and sporting enterprise. In 1924, Austria was the first country outside Britain to create a professional league. Others followed suit: Czechoslovakia (1925), Hungary (1926), Italy (1928), Spain (1929), Argentina (1931), Brazil (1933), and the Soviet Union (1936). International competitions became fixtures in the football calendar: the Copa América (1916), the Mitropa Cup (1927), and the World Cup (1930).

More money circulated in the game. Goalkeeper Ricardo Zamora was the first star of Spanish football. The hero of Spain's victory at the 1920 Olympics, *El Divino* (the Divine One), was alive to football's commercial possibilities. Before the tournament, Zamora's highest match bonus was 25 pesetas. In 1921 he played exhibition matches for 1,000 pesetas. In 1922 he moved from Barcelona to city rivals Espanyol for 2,000 pesetas a month and a signing-on fee of 25,000 pesetas, the kind of illicit payment (*marronismo*) also common in Argentinean football in this period. The transfer signalled the death knell of amateurism. The Spanish FA repealed its initial ban on Zamora, who was too popular and talented to be omitted from the national team. Football was professionalized in 1926. By then, Zamora was an international celebrity and football an integral part of Spanish popular culture, alongside cinema and bullfighting. The goalkeeper endorsed alcoholic drinks, starred in a movie, and did lucrative tours of Europe and South America with Espanyol.

Zamora, of course, was atypical. In many parts of the world, footballers' economic status did not change significantly until the late twentieth century. The introduction of professionalism in England (1885) was designed to limit players' bargaining powers not to open the financial floodgates. The average professional had a short, precarious career. At Barnsley FC in South Yorkshire in the 1950s, most of the playing staff of thirty-eight still needed side jobs. One senior player sold his own brand of detergent. Many of the reserves worked in local mines.

After the Second World War, football slowly entered new commercial waters. Insurgent forces, most notably television, challenged the game's long-standing reliance on gate receipts as the primary source of income. Players sought to benefit from the changing landscape. In England this was symbolized by the abolition of the maximum wage in 1961. Though the lives of many professionals were not greatly affected, the top of the game was transformed. Manchester United winger George Best personified the modern celebrity footballer. Dubbed "the fifth Beatle" by Portuguese newspapers in 1966, his fame transcended the game, intersecting with various elements of 1960s popular culture: nightclubs, boutiques, restaurants, music (he appeared on *Top of the Pops* in 1965), and advertising. Best, like Zamora in a previous generation, was in some respects an anomaly. But he symbolized an era when the earnings of elite footballers began to separate them from the people who watched them play. Wages in Italy and Spain followed a similar trajectory, and at earlier dates. Real Madrid spent 40 per cent of its annual revenue in the negotiations that brought Alfredo Di Stéfano to the club in 1953.

In the more conservative Bundesliga, founded in 1963, low wages contributed to a series of financial scandals (discussed below). The West German competition was ahead of the commercial curve in other respects. In 1973, it became the first major European league to allow shirt sponsorship, when Eintracht Braunschweig took to the field advertising the liquor company Jägermeister. The DFB had opposed Braunschweig's move before conceding to market realities. Other countries soon followed suit: England in 1977, Italy in 1978, Spain in 1982, and Brazil in 1983. From FIFA downwards, commercial possibilities opened up. In 1980 the Intercontinental Cup, contested since 1960 between the champions of Europe and South America, was relocated to Japan under the sponsorship of Toyota.

The new football economy that began to emerge in the 1960s, a decade of rising wages and increased TV coverage, was not always as new as it seemed. Most footballers remained on the poorer side of what economists termed a dual labour market, far from the riches of superstars such as George Best. Even Best, as Arthur Hopcraft noted in a sympathetic and perceptive portrait in 1968, was a less remote figure than he at first seemed: "It is only because the pay and working conditions of leading professional footballers were until recently those of moderately skilled factory helots that [he] and his contemporaries look so excessively immodest and affluent."[1]

Wealth at the top of the game failed to mask problems elsewhere. As Brazilian star Pelé became a global commercial icon, the game that he played and marketed so brilliantly became increasingly unattractive. With exceptions such as Italy, football declined steeply as a live spectator sport in the 1970s and 1980s, particularly in north-western Europe—and television was not yet willing or able to fill the empty space. The reasons for this decline ranged from appealing leisure alternatives (including, of course, television) to the rise of hooliganism (see Chapter 8). The result in England, the *Sunday Times* newspaper dismissively claimed in 1985, was "a slum game played in slum stadiums watched by slum people."[2] The idea that football would become, less than a decade later, a cash cow for global businesses—not least for the organization that published the *Sunday Times*, Rupert Murdoch's News Corporation—seemed absurd.

Outside elite competitions in Western Europe and, to a lesser degree, South America, the pace of economic change was slower. The privatization of African football only began in the 1980s. After the Cameroonian Issa Hayatou became Confederation of African Football (CAF) president in 1987, the continent's major international tournament, the Cup of Nations, was opened to sponsorship from FIFA stalwarts such as Adidas and Coca-Cola. Commercial development, though, from television coverage to shirt sponsorship, remained limited.

The same was true, albeit for political rather than economic reasons, in Eastern Europe. Behind the Iron Curtain, the commercial imperatives of capitalist football were, in theory at least, rejected. Even under Yugoslavia's "self-management socialism," in which consumer society was relatively open to outside influences, the introduction of professional football in the late 1960s was framed in terms that separated it from Western practices. In countries such as East Germany, the Western model was explicitly rejected. The collapse of communism in the region between 1989 and 1991 over- turned socialist complacencies. It opened Eastern Europe, like the rest of the world, to football in the age of neo-liberalism.

If there was an economic revolution in football, it can be located in the game's globalization since the 1990s. Many statistics illustrate the point. FIFA's total income between 1979 and 1982 was US$70 million. Between 2007 and 2010, it was US$3 billion, a more than fortyfold increase. In 1990 Italian Roberto Baggio controversially joined Juventus from Fiorentina for a world record transfer fee of 8 million Euros. In the summer of 2017, when Brazil's Neymar moved from Barcelona to Paris Saint-Germain, the new world record was 222 million Euros, more than twenty-five times what Baggio had cost twenty-seven years earlier.

Startling commercial growth fostered startling levels of inequality. In 2006/07 the total value of Europe's football market was an estimated 13.6 billion Euros. The five biggest leagues, in England, France, Germany, Italy, and Spain, generated more than half of this amount (7.1 billion Euros). The chief driver of increased wealth and its increasingly unequal distribution was television. In 1984, English football earned 2.4 million Euros from its free-to-air contracts with the BBC and ITV. The deal negotiated between the Premier League and satellite company Sky for the 2007–10 period was over a thousand times more valuable, at 2.7 billion Euros. Over an eight-year period, the total value of two television deals in Eastern Europe's largest post-communist market, Russia, was 25 million Euros. Outside Europe, TV contracts were even more modest. Nigeria's record-breaking deal in 2005, for example, was worth US$2 million. The neo-liberal turn created, sometimes quite literally, less equal playing fields. When a new ground was built in the Ukrainian resort town of Slavs'ke before the 2012 European Championship (which Ukraine cohosted with Poland), it was built on public land, but quickly privatized. The pristine pitch was ring-fenced and guarded by a security company. Few locals could afford the fees required to use the facility. As a consequence, it mostly lies unused—in contrast to the Soviet era, when venues such as Kiev's Respublikansky Stadion hosted fitness classes as well as football matches and, like public squares, were open to everyone.

Inequalities manifested themselves in multiple ways. There were transcontinental discrepancies, most notably the growing gap between West European and South American football, itself reflective of the socio-economic divide between the Global North and the Global South. There were regional discrepancies, for example between Western and Eastern Europe (as illustrated by the clubs who dominated UEFA's European Cup after its 1992 rebranding as the Champions League) or between the wealthiest African leagues (above all, South Africa's Premier Soccer League) and impoverished counterparts elsewhere on the continent. There were imbalances in national competitions, as seen in the gulf separating transnational super clubs such as Bayern Munich or Barcelona and Real Madrid from their German or Spanish competitors. Finally, a funding chasm separated elite men's football from women's football and the amateur game. In an age of unprecedented wealth at the top of English football, the number of adult recreational players dropped from 2.02 million in 2005 to 1.84 million in 2014.

Football's commercial revolution has not gone unchallenged. Supporters' groups have resisted "hyper-commodification," from the Liverpool fans who staged a walkout during a game in 2016 in protest against rising ticket prices to the hardcore "cheering club" (*porra*) supporters of Mexico City's Pumas, who campaigned against Nike's influence on the club in the early 2000s. Nor has football necessarily, or consistently, caused the economic transformation often ascribed to it. The oft-repeated argument that "money has ruined football" may have currency at the top of the men's game, but it is neither entirely new nor entirely correct. For most players and spectators, the game's fundamentals have altered little since the late nineteenth century. If money has changed football, it might also be claimed that football—a game where profit means little without trophies or promotions—has changed money. It remains difficult to monetize even the biggest clubs as one might monetize global businesses such as Apple. Twenty-first century football is hardly the model student of neo-liberal economic orthodoxy.

From Amateurs to Professionals

Modern football's roots as an amateur pastime for social elites shaped the contested emergence of professionalism. The codified version of the game hammered out in debates at Cambridge University, public schools, and English FA headquarters was quickly localized and nationalized in the late nineteenth century. It thereby spread far beyond privileged confines. The elites, many of whom remained stakeholders in football associations and clubs, rarely welcomed the noisy intrusion of the masses. The FA's decision to professionalize English football in 1885, as already noted, was about limiting not escalating wage demands. The wave of professionalization after the First World War was motivated by similar damage-limitation strategies. In places such as Argentina, Brazil, and Uruguay, this was a class struggle between players from largely modest backgrounds and the elites who ran the game. Following a players' strike in 1931, Argentina became the first country outside Europe to adopt professionalism. Players, like their counterparts in England in 1885, won the right to be paid openly, but they did not gain freedom of contract (i.e., the right to decide when they might leave a club and where they might go).

Advocates of amateurism did not go quietly into the night. When the Yugoslavian FA introduced professionalism in 1935, parts of the kingdom opposed the move. Hostility in Slovenia came largely from the nationalist Sokol gymnastics movement, which saw football as a morally inferior, violent rival to its own amateur clubs and programs. In Austria, the prime opponent of the switch to professionalism in 1924 was the social-democratic Amateur Footballers' Association, which sought, like workers' sports organizations elsewhere in Europe, to mobilize proletarian support for selfless socialist amateurism. Attempts to create a "red" football culture, though, were doomed, given the sport's popularity in Vienna. Neither left nor right could ultimately prevent athletes from being paid. FIFA had adhered to amateurism in the 1920s, but stopped regulating it in 1932, returning any problems to national associations. By 1937, an estimated two-thirds of Austria's professional footballers came from two working-class districts of Vienna, Favoriten and Floridsdorf.

No leading football nation resisted professionalism longer than Germany. West Germany only introduced a professional league in 1963. The East German Oberliga was founded in 1949. Nominally home to socialist amateurs, it had some of the trappings of professional competition in the capitalist West, but fully professional structures only arrived in 1991, after communism's collapse and the eastward extension of the Bundesliga. Suspicion of professionalism crossed epochs and ideologies. The conservative DFB leadership voted in 1925 to boycott matches against countries such as Austria, Czechoslovakia, and Hungary where football had been professionalized. Much of its subsequent support for Nazism came from the Hitler regime's (nominal) opposition to professional football. The post-1945 communists in East Germany predictably condemned the capitalist structures and wage slavery of the professional game. More surprisingly, hostility to professionalism survived in prosperous, capitalist West Germany. When Hamburg striker Uwe Seeler refused a lucrative move to Inter Milan in 1961, he was widely praised for his humility and loyalty.

Fulminations against professionalism hid more complex realities. In the Weimar Republic (1919–33), the DFB's business concerns and political convictions were not easily separated. The result was an economic system full of double standards. While the DFB profited handsomely from match ticket sales, players were denied the same benefits. In 1930, Schalke, a popular team from the coal-mining region of the Ruhr, was accused of making illegal payments to fourteen players. The players were banned. Schalke contested the 1930/31 season with a reserve squad. It was no accident that when the authorities acted to defend amateurism, it targeted a club from a working-class city (Gelsenkirchen) mired in economic depression, where players and fans saw the game as a means of escape from life down the mines.

Money was no less a minefield in East German football. Like the DFB in the Weimar and Nazi eras, the East German FA publically rejected the mercenary practices of professional sport. There were no transfers, only state-sanctioned "delegations." Even the best players, according to the party line, were amateurs, with jobs in the state organizations (such as the police and the railways) that ran football clubs. Money was the elephant in the room. When writer Erich Loest spent time with the Lokomotive Leipzig team, as research for his 1969 novel *Der elfte Mann*, he noted that, once a month, a man called "Uncle" paid the players out of a large suitcase full of cash. "The *Oberliga* players of the GDR were professionals, everyone knew it, and nobody talked about it."[3]

The German Democratic Republic (GDR) kept up the pretence of amateurism longer than other socialist states, but even communist hardliners accepted de facto professionalism as the price to pay for competing on the international stage. For all that players in Eastern Europe made less than their counterparts in the West, high-earning celebrities thrived on both sides of the Cold War divide. In the early 1950s, the Yugoslav authorities condemned football's slide toward professionalism. Ineffective "Courts for the Protection of Amateurism" were established to hand out life bans to players who were paid to play. By the late 1960s, the regime had bowed to the inevitable and introduced professionalism. Star players such as Dragoslav Šekularac and Mustafa Hasanagić, like their peers in England and West Germany, were already pop cultural icons, appearing in movies and making records.

Economic pressures led the transition from amateur to professional football, but never in isolation from political and societal factors, such as class and race. Socialist ideals of amateurism—whether from the Soviet Proletkultists who rejected all forms of capitalist sport or the English socialists who sought to outflank "gentlemanly amateurism"—lost out to a commercialized model of professional sport. But the workers' sport movement did not go down without a fight. When Brazil introduced professionalism in 1933, it was tied to attempts by Getúlio Vargas's government to forge a multiracial Brazilian identity. Black and mixed-race players soon featured prominently in the national team and at leading clubs in Rio de Janeiro and São Paulo. Professional football arguably served as a form of black emancipation.

In contrast to South America and Central Europe, much of north-western Europe—Germany, the Netherlands, and Scandinavia—resisted professionalism. These were affluent capitalist societies, in which hostility to the idea of paying athletes was anchored in fiscal and social conservatism. When the Dutch FA reluctantly allowed professionalism in 1954, its hand was forced by players and coaches frustrated by the backward state of Dutch football.

Where did the path to professionalism eventually lead? The modern superstar footballer, such as Lionel Messi or Cristiano Ronaldo, has an earning capacity to rival international film and pop stars. David Beckham married a pop star, wore a sarong, and cashed in on almost any commercial opportunity. Beckham's fame transcended the global game. It suggested new forms of masculinity (see Chapter 5) and confirmed the entrance of elite footballers into the world of the super rich. Though his performances for Manchester United and Real Madrid were characterized by an impeccable work ethic, Beckham, rightly or wrongly, came to stand for the excess consumption that accompanied football's commercial revolution.

Beckham's was an extreme case, but the pattern after the 1990s was unmistakable. Top clubs spent more on wages. Players, in turn, became increasingly remote from real-world economic realities. Wage bills in the English Premier League more than quadrupled between 1993/94 and 2002/03. It was a similar story in Spain's La Liga. Wage inflation was a key factor in European football's economic crisis in the early to mid 2000s. As salaries consumed up to 90 per cent of turnover, many high-profile clubs— Fiorentina and Napoli in Italy, Borussia Dortmund in Germany—filed for bankruptcy. Top players emerged unscathed. In 2018, one of the world's biggest spenders, Paris Saint-Germain, paid 332 million Euros in wages. The highest earner, Neymar, took home 600,000 Euros per week.

Beneath the thin crust of wealth, the narrative of professionalization— and the economic status of the modern footballer—looked very different. Extractive relations between the Global North and the Global South meant an exodus of elite players from Africa and South America to Europe, chronic indebtedness and underinvestment, and vast inequalities. For those who stayed at home, football was often a precarious livelihood. In the early 2000s, almost 90 per cent of Brazil's 23,000 professionals earned less than £100 per month. Average earnings in Brazil's top division were no more than double the national minimum wage. In 2004, Uruguayan footballers, many of whom earned less than US$50 per month, went on strike. They demanded, and eventually received, a minimum monthly wage of US$400. Similar strikes occurred in Argentina and Chile. Not only were wages low in such countries, they were not always paid. Nigerian football was professionalized in 1990. Labour conditions worsened, as players lost state protection from both free market practices and inept or corrupt management. Players at clubs such as Enugu Rangers and Sunshine Stars went on strike to claim unpaid wages, signing-on fees, and bonuses. In 2013, the players' union claimed that Nigerian clubs owed players and coaches 888,803 million naira (approximately US$2.5 million). In such circumstances, it is easy to imagine how footballers might be tempted to supplement their incomes illegally. Corruption, though, sprang more often from wealth than poverty.

Scandals

In July 2006 in Berlin's Olympic Stadium, Italy defeated France on penalties to win the World Cup for the fourth time. Joyous celebrations could not keep a darker story out of the news. Shortly before the tournament, police uncovered evidence of a match-fixing scandal centred on Italy's richest and most successful team, Juventus. *Calciopoli*, as the scandal came to be known, revealed a murky world where club and match officials colluded to ensure that certain referees were picked for certain games. The football federation's investigation was published less than two weeks after the win in Berlin. Juventus was relegated to the second division and stripped of the last two *scudetti* (league titles). Three other clubs, AC Milan, Fiorentina, and Lazio, received lesser punishments. Subsequent revelations suggested that the corrupt system led by disgraced former Juventus general director Luciano Moggi went much further, and lasted much longer, than the 2006 scandal revealed. Italian football, historian John Foot concluded, had become akin to American professional wrestling: hugely popular but "violent, over-the-top, ridiculous, hysterical and completely fake."[4]

Calciopoli resulted from the vast sums that flowed into Italian football from the 1990s onwards. The chief recipient, Juventus, used its financial power to build the "Moggi system," controlling match officials, journalists, and player agents. However, bribery and match-fixing had a much longer history in Italian football. Torino was stripped of the league championship in 1927 for allegedly bribing Juventus defender Luigi Allemandi ahead of a game between the Turin rivals. During the 1960s and 1970s, Italian clubs such as Inter Milan attempted to bribe officials in European competitions. In 1980, an illegal gambling scandal (Totonero) broke. It involved thirty-three Serie A players, bookmakers, and two match fixers. Though the players accused of selling matches for money escaped prosecution ("sporting fraud" only became a criminal offence in 1989), they were banned from football for between three months and six years. AC Milan and Lazio, the two clubs most heavily implicated, were relegated to Serie B. These scandals, spanning almost a century of football, were the tip of the iceberg. The notorious fixer and Perugia president Luciano Gaucci once remarked, "Eighty per cent of the games in Italy are fixed."[5]

Italy was not alone. Corruption in the modern game has been an international phenomenon. Through illegal gambling syndicates, it has become increasingly transnational too. UEFA reported in 2007 that Asian betting companies regularly manipulated top-flight games. A ninety-six-page dossier noted corruption in Europe's domestic leagues and in UEFA competitions, involving clubs from Italy, the Czech Republic, Georgia, and Greece. Twenty-six matches were allegedly fixed between 2005 and 2007.

Corruption has touched all of the sport's actors, from powerful institutions to players, referees, coaches, administrators, and viewers. It has transcended political borders—there were, for example, match-fixing scandals in communist Yugoslavia and capitalist West Germany in 1965—and historical epochs. There was no age of innocence. In 1915, as sportsmen were mobilized for the "Great Game" of the First World War, seven players from Liverpool and Manchester United received lifetime bans for illegally gambling on a match between the two teams. Relegation-threatened Manchester United won by the prearranged scoreline, 2–0. Once the goals were scored, the ball was persistently kicked out of play. Liverpool missed a penalty. A Liverpool player not in on the scheme was shouted at for almost scoring late in the game.

In the history of football corruption, there are more grey areas than smoking guns. Suspicion clouded Argentina's 6–0 win over a talented Peru side at the 1978 World Cup, a result which allowed the hosts to advance to the final on goal difference. Peru fielded four reserves and played poorly. Argentina sent 35,000 tons of grain to its fellow junta in Peru and unfroze US$50 million in bank credits. It probably sent arms too. However, there is no hard evidence that bribes, rather than trade deals, were made. Recent scandals at FIFA (discussed below) show that corruption can be hard to prove and even harder to analyze.

In April 1971, Horst-Gregorio Canellas, a banana exporter and president of the recently relegated Bundesliga club Kickers Offenbach, played an audio tape to DFB officials at a garden party. The contents were sensational. Canellas had recorded phone conversations with players from Hertha Berlin and Cologne in which they offered to throw matches in Offenbach's favour for large sums of money. Subsequent DFB investigations found that eight matches during the 1970/71 season were fixed. Fifty-two players from seven clubs—including most of the squads of Eintracht Braunschweig, Hertha, and Schalke—were found guilty of taking money to throw games. Among the eight coaches and officials punished for their roles in the scandal was the whistle-blower himself, Horst-Gregorio Canellas.

Was the 1971 scandal produced by an unjust system in which players were short-changed by the hypocritical DFB, which (as in the Weimar and Nazi eras) filled its coffers while guarding against unfettered professionalism? Or was it a case of players' greed? In West Germany as elsewhere, individual corruption was not easily separated from systemic issues. The 1965 match-fixing scandal in Yugoslavia centred on Bosnian team Željezničar Sarajevo, which threw two matches against relegation-threatened teams from Croatia, Hajduk Split and Trešnjevka Zagreb. Financial inducements were bound up with the complexities of nationalist politics in multi-ethnic Yugoslavia. Hajduk was one of the country's most popular teams and a potent symbol of Croatian nationalism. The Željezničar striker, and later Yugoslav national team coach, Ivica Osim, who was banned for his role in the affair, recalled the pressure on his team to ensure that Hajduk won.

In apartheid South Africa, the dispute in the blacks-only Durban and District African Football Association (DDAFA) during the 1950s focused on controversial businessman Henry Ngwenya. Ngwenya siphoned gate-receipt money to fund a patronage network that modernized Durban football. He hired professional coaches, organized overseas tours, and awarded match-day catering contracts to his restaurant. Ngwenya reinforced his power base with populist campaigns that pitted working-class, Zulu-speaking officials against the educated, English-speaking "elites" on the DDAFA executive who, rightly, questioned his financial probity. Ngwenya's abuse of power was not only about individual corruption. It revealed class and race tensions that impeded the development of black South African football. By 1960, the once powerful DDAFA was falling apart.

Henry Ngwenya was a product of the limited opportunities for black advancement in apartheid South Africa. "Big men" like him, frequently from business backgrounds, were ubiquitous in the modern game. Used to getting their way, they frequently overstepped the line between acceptable and unacceptable practices. Bernard Tapie combined business, football, and politics to become one of France's richest men. In 1986 he became chairman of one of the country's biggest clubs, Olympique de Marseille. In 1989 he entered parliament as a socialist deputy. In 1990 he purchased Adidas. Under Tapie's leadership, Marseille spent heavily. It won the league title five years in a row (1989–94) and in 1993 became the first French club to win the European Cup. Things quickly collapsed. Tapie was accused of offering bribes to Valenciennes players before a league match in the 1992/93 season. A subsequent criminal investigation into Tapie's activities as Marseille chairman found him guilty of bribery, tax evasion, and false accounting. He was declared bankrupt and sent to prison.

The commercial interests underpinning corruption did not always have such recognizable faces as Bernard Tapie. Individuals emerged as the central figures in news stories on scandals, but they were symptomatic of deeper problems. In 2005 São Paulo police accused one of Brazil's top referees, Edilson, of agreeing to throw more than twenty league matches. In the same year, a scandal broke in German football. Second division referee Robert Hoyzer was imprisoned for his role in fixing league and cup games. Hoyzer became the public face of the 2005 scandal, but other referees were involved too. The match-fixing organizers were members of a Croatian gambling syndicate with ties to organized crime. Edilson's case was one among many in a football culture of corrupt co-dependencies, which included players, referees, administrators, and the media. Multiple government inquiries into match-fixing, tax evasion, and money laundering revealed the rotten core of Brazilian football. They implicated successive heads of the football federation as well as national team coach Vanderlei Luxemburgo. The chair of a 2001 Senate inquiry noted that "there is hardly a form of illegal activity that we haven't come across."[6]

Amid hand-wringing from the media and politicians, there have been regular calls to "clean up" football. Between 2004 and 2006, there were match-fixing scandals in twelve countries. They included Brazil, Italy, and Germany (as discussed above), as well as Finland, Greece, China, and Thailand. Corruption got so bad in Ukraine that the football association imported match officials to ensure that games were run cleanly. In 2013, Interpol's football anti-corruption unit identified an Asian crime syndicate that was accused of fixing 380 matches in Europe and 300 more worldwide.

Transparency, though, is easier to discuss than enact. There are four problem areas. First, stronger regulation has its dark side in the form of increased surveillance and social control. Second, some argue that transparency runs counter to the logic of football culture. This is a game built on subjectivity and a ruthless quest for advantage that includes a range of questionable activities, from diving for a penalty to doping and match-fixing. Third, the global availability of online gambling—weakly policed, hugely popular (especially in Asia), and with opportunities to bet, in theory at least, on any aspect of any professional match around the world—has shifted the goalposts. In deregulated markets where transnational corporations often hold more sway than national governments, fiscal accountability can seem impossible to achieve (and, for many stakeholders, undesirable). Fourth and finally, transparency requires transparent institutions. It is hard to imagine greater probity when many of the biggest scandals involve the organization that runs the world game.

There is insufficient space in this short book to list the corruption allegations that have dogged FIFA since João Havelange took office in 1974. They have involved FIFA sponsors—both as accomplices and victims. Adidas, for example, played kingmaker by supporting Havelange in the 1974 presidential election, while MasterCard was awarded US$90 million in 2006 after a US court ruled that FIFA had lied during contract negotiations. FIFA scandals have implicated high-ranking executives, many of whom, like the disgraced Trinidadian president of the Confederation of North, Central

America and Caribbean Association Football (CONCACAF), Jack Warner, were influential figures in regional confederations. They have circled back to FIFA's marketing partner from 1982 until its collapse in 2001, the Adidas-backed Swiss company, International Sport and Leisure. Investigations have revealed the depth and breadth of FIFA's global network of graft: vote rigging in presidential elections and World Cup bids, false expense claims, bribery, tax evasion, embezzlement, and the illegal sale of World Cup tickets. The dam broke in 2015, when US prosecutors announced the results of an investigation into fraud and money laundering. Seven FIFA executives were arrested in Zürich in May. Further arrests followed around the world. Among those charged were former FIFA vice-presidents; heads of CONCACAF and CONMEBOL; heads of the Venezuelan, Nicaraguan, Brazilian, Costa Rican, and Cayman Islands football associations; and the American sports marketing company, Traffic. The 2015 scandal revealed the sleazy elements in football's story of globalization. Mired in corruption allegations since taking office in 1998, FIFA President Sepp Blatter was finally forced to resign.

Owners, Sponsors, and Television

For much of its history, Liverpool FC, like most clubs around the world, was locally owned. Founded in 1892, the club had John Houlding as its original chairman. A brewer and landlord in the Liverpool 4 district, Houlding owned the Anfield stadium that became Liverpool's home. After Houlding died in 1902, club ownership passed to a group of modestly wealthy local businessmen. There it remained for much of the twentieth century. There was a rotating cast of chairmen, the two most successful of whom, T.V. Williams (1956–64) and John Smith (1973–90), helped the club to become a dominant national and international force.

Liverpool's supremacy ended in the 1990s, just as the English game was transformed via television money and the Premier League into a lucrative product. Poor results, the success of rivals Manchester United, and the arrival in English football of Russian oligarch Roman Abramovich (who bought Chelsea in 2003) encouraged the club to seek outside investment. In 2007, Chairman David Moores—whose retail and football betting empire, Littlewoods, had supported the club for over fifty years—sold the majority of his shares to American businessmen Tom Hicks and George Gillett. Both men had dabbled in North American sports team ownership. Neither had much football experience. This was emphasized in Gillett's early description of the club as a "franchise" and Hicks's later comparison of the purchase of Liverpool to the leveraged buyout of the breakfast cereal company Weetabix. The takeover was built on a financial house of cards. Three years of turmoil ensued. The two businessmen fell out. They clashed with their creditors. Supporters mobilized against the American "cowboys" (see Chapter 9). In 2010, after much High Court wrangling and with bankruptcy imminent, Hicks and Gillett's creditors forced through the sale of the club to New England–based sports investment company and owner of the Boston Red Sox, Fenway Sports Group. FSG brought financial stability and a savvier exploitation of Liverpool's global commercial potential. Success on the field eventually followed. Under manager Jürgen Klopp, Liverpool reached the Champions League final in 2018 (losing to Real Madrid) before claiming its sixth European Cup with a 2–0 win over Tottenham Hotspur in 2019.

Liverpool's story was a familiar one in the early years of the twenty-first century. The campaign against George Gillett and Tom Hicks ran almost concurrently with an anti-ownership mobilization at Manchester United in response to the 2005 takeover of the club by American businessman Malcolm Glazer and his family. Manchester United continued to win trophies under foreign ownership, but Glazer's financial strategy, which leveraged acquisition debts onto the club, was unpopular. Elsewhere, Austrian energy drink company Red Bull effaced the lines between ownership and sponsorship. Between 2005 and 2009, Red Bull purchased and renamed clubs in Austria, Brazil, Germany, and the United States.

Red Bull's acquisition of the playing rights of the small German club SSV Markranstädt, and the club's rapid transformation into the wealthy and successful Bundesliga club RB Leipzig, was rightly criticized for cynically manoeuvring around DFB rules on club licensing. Corporate ownership of German teams, though, was not new. Employees of one of the world's largest pharmaceutical companies, Bayer, founded Bayer Leverkusen in 1904. VfL Wolfsburg emerged after 1945 from a works team at the local Volkswagen factory.

Company clubs exist throughout football. From 1928 to 2015, the car manufacturer Peugeot owned the French club FC Sochaux. The company openly paid Sochaux's players, created a breakaway competition (the Peugeot Cup) in 1930, and effectively forced the French federation to introduce a professional league in 1932. The "Old Lady" of Italian football, Juventus, is the most famous works team of all. Since 1923, the club has been owned by one of Italy's largest companies, the car manufacturer FIAT. FIAT symbolized Italian capitalism, just as Juventus symbolized Italian football. The club built a huge following among southern immigrants who came to Turin after the Second World War to work in FIAT factories.

Corporate ownership of a different sort existed behind the Iron Curtain. In communist countries, where private business was outlawed or marginalized, state-run industries and institutions supported football clubs. This became a transnational model of sorts, as Soviet club names were exported to Eastern Europe after 1945. The most infamous example was Dinamo/Dynamo, the name given to police clubs from Moscow to East Berlin. Dynamo teams were sometimes unpopular, usually successful, and always controversial. The head of the Soviet secret police between 1938 and 1945, the Georgian Lavrentiy Beria, was a football fan. He became, in Robert Edelman's words, "the Soviet equivalent of a meddling capitalist team owner," a combination of J. Edgar Hoover and George Steinbrenner in one intimidating package.[7] When his favourite team, Dinamo Tbilisi, lost a cup semi-final to Spartak Moscow in 1938, Beria ordered that the game be replayed—three weeks *after* Spartak won the final. After Spartak won the semi-final for a second time, even Beria accepted defeat.

Party bosses like Beria often acted as "local patriots," trying to ensure victory for their team by hook or by crook. For all of the influence exerted by powerful corporate entities (whether capitalist or communist), club ownership around the world has been, and remains, overwhelmingly local in its composition and interests. For every super-rich club such as Manchester City—owned since 2008 by the Abu Dhabi Investment Group—there are thousands of clubs in local hands. In countries such as Germany and Spain, an associative ownership model has ensured that even large clubs such as Bayern Munich and Barcelona remain embedded in large, primarily local sporting communities. Lower down the food chain, overseas ownership is rare. Of the twenty-four professional clubs in League Two, English football's fourth tier, only two, Blackpool and Coventry City, were owned or partly owned by foreign investors in 2018. More clubs (three) were owned by supporters' trusts (i.e., by fans themselves).

In recent decades, there has been considerable and often successful resistance against incompetent, unaccountable, and corrupt club owners, whether local or foreign. AFC Wimbledon was founded in 2002 after the original Wimbledon FC was relocated from South London to Milton Keynes (90 kilometres north) and renamed MK Dons—a rare case of North American–style franchise relocation that was widely resented. After starting life in the ninth tier of the football pyramid, AFC Wimbledon competed in League One in the 2018/19 season, one division higher than the upstart MK Dons. In protest against the Glazer takeover at Manchester United in 2005, supporters' groups formed FC United of Manchester. Kitted in green and gold, the colours of the Newton Heath team that preceded Manchester United, the breakaway club rose steadily through the ranks of semi-professional football.

Fan ownership models in Manchester and Wimbledon have global imitators. There are supporter-owned clubs in Australia, Japan, Indonesia, and Mali. Involvement can take a variety of forms, some more altruistic than others. It remains vulnerable to outside commercial interests—and, increasingly, to the challenges of the digital age. Hapoel Kiryat Shalom FC, a lower-league club in the Israeli capital Tel Aviv, made headlines in 2007 when it became the first interactively managed (though not interactively owned) football team. Supporters voted free online on all manner of issues, including team selection, via the company, Web2Sport, that had purchased the club. The system, predictably, was open to abuse. Fans of rival teams were accused of substituting Hapoel's striker during games. Web2Sport closed in 2008, as the high-tech market crashed during the global economic crisis.

For much of the first century of football's existence, sponsorship was tied to players not clubs. In the 1920s, for example, Spain's goalkeeper Ricardo Zamora was the face of the drink Anís Zamora, while Everton striker Dixie Dean sold Player's cigarettes. Recompense was usually modest, even for the biggest stars. Commodification gathered pace in the 1960s, even in unlikely places. A 1965 magazine advertisement shows a smiling Difference Mbanya, captain of the black South African team Moroka Swallows, alongside a bottle of beer and the message "Guinness gives me POWER—keeps me scoring."[8] In subsequent decades, advertising became more visible in the stadium, via hoardings and shirt sponsorship.

Football's sponsorship revolution began in the 1990s. Deals got bigger and more transnational. Stadiums no longer sold only pitch-side advertising and corporate boxes. They sold themselves, via the granting of stadium "naming rights" to commercial partners. The world's leading clubs no longer had one sponsor but an army of backers. Barcelona had no shirt sponsor before 2006 and was then sponsored by UNICEF until 2011. In 2018, the club's website listed no fewer than forty-seven sponsors. These ranged from "main sponsors" Nike (US) and Rakuten (Japan) through "premium" and "official" partners to a swathe of "regional partners." Such corporate support helped Barcelona to increase its annual wage bill by 42 per cent, becoming the first club in world football to break the 500 million Euro mark in payments to players.

The dense web of commercial networks created conflicts of interest. The 1998 World Cup final pitted French star Zinedine Zidane against Brazil's brilliant striker Ronaldo. It also pitted France's kit sponsor, Adidas, against Nike, which had in 1996 signed a ten-year deal with the *seleção* worth £250 million. On the morning of the game, Ronaldo—the face of Nike's pre-tournament advertising campaign—suffered a seizure. He was medicated and initially declared unfit for the final that evening. When the game kicked off, though, Ronaldo was in Brazil's line-up. France won 3–0. Zidane scored twice; a struggling Ronaldo barely touched the ball. Rumours that Nike forced Ronaldo to play were denied by both company and player. This did not prevent a parliamentary inquiry into Nike's powerful role in Brazilian sport. Its findings on the 1998 World Cup final were inconclusive. Corporate collusion was not proved, but it was not disproved either.

Such stories suggest that football's hyper-commodification has long since gone into overdrive. A cartel of West European clubs (self-styled in the early 2000s as the G-14) dominates the commercial and sporting landscape. It monopolizes global competitions and global sponsors. It maintains a controlled degree of "uncertainty of outcome," while excluding outsiders and maximizing profits.

Partly in response to this cartelization and to the "financial doping" that it permitted, Europe's governing body, UEFA, introduced financial fair play (FFP) regulations in 2010. FFP sought to ensure that teams entering UEFA competitions adhered to a "break-even rule." This meant spending no more on wages and transfers than they earned from "football-related activities." Early research suggests that, far from redressing competitive imbalance, FFP cemented the advantages of elite clubs skilled in creative accounting and wealthy enough to brush off meagre fines or temporary transfer bans. Those most heavily penalized under the new system for "overdue payables" (i.e., unpaid debts) were not super-rich clubs, such as Chelsea or Manchester City, but smaller, insolvent clubs from countries with weak national associations. Serbia's Partizan Belgrade, for example, received a one-year ban from UEFA competitions in 2017 for contravening FFP regulations. It was overturned on appeal to the independent Court of Arbitration for Sport. Such clubs tended to survive, but they rarely made money. In an era of great wealth creation, and even greater wealth inequality, football remained an unusual kind of business.

What made football so attractive to multinational sponsors and wealthy investors? The short answer was television. FIFA's television revenues for the 1978 World Cup in Argentina were US$40 million. The combined

TV revenues for the 2002 and 2006 tournaments (in Japan/Korea and Germany, respectively) were almost fifty times higher, at US$1.7 billion. Similar increases marked other international competitions. Revenues from the 1960 European Cup final were 8,000 Euros. The 2005/06 Champions League tournament earned more than 400 million Euros—50,000 times the 1960 figure—in TV and sponsorship deals.

Domestic competitions experienced the same boom, as television deals moved from free-to-air packages (prevalent until the 1980s) to pay-TV and cable providers. Television rights for the German Bundesliga were worth 40 million Deutschmarks in 1988/89. The five-year deal that the DFB signed with KirchMedia in 1992 was worth 700 million DM, or 140 million DM per season. In England in 1984, top-flight clubs earned 2.6 million Euros per season from TV deals with free-to-air providers. The three-year domestic TV deal signed with cable TV provider Sky in 2001 was worth 1.46 billion Euros (or more than 485 million Euros per season).

The glut of television money often exacerbated inequalities. In Spain until 2016, clubs negotiated separate rather than collective television deals. Spain's two largest clubs, Barcelona and Real Madrid, signed seven-year deals with Mediapro in 2007 worth 1 billion and 1.1 billion Euros, respectively, far outstripping the deals arranged by smaller clubs. This had knock-on effects on clubs' spending on wages and transfers, reinforcing competitive imbalance in La Liga. Between 2007 and 2016, only Atlético Madrid (once in 2013/14) broke the stranglehold the "Big Two" had on the league title.

Domestic inequalities paled alongside international ones. Since the 1990s, television money has played the primary role in separating Europe's biggest leagues (in England, France, Germany, Italy, and Spain) from smaller competitions, many of which (in the Netherlands and Scotland, for example) previously punched above their weight. TV rights generated half of the total income in the "big five" leagues in 2004. In smaller competitions, they accounted for 13 per cent of total income. Belgium's best-performing teams, for example, earned 1.1 million Euros of TV money per season. Television netted England's richest club, Manchester United, 83.6 million Euros per season.

Outside Europe, the discrepancies were greater. The sale of international broadcasting rights for the behemoth of televised football, the Premier League, popularized English football in such countries as Indonesia and Thailand. It left less space on television, and in the public imagination, for lower-standard, cash-strapped domestic leagues. In Africa during the

1990s, transnational satellite channels such as Supersport (English) and Canal Horizon (French) significantly increased the number of European matches shown on television, especially as top leagues were importing so many African players. The results, as one Nigerian sportswriter noted, were clear: "When you look at the stadiums you'll find that the stands are virtually empty, while the bars and the joints that have satellite TV are full. People will pay to watch the Premier League on TV but not to watch Nigerian football live."[9] For many scholars, this marginalization of local competition, both as live and television spectacle, was a form of cultural imperialism. Global football's premier competitions were at once the life-blood and death knell of the world game.

Notes

1 Arthur Hopcraft, *The Football Man* (1968; London: Aurum Press, 2006), 18.

2 Quoted in Goldblatt, *The Ball Is Round*, 452.

3 Quoted in Alan McDougall, *The People's Game: Football, State and Society in East Germany* (Cambridge: Cambridge University Press, 2014), 67.

4 Foot, *Calcio*, 534.

5 Quoted in Foot, *Calcio*, 240.

6 Quoted in Larry Rohter, "Huge Soccer Scandal Taints National Obsession of Brazil," *New York Times*, May 24, 2001, https://www.nytimes.com/2001/03/24/world/huge-soccer-scandal-taints-national-obsession-of-brazil.html (accessed 18 April 2018).

7 Robert Edelman, *Spartak Moscow: A History of the People's Team in the Workers' State* (Ithaca, NY: Cornell University Press, 2009), 118.

8 Peter Alegi, *Laduma! Soccer, Politics and Society in South Africa, from its Origins to 2010*, 2nd ed. (Scottsville: University of Kwa-Zulu Natal Press, 2010), 97.

9 Gerard Akindes quoted in Alegi, *African Soccerscapes*, 107.

4 | Competitions

At first glance, much more than decades and continents seem to separate the first World Cup, held in Uruguay in 1930, and the nineteenth edition of the tournament, hosted by South Africa in 2010 (see Table 4.1). FIFA's inaugural global competition featured thirteen teams. Only four came from Europe, often without their best players. In the shadow of the Great Depression, many European nations cried poverty. Italian newspaper *La Gazetta dello Sport* devoted just twenty lines of print to the final of a high-scoring tournament. One hundred thousand people watched Uruguay's 4–2 win over Argentina at the Estadio Centenario in Montevideo. The tournament's average attendance was a little under 33,000. Eight cameramen filmed the final, but it was largely a radio and print media event. The tournament made FIFA a modest profit, enough to encourage a repeat in Italy four years later. Beyond the bidding process, though, FIFA's involvement in the first World Cup was minimal.

The 2010 World Cup, the first in Africa, featured thirty-two teams, drawn from all six continental federations. The best teams and best players were present. There was saturation media coverage of a low-scoring tournament. South Africa became the first host country to fail to reach the knock-out stages. The dour final between Spain and the Netherlands featured fourteen yellow cards but only one goal, as Andrés Iniesta's extra-time strike in Johannesburg's Soccer City Stadium crowned Spain world champions for the first time. Average attendance was just under 50,000, but ticket allocation was widely criticized. Black, working-class South Africans saw

TABLE 4.1 World Cups, 1930–2018

Year	Host	Winner	Runner-Up	Participants	Goals per Game	Average Crowd
1930	Uruguay	Uruguay	Argentina	13	3.9	32,808
1934	Italy	Italy	Czechoslovakia	16	4.1	21,352
1938	France	Italy	Hungary	15	4.7	20,872
1950	Brazil	Uruguay	Brazil	13	4.0	47,511
1954	Switzerland	W. Germany	Hungary	16	5.4	29,561
1958	Sweden	Brazil	Sweden	16	3.6	23,423
1962	Chile	Brazil	Czechoslovakia	16	2.8	27,911
1966	England	England	W. Germany	16	2.8	48,847
1970	Mexico	Brazil	Italy	16	3.0	50,124
1974	W. Germany	W. Germany	Netherlands	16	2.6	49,098
1978	Argentina	Argentina	Netherlands	16	2.7	40,678
1982	Spain	Italy	W. Germany	24	2.8	40,571
1986	Mexico	Argentina	W. Germany	24	2.5	46,039
1990	Italy	W. Germany	Argentina	24	2.2	48,388
1994	USA	Brazil	Italy	24	2.7	68,991
1998	France	France	Brazil	32	2.7	43,517
2002	Japan / S. Korea	Brazil	Germany	32	2.5	42,268
2006	Germany	Italy	France	32	2.3	52,491
2010	S. Africa	Spain	Netherlands	32	2.3	49,669
2014	Brazil	Germany	Argentina	32	2.7	52,918
2018	Russia	France	Croatia	32	2.6	47,371

Source: Adapted from https://www.fifa.com/fifa-tournaments/archive/worldcup/index.html.

more games in FIFA-sponsored fan parks than in stadiums. World football's governing body tightly controlled proceedings, from the US$3.2 billion sale of broadcasting rights (up 30 per cent from the 2006 tournament in Germany) to the final totting up of profits. For a US$326 million outlay, FIFA returned tax-free profits of US$4.2 billion.

So far, so different. Yet there were continuities. They reflected the mix of nationalist self-promotion and transnational economic and cultural exchange that has characterized the World Cup in every phase of football's globalization. In Uruguay in 1930 and South Africa eighty years later, international competition served as a showcase. The 1930 tournament celebrated 100 years of Uruguayan independence. This was reflected in the name given to Juan Scasso's showpiece modernist stadium, the Estadio Centenario, and in the wild celebrations that followed victory over Argentina in the final. In South Africa in 2010, the tournament confirmed a rehabilitation process begun in 1995, when the country's white-dominated rugby team hosted and won the World Cup and the country's first black president Nelson Mandela donned a Springboks jersey for the trophy ceremony. A sporting pariah during the apartheid era (see Chapter 6), South Africa could now parade its credentials as a modern nation, capable of running world-class sports events.

Both the 1930 and the 2010 tournaments shaped and reflected transnational connections. FIFA's awarding of the 1930 World Cup to Uruguay broadened football's previously Eurocentric geopolitical base. The final revealed the fierce rivalry between Argentina and Uruguay but also the cross-border exchanges that announced *fútbol rioplatense* (River Plate football) as international football's new standard bearer. Eighty years later, Africa's first World Cup was saturated in pan-African acts and symbols, from the "Africa Unity" kits designed by Puma for the four African teams that it sponsored to the upsurge of local support for the only African team to reach the elimination rounds, Ghana.

Football's global appeal was always embedded in international competition. This allowed players, coaches, and supporters to cross borders. It transformed football as a media spectacle, creating and costing billions of dollars. Little compares to the scope and popularity of football showpieces. The Venice Biennale, one of the world's biggest art exhibitions, had 501,000 visitors in 2015. The annual Hajj pilgrimage attracts 2 million Muslims to the holy city of Mecca in Saudi Arabia. The 2014 World Cup in Brazil had total crowds of 3.43 million. Another 3.2 billion people watched on television.

Focusing primarily on the World Cup, this chapter examines the history of football competitions—how they have been played and organized, how they have been mobilized for political purposes, and how they have shaped and reflected international developments in and beyond sport. It begins with the early years of international competition, as administrators, coaches, and players forged transnational connections. The chapter then focuses on the globalization and politicization of international competition between the early 1930s and the early 1950s. The third section examines the proliferation and commercialization of international competition from the mid-1950s onwards. The chapter concludes with a critique of contemporary football mega-events, beginning with the 1994 World Cup in the United States. It highlights international competition's role in replicating global inequalities, as well as in reinforcing national and, increasingly, post-national identities.

The Early Years, circa 1872–1930

International competition is almost as old as football itself. The first official match, between England and Scotland, took place near Glasgow in 1872. By the end of the decade, Scotland games against the "Auld Enemy" drew crowds of more than 20,000 and required bigger stadiums. Matches were played between women's teams from the same countries in 1881 and, four years later, between men's teams representing Canada and the United States. Football debuted at the Olympics in Paris in 1900. Two years later in Vienna, Austria and Hungary contested the first international match outside Britain. Cross-border encounters between clubs were equally important. Teams from Ontario played American teams at least thirty-seven times between 1884 and 1891. British clubs toured near and far. The London amateur side Corinthians visited South Africa in 1897, winning 21 of the 23 matches that it played. A year later, Scotland's leading amateur club, Queen's Park, undertook the first of three summer tours to Denmark.

Queen's Park and the Corinthians symbolized an era in which international tours were an elite privilege, for the leisured classes and "gentlemen players" only. These footballers, so the story goes, played for the love of the game, evangelizing amateur ideals of fair play. The reality behind this idealistic portrait, as recent research has shown, was more complicated. For its first tour of Denmark in 1898, ostensibly to attend an amateur sports festival, Queen's Park demanded an appearance fee of at least £100. The Corinthians toured Europe, South Africa, Brazil, and North America between 1897 and 1914 and depicted their brand of amateurism in similarly mercenary terms. National federations and host clubs soon grew tired of the club's demands. They realized that better options were available—namely, professional clubs.

From Brazil to Denmark, the next wave of British football tourists was professional. The sports tour was a pre-season or end-of-season ritual that featured in many players' autobiographies. Encounters were often unbalanced. For visiting British teams, tours were money-making and recreational ventures, not opportunities to learn about how other countries played. The highlight of Scottish clubs' pre-1914 tours of Denmark was usually not a match but the trip to Copenhagen's Carlsberg brewery. Host countries, in contrast, soaked up British playing and coaching expertise in order to raise domestic standards.

A lively traffic in international matches predated FIFA's founding in 1904. These were mostly stand-alone "friendly" or exhibition encounters, at best part of a series of tour games in different cities. South America was the trailblazer in creating international tournaments, competitive spectacles with structure and prestigious prizes. The region was an early beneficiary of globalization, as football was diffused from its European heartlands via education, trade, and tours. South American football soon left the "old continent" in its wake. A competition between club teams from Argentina and Uruguay, the Copa Aldao, was first contested in 1916. In the same year, Argentina hosted the world's first transcontinental championship for national teams, the Copa América. As a result of the success of the four-team tournament involving Argentina, Brazil, Chile, and Uruguay, a regional confederation (CONMEBOL) was founded. Both tournament and confederation built transregional connections that outlasted more than a century of political divisions and economic crises.

Europe slowly heeded this football revolution. At the 1924 Paris Olympics, Uruguay's performances transformed the sport's international standing. Sixty thousand people watched *La Celeste* defeat Switzerland 3–0 in the final. Another ten thousand were locked outside the stadium in Paris. Gate receipts for this one match accounted for almost 10 per cent of the takings for the Olympics. Spanish journalist Enrique Carcellach was one of many European observers to rhapsodize about the victors: "I did not suspect football could be brought to this degree of virtuosity, this artistic limit."[1] Uruguay repeated as Olympic champions four years later in Amsterdam, after a titanic two-game struggle with Argentina. Two hundred and fifty thousand ticket requests for the first game, held in a stadium with a forty-thousand capacity, came from across Europe. Following a 1–1 draw, a quarter of the adult Dutch male population applied to watch the replay. FIFA could hardly fail to notice Uruguay's brilliance or football's potential as a spectator sport. Two years later, the first World Cup was held, fittingly, in the country that did the most to internationalize football.

In terms of international club competition, the pioneers came from the other hotbed of world football after 1918, Central Europe. In the prewar Habsburg Empire, the football cultures of Austria, the Czech lands, and Hungary cross-pollinated, creating relationships that outlived the political system in which they were born. The short-passing "Danubian School" of the 1920s came to be associated with Austria's *Wunderteam*, but it was a cross-border phenomenon. The Mitropa Cup, first played in 1927, concentrated on clubs from Vienna, Prague, and Budapest. It was also open to clubs from Italy, Romania, Switzerland, and Yugoslavia. Played every year between 1927 and 1939, the tournament anticipated the European club competitions introduced thirty years later. In an age of rising nationalism, it illustrated football's power as a transnational model of belonging, rooted in shared interests and shared rivalries.

Globalizing (and Politicizing) International Competition, circa 1930–54

By the 1930s, governments of all political stripes recognized the benefits of elite sport. International competitions proliferated. No longer small-scale festivals, they became global events that attracted fans, media, and politicians alike. This was true, most obviously, of the Olympics and the World Cup. It applied to many other competitions, from the transatlantic boxing bouts between American Joe Louis and German Max Schmeling (1936 and 1938) to the Workers' Olympics organized by the Socialist Workers' Sport International in Vienna (1931) and Antwerp (1937) and the quadrennial Women's World Games run by Alice Milliat's International Women's Sport Federation between 1922 and 1934. The propaganda opportunities afforded by international sport were not lost on Europe's dictators. More ink has been spilled on the 1936 Olympics in Berlin than on any other sports event. Hitler attended his first and only game during the football tournament, Germany's shock loss to Norway. But the sport's role in the Olympics—and in Leni Riefenstahl's epic documentary about the games, *Olympia* (1938)—was minor.

Two years earlier, football provided a more extensive testing ground for the interplay between authoritarianism and sport. Hosted by fascist Italy, the 1934 World Cup was the first international football tournament designed as a stage-managed, politicized spectacle. Stadiums such as the Littoriale (Bologna) and the Giovanni Berta (Florence) showcased new architecture (see Chapter 7). Hundreds of thousands of stamps, postcards, cigarette packets, and posters—the latter designed by Mussolini's friend, the Futurist Filippo Marinetti—advertised the tournament. Tourism was encouraged, as travellers from neighbouring countries benefited from subsidized rates for transport and accommodation. The state radio broadcaster sold rights to audio commentaries to European and South American stations. Sixteen teams participated: twelve from Europe, two from South America, the United States, and Egypt.

The political aim in 1934 was clear: to use football as an international platform for Italian fascism. Italy's ascension to the summit of the global game made this task easier. Bologna won the Mitropa Cup in 1932 and 1934. The national team was bolstered by the cosmopolitan experience of Anglophile coach Vittorio Pozzo and the influx of *rimpatriati* from Argentina and Uruguay (see Chapter 2). Ahead of the final, Mussolini asked, "How can Italy not be the champions?"[2] Was this a political threat or a sporting boast? Some historians argue that the home-field advantage in 1934 was nothing unusual. Others claim that corrupt match officials in the pocket of the Italian Football Federation enabled Italy's progress to the title.

Disentangling the sporting and political elements in Italy's triumph is not easy. The fact that the Italian team retained the world title in a hostile environment, Popular Front France in 1938, speaks to the quality of the players at Pozzo's disposal. Echoing fascist rhetoric, Pozzo praised the players' patriotic devotion to duty and discipline. This was a victory, he claimed, for "moral fortitude, the spirit of self-denial, [and] firm willpower."[3] Politics undoubtedly shaded into play in 1934. Italy's most controversial match, the quarter-final victory over Spain in Florence, sparked protests from all corners of the divided Spanish Republic. Spaniards wrote to the "bandit" Mussolini, decrying the corrupt refereeing that handed Italy a bruising 1–0 win. Intrigue coloured the semi-final win over Hugo Meisl's *Wunderteam* as well. Following brutal clashes between government forces and socialists in "red Vienna" in February, a pro-fascist government had come to power in Austria in May. The Austrian consulate, keen to placate its new Italian ally, allegedly warned the team not to try too hard. Italy, with another sympathetic referee in place, won 1–0. The final was against Czechoslovakia, one of the states with most to fear from Mussolini's plans for a Danubian sphere of influence. In front of a partisan crowd of 50,000 at Rome's PNF National Stadium, Italy again benefitted from favourable officiating—most notably a missed handball in the build-up to Angelo Schiavio's decisive goal—to win 2–1. National destiny was fulfilled, by fair means and foul.

Despite the controversies, and the poor crowds for games not featuring Italy, FIFA regarded the 1934 World Cup as a success. The tournament showed that the World Cup was here to stay. For most of the next twenty years, though, attempts to build on the 1934 spectacular were stymied. The 1942 tournament, slated for Berlin, was cancelled. FIFA activities and resources were stripped to the bone during the Second World War. No tournament took place in 1946. The 1950 tournament in Brazil, the first World Cup for twelve years, marked FIFA's re-emergence as a global actor.

The dramatic finale, the national trauma of Brazil's 2–1 defeat to Uruguay in the Maracanã Stadium, obscured the modesty of much of what preceded it. Only thirteen teams appeared for the sixteen-team tournament. The tournaments in Switzerland in 1954, Sweden in 1958, and Chile in 1962 were the last small World Cups. The modest 1954 tournament in neutral Switzerland made for a fascinating contrast with the politicized bombast of the World Cup in Italy twenty years earlier. Affluent and politically stable, Switzerland provided FIFA with a safe pair of hands. In terms of goals per game, the 1954 competition was the most entertaining World Cup in history. It featured two famous matches involving the great Hungarian side of Puskás, Kocsis, and Hidegkuti: the violent 4–2 quarter-final win over Brazil and the shocking 3–2 loss to West Germany in the final at Bern's Wankdorf Stadium. The host nation provided an undemonstrative backdrop to these sporting dramas.

The World Cup was back on track by the mid-1950s, but FIFA's showpiece tournament was not yet a global spectacle. Low participation rates were partly due to travel logistics in an era before long-haul flights were readily available. When England made its World Cup debut in 1950, the thirty-one-hour plane trip to Brazil took in stopovers in Paris, Lisbon, Dakar, and Recife. Low rates also resulted from the inequities of FIFA geopolitics. For non-European teams, withdrawal or non-participation could often be justified on economic and political grounds. It was not until the 1958 competition in Sweden, the first World Cup to be extensively televised, that a truly international field was assembled, with no noticeable absentees. The Swedish edition pointed backwards as well as forward. Many matches took places in small towns—Halmstad, Sandviken, and Uddevalla—where the stands were wooden, the pitches bumpy and patchy, and local commercial and media interest minimal.

Aside from the World Cup, the paucity of international competition in the early postwar period was striking. The Mitropa Cup was in decline. The Copa América was contested irregularly for much of the 1940s and 1950s, and the Copa Aldao was abolished in 1955. This modest schedule, though, would soon become a thing of the past.

The Proliferation of International Competition, circa 1955–92

A golden age of international competition began in the mid-1950s. Between 1955 and 1967, ten major tournaments were founded. UEFA introduced its three European club competitions—the European Cup, the Inter-Cities Fairs (later UEFA) Cup, and the Cup Winners' Cup—between 1955 and

1956. Sudan hosted the first Africa Cup of Nations in 1957, three years before UEFA launched its continental tournament for national teams, the European Championship. Also in 1960, CONMEBOL introduced a continental championship for South American clubs, the Copa Libertadores. The inaugural winners, Uruguay's Peñarol, played European Cup winners Real Madrid in the first Intercontinental Cup later that year. El Salvador claimed CONCACAF's first Championship of Nations in 1963. The first African Champions Cup was won by Cameroonian club Oryx Douala in 1964. Three years later, Israel's Hapoel Tel Aviv became inaugural winners of the Asian Club Championship.

Various factors encouraged the abundance of international competitions. Peace and economic growth created the preconditions for increased sporting exchange. Air travel became cheaper and more accessible, allowing teams to reach distant destinations quickly and in relative comfort. New continental confederations—the AFC and UEFA in 1954, CAF in 1957, and CONCACAF in 1961—wanted to make their mark with new tournaments, as CONMEBOL had done in 1916. New tournaments shaped and responded to increased media coverage of football, particularly via television. Floodlights enhanced the televised spectacle. The first floodlit international match, between England and Spain, took place at Wembley in 1955. Across Europe, the new and powerful lighting system helped to cement midweek evenings as a fixed place in the calendar for international encounters.

The founding in 1957 of an African football confederation coincided with the wave of decolonization that swept the continent between the late 1950s and the mid-1960s. CAF was more than a sports organization. It was a groundbreaking transnational institution formed six years before the creation of the continent's major pan-African political body, the Organization of African Unity (today's African Union).

CAF quickly sought a regular showpiece tournament for the continent's national teams. The first Africa Cup of Nations coincided with CAF's launch in Khartoum in 1957. It featured only three teams, Egypt, Ethiopia, and Sudan (CAF's fourth founder member, South Africa, was excluded due to apartheid). As decolonization built momentum, this CAF competition gained in sporting and political importance. Ghana's pan-African president, Kwame Nkrumah, saw football as a means of building national and continental solidarity. Nkrumah and his sports chief Ohene Djan built infrastructures and teams that promoted Ghanaian identity. Loosely modelled on Real Madrid, Nkrumah's Real Republicans Sports Club was founded in 1961. It had the pick of Ghana's best players. Other clubs, most conspicuously Asante Kotoko, protested against perceived favouritism toward Nkrumah's super club. Despite powerful backers, Real Republicans never won the league championship. The club was disbanded in 1966, after a coup ousted Nkrumah from power.

The super-club strategy was more effective on the international stage. Under Nkrumah's direction, the national team adopted the nickname Black Stars. This was an homage to the shipping line between Africa and the rest of the world, started in 1919 by Jamaican pan-Africanist Marcus Garvey. Both shipping line and team were meant to foster transnational black pride. International tournaments became vehicles for Ghanaian patriotism and pan-Africanism, and the Black Stars became ambassadors for Nkrumah's dual message. In 1960, Ghana defeated Sierra Leone to win the Kwame Nkrumah Gold Cup, a tournament designed to promote African unity through football. Three years later, Ghana hosted the Africa Cup of Nations. Based throughout the tournament in the capital city, Accra, with a squad dominated by players from Real Republicans, the Black Stars progressed to the final. There, in front of 40,000 spectators at the Independence Stadium, the hosts defeated Sudan to claim the continental crown for the first time. Nationwide celebrations followed. A photograph of Nkrumah with the victorious team was said to decorate almost every home. Two years later in Tunisia, Ghana retained the title. In between, Nkrumah pushed CAF to create a Champions Cup for African clubs. Accra hosted the first final in 1964, shortly after Nkrumah became the first world leader to hold an official audience with newly crowned world heavyweight boxing champion and emerging pan-African hero, Muhammad Ali. Authoritarian tendencies led to Nkrumah's fall in 1966, but his national and continental influence on football was profound.

The 1963 tournament was a modest event. There were six teams. Matches were played in the country's only two suitable stadiums, in Accra and Kumasi. In subsequent decades, the Africa Cup of Nations modernized and expanded, albeit at a slower pace than equivalent competitions in Europe and South America. By the 1992 tournament in Senegal, sixteen teams competed for the trophy. The rising tide of commercialism reached Africa's premier tournament. The long-standing CAF president, Ethiopia's Yidnekatchew Tessema, a pan-Africanist sceptical about market forces and professionalism, died in 1987. His replacement, the Cameroonian Issa Hayatou, opened the Africa Cup of Nations and the Champions Cup to business. Television rights were sold to the highest bidder. Corporate sponsorship brought the Cup of Nations into line with other big international tournaments. FIFA's long-standing partner, Coca-Cola, was official sponsor of the 1996 competition in South Africa. In Africa, as elsewhere, football entered the era of the sports mega-event.

UEFA was created in 1954 not only to safeguard Europe's privileged place in football's world order but to develop enduring continent-wide structures for the game. The head of the French football federation Henri Delaunay, a key figure in UEFA's founding, wrote an essay that year advocating "a Europe of football." In contrast to the supranational economic and political bodies born in the same period—most notably, the European Economic Community (1957)—UEFA was a European rather than West European entity. The strongest commitment to Europeanization came from behind the Iron Curtain.

UEFA's new competitions faced teething problems. The English FA refused to enter league champions Chelsea in the inaugural European Cup in 1955, claiming that it interfered with the domestic schedule. Clubs from Denmark, Hungary, and the Netherlands also declined participation. Of the sixteen countries represented in the draw, it was Spain that emerged victorious, as Real Madrid defeated France's Stade de Reims in the final in Paris in 1956. Delaunay's brainchild, the European Nations' Cup, also had notable absentees. Citing reasons that ranged from a crowded international calendar to the reopening of wounds from the Second World War, heavyweights of West European football, including England, Italy, and West Germany, refused participation in the inaugural competition. Stretched out over two years, with a final round in France in 1960, the tournament concluded with the Soviet Union beating Yugoslavia to become the first European champions. Only 18,000 watched the final in Paris.

The quadrennial European Championship, as the Nations' Cup was generally called by the late 1960s, was a slow burner. The 1972 and 1976 championships suffered financial losses. The eight-team tournament in Italy in 1980 was a miserable spectacle. Warm weather, high ticket prices, and hooliganism contributed to what one British newspaper called the "football melancholy" on display. Average attendance was barely 25,000. The turning point came in France four years later. The first globally memorable European Championship, it featured brilliant attacking teams, most notably the hosts and victors, France; increased television coverage; and fan cultures increasingly willing to cross borders. A large, popular Danish contingent followed the progress of Sepp Piontek's "Danish Dynamite" to the semi-finals. By the 1992 event in Sweden, the European Championship—though still in the World Cup's shadow—had become a big tournament in its own right.

The key tournament in Delaunay's "Europe of football" was the continent's premier club competition, the European Cup. Spain's Real Madrid won the first five European Cups, playing a devastating brand of attacking football centred on the international strike force of Alfredo Di Stéfano and Ferenc Puskás. In the team's signature performance, the 7–3 victory over Eintracht Frankfurt in the 1960 final at Glasgow's Hampden Park, Di Stéfano scored three times and Puskás four. The chief football writer at the *Liverpool Echo* newspaper was not alone in documenting how the game caught the imagination: "The strolling artistry of this superb team made us all realize how the game in Britain has retarded as the Continentals and others have become far superior to anything we have here ... Everywhere I go I hear people discussing this match and the sheer thrill and entertainment of the Spanish side."[4]

The European Cup provided new and regular opportunities for international exchanges. These exchanges often transcended Europe's postwar political divisions, even as various sides claimed football victories as political ones. In 1959, one of Franco's ministers, José Solís, told the Real Madrid team, "People who hated us understand us now, thanks to you ... Your victories are a legitimate source of pride for all Spaniards, at home and abroad."[5] The impact of Franco's white-shirted football ambassadors in easing hostility toward Franco's dictatorship, like the impact of Benfica's European Cup wins on the legitimacy of Portugal's António Salazar, is hard to measure. But the transnational impact of great European clubs and players was undeniable. In communist East Germany, the football association sang the aging Alfredo Di Stéfano's praises in 1964. Seven years later, when Dynamo Dresden travelled to the Netherlands to play Ajax in the European Cup, officials admired the hosts' fluent play. The Ajax system, soon known to the world as "total football," had a revolutionary impact in the 1970s, as the Amsterdam club won three successive European Cups (1971–73).

More than UEFA, it was the French newspaper *L'Équipe* that drove the creation of the European Cup in 1955. But it was television not print media that turned the competition into a transcontinental phenomenon. Like UEFA competitions and floodlights, televised coverage began in the 1950s. Broadcasts transformed the historical record. Football's past became increasingly visual, as television became a mass activity. The 1960 final at Hampden Park, the first to make an indelible mark in European collective memory, was the first to be broadcast live across the continent. Later standout teams had a similar impact. English writer David Winner was fourteen when he first heard of Ajax from a Greek friend at his London school. His friend saw the Dutch side defeat Panathinaikos at Wembley to win the European Cup for the first time in 1971. By the 1972 final, which saw Ajax retain the trophy with a 2–0 win over Inter Milan, Winner, watching live coverage from Rotterdam, was hooked: "Ajax played with a gorgeous, hyper-intelligent swagger. They ran and passed the ball in strange, beguiling ways, and flowed in exquisite, intricate, mesmerizing patterns around the pitch ... Ajax were like beings from a quite different, more advanced football civilisation."[6] The combination of the European Cup and television gave football glamour, a sprinkling of magic that rubbed off on the game wherever it was played or watched.

In the Cold War era, popular interest in European club football did not reach saturation point. Even into the late 1980s, live television coverage was reserved for the final rounds of UEFA tournaments. Attendance was often poor. The nadir was the 1974 final of the least prestigious club competition, the European Cup Winners' Cup. Only 5,000 people saw Magdeburg's shock 2–0 win over AC Milan in Rotterdam's De Kuip Stadium (capacity 55,000). Four years earlier, fewer than 8,000 people watched Manchester City defeat Górnik Zabrze in Vienna's Prater Stadium (capacity 90,000) to win the same trophy.

UEFA's flagship event was not immune. A series of European Cup finals in the late 1970s and early 1980s were played in front of small crowds at prestigious stadiums. Part of the problem was football's hooligan-blighted image (see Chapter 8). Part of it was the unheralded status of many of the teams who reached the final. Finalists between 1978 and 1991 included Nottingham Forest, Malmö, Aston Villa, Steaua Bucharest, PSV Eindhoven, Porto, and Red Star Belgrade. Europe's wealthiest clubs grumbled about a competition that regularly threw up such surprise contenders. Under the threat of a breakaway, UEFA overhauled its elite competition. In the 1992/93 season, the European Cup became the Champions League, with group stages (mini-leagues) scheduled before the knockout rounds. From 1997 the continent's top eight leagues were allowed to enter a second team in the tournament. The Champions League, no longer just a competition for champions, was en route to becoming a global behemoth, dominated by a small set of wealthy West European clubs.

International Competition since the 1990s

The opening ceremony for the 1994 World Cup, the first to be held in the United States, took place in front of 67,000 people at Chicago's Soldier Field. The climax saw singer Diana Ross belt out her hit "I'm Coming

Out." She then ran down the pitch past a group of dancers to take a penalty kick. Her shot into the net would symbolize the start of both the tournament and America's coming-out party as a soccer nation. Ross missed the penalty, sending the ball embarrassingly wide. To make matters worse, the goal—set up to "explode" when Ross's shot hit the net—collapsed anyway. It was an inauspicious start.

As a metaphor for the United States' awkward relationship with football, Diana Ross's penalty miss was hard to beat. In fact, USA '94 was, by most measures, a success. Beyond the usual categories of profit, attendance, and viewing figures, recent research has emphasized the tournament's social impact, boosting an already impressive grassroots soccer program (for men and women) and subtly changing perceptions of the country's large, football-loving Latino migrant communities. What is most interesting about the opening ceremony, missed penalty or not, is what it said about the World Cup's arrival as a global mega-event. Before the first match at the 1966 World Cup in England, schoolboys paraded around Wembley with the flags and national colours of the sixteen participating teams. By 1994, the sense of spectacle and celebrity was far greater. In addition to Diana Ross, President Bill Clinton gave a speech. TV presenter Oprah Winfrey ran proceedings. There were singers, dancers, confetti, balloons, and a football-shaped stage. This was less, as snobbier critics suggested, US "razzmatazz" on lurid display than a reflection of FIFA's increasingly showy commitment to the World Cup as spectacle.

During the 1958 World Cup in Sweden, a rope hung between wooden poles was all that separated the crowd from the pitch at the France-Paraguay game in Norrköping. Despite television's inroads, subsequent tournaments kept something of this modest scale. England's sole World Cup win, on home soil in 1966, became a central, often nostalgic element in the national psyche. At the time, though, the tournament hardly looked like the patriotic celebration of later legend. When Prime Minister Harold Wilson appointed Denis Howell as Minister for Sport in 1964, Howell had to remind him that England was about to host the World Cup. England's early matches in the tournament did not sell out. World Cup fever only took hold in the tournament's latter stages.

The 1974 World Cup in West Germany marked a turning point in the tournament's evolution to mega-event status—less for what happened on the pitch than because of João Havelange's election as FIFA president. Havelange turned FIFA into a global commercial organization. His mandate took time to take effect. It was not until the 1982 World Cup in Spain that a twenty-four-team tournament was debuted, with additional places for CAF, AFC, and CONCACAF teams and bespoke sponsorship deals for multinational corporations. The pitch invasion that followed Argentina's win over West Germany in the 1986 final in Mexico was a farewell of sorts to the old (dis-)order. Beginning in the 1990s, all World Cup games, not just the final, were better policed and better designed for television consumption. The World Cup in Italy in 1990 reflected a game, and a world, on the brink of transformation. The fall of communism and the end of the Cold War cleared the path for neo-liberalism. Havelange's commitment to globalization and commercialization found the right historical moment. Sponsorship and broadcasting deals took off. Hooliganism, a media obsession in the 1980s, slipped off the public radar. Fans became consumers, as higher ticket prices and all-seater stadiums changed the spectator demographic. The sport gradually became safer, more expensive, and more fashionable—in short, a more suitable staging ground for lucrative international competitions.

No World Cup featured a lower goals-per-game average than Italia '90. The football was so negative that FIFA introduced the back-pass rule in 1992, to prevent goalkeepers from time wasting by picking up the ball after it was passed to them. But the tournament's technical paucity paled alongside its economic and cultural significance. Italia '90 was, at the time, one of the world's biggest television events, watched by a cumulative audience of 27 billion viewers in 167 countries. In England, New Order's "World in Motion" and Luciano Pavarotti's aria "Nessun dorma" ("None Shall Sleep") became the soundtrack of a football renaissance. The tears of midfielder Paul Gascoigne overshadowed the England team's performance in reaching the semi-finals. Gascoigne's display of emotion, after receiving a yellow card in the loss to West Germany, heralded a new, more vulnerable, and better-paid masculinity. Pete Davies's account of Italia '90, *All Played Out*—one of the decade's first and best examples of football writing—captured the zeitgeist but underestimated the inflation ahead: "The World Cup's grown so big (some would say bloated) that it's become a whole alternative world unto itself: Planet Football, an unreality zone of media and marketing mayhem, a land of hysterical fantasy."[7]

As football's stock rose, the World Cup spectacle only got bigger. In France in 1998, the tournament expanded from twenty-four to thirty-two teams, introduced the first public screening of matches, and made handsome profits for FIFA and its thirteen multinational corporate partners. By the 2014 World Cup in Brazil, for an outlay of US$2.2 billion, FIFA made profits of US$4.8 billion. The vast majority came from the sale of television and marketing rights. In 2017, FIFA announced that the 2026 World Cup, awarded a year later to the joint bid from Canada, Mexico, and the United States, would feature forty-eight teams and eighty games. It was estimated that the expanded (some would say bloated) format would place an extra US$1 billion in FIFA coffers.

The growth of the World Cup and the Olympics has triggered debates about the costs and benefits of the sports mega event, a term used to denote large, expensive, and international multi-day sports competitions. With no bid for the World Cup or Olympics free of promises about "legacy building," discussion has focused on the economic impact of hosting. There is scepticism about the mega-event's role in promoting a "virtuous cycle" of sport. This model, adopted by every bidding country, argues that success in elite competition drives increased grassroots sports participation.

Particularly since the 9/11 terrorist attacks on the United States, academics have examined the increased securitization of mega-events. UEFA used more than 15 kilometres of tarpaulin at the 2008 European Championship, cohosted by Austria and Switzerland, to create restricted-access sites across the host cities, from the stadiums themselves to team hotels. Such spatial demarcation is exemplified by FIFA-sponsored public viewing areas, introduced at the 1998 World Cup in France and now common at all major football events. In these heavily policed spaces, where crowds gather to watch broadcasts of live matches, what is the relationship between sport and surveillance? Do public viewing areas reflect a "transnational public sphere"? Or are they, and the mega-events that they screen, emblematic of what Guy Debord called the "society of the spectacle," places where "all that once was directly lived has become mere representation"?[8]

The 2002 World Cup in Japan and South Korea was the first World Cup in Asia and the first to be cohosted. The partnership was historically charged, given that Korea was a Japanese colony between 1910 and 1945. The tournament played a limited role in reconciling the two countries but a stronger one in fostering national pride among South Koreans. Seven million people were in the streets to watch the 1–0 semi-final loss to Germany, the largest public gathering in South Korea since pro-democracy protests in the early 1980s.

The tournament featured FIFA gigantism on an unprecedented scale. Built at a cost of US$7.3 billion, sixteen of the twenty stadiums were new, as the cohosts competed in an architectural arms race. Television rights were sold to private broadcasters for US$800 million. Based in two countries with strong electronics and telecommunications industries, the 2002 World Cup reached new levels of high-tech expertise and mass marketing. It was efficiently run and, by most accounts, a success. The goals-per-game average was lower than in France or the United States. Much of the tournament drama centred on the celebrity of David Beckham and South Korea's surprise performance rather than on the quality of the football.

What are the legacies of such a mega-event? Metrics can be difficult, and can support a variety of political agendas. The tournament contributed to a modest upturn in the global performances of Asian sides. Both Japan and South Korea qualified for the knockout stages of the 2010 World Cup in South Africa. However, no AFC team won a game at the 2014 World Cup in Brazil. Beneath the apex of the game, the tournament shaped perceptions of the "W" (as in World Cup) generations in South Korea, the young people who took over public spaces and remade Korean nationalism in the summer of 2002. But little evidence supported the "growth machine" argument that hosting a sports event boosts economic performance. Many of the stadiums built for the 2002 tournament became white elephants. Japan's ten state-of-the-art venues, heavily subsidized by taxpayers, cost far more than they could generate. The country was left with a host of oversized arenas, with seating capacities 200 per cent larger than was required for domestic league matches.

A growing body of evidence suggests that World Cups and other sports mega-events, which prioritize spectacle and consumption over play, do not grow grassroots sport. They may, in fact, have the opposite effect. A 2006 FIFA survey showed that the number of AFC registered players, 85,176, was proportionately, and by a considerable distance, the lowest of any FIFA confederation, accounting for just 0.00003 per cent of the continent's population of almost 3.9 billion. Stadium use and participation figures at the very least raised questions—as they have after many World Cups or Olympics—about the long-term benefits of 2002 for football in South Korea and especially Japan. A major tournament's impact often appears to be ephemeral and expensive.

At the pinnacle of the world game, the mega-event shows no sign of slowing down. The Champions League final is no longer just a football match. It is an incessantly marketed sports festival akin to the Super Bowl, but with larger viewing figures. At the 2017 final in Cardiff between Juventus and Real Madrid, pre-match entertainment came from one of the world's biggest pop bands, the Black Eyed Peas. The previous year in Milan's San Siro Stadium, it had been another global star, Alicia Keys.

The World Cup, the Champions League final, and other showpieces cast a long shadow over contemporary football and over contemporary scholarship on the game as a global spectacle. But alternative narratives, and competitions, exist. Many events that have followed the template of the behemoths do not compete on the same financial plane. The African Champions League—as CAF renamed its flagship club competition, the African Champions Cup, in 1997—was based on the UEFA Champions League. Television income, though, was less than 1 per cent that of its money-spinning role model. FIFA's other global competitions—the Futsal (indoor) World Cup, the Beach Soccer World Cup, and various junior tournaments—bring in a tiny fraction of the revenues earned by the World Cup. Average attendance at the 2016 Futsal World Cup in Colombia was 2,684. At the outdoor men's tournament in Brazil in 2014, it was 52,918. The Women's World Cup came under FIFA's remit in 1991, but remains the poor cousin of its male counterpart. Total FIFA prize money for the 2014 Men's World Cup in Brazil was US$576 million. For the Women's World Cup a year later in Canada, it was US$15 million. Such geographical, racial, and gender inequalities characterize profit and spectacle in the contemporary game. Disability adds another layer to the discussion. Football did not join the Paralympics until 1984. As of the 2016 Games in Rio, there was no women's presence in the two football competitions, a seven-a-side tournament for athletes with cerebral palsy and a five-a-side tournament for the visually impaired.

Not all global football events are created equal. Nor are they all designed with profit in mind. The Homeless World Cup was first held in the Austrian city of Graz in 2003. It had 144 participants from eighteen countries. Organized annually since then by a Scottish-based social organization, it has become an international means of raising money for and awareness of homelessness. Can sport be an effective means of tackling social exclusion? Fieldwork on the United Kingdom team that played in the 2003 Homeless World Cup did not reach uplifting conclusions. Under pressure on and off the field—from the quality of other competing teams and the relatively large crowds at a well-organized event—the squad struggled. One player began binge drinking. After 10–0 and 9–1 losses, and some barracking from the crowd and commentators, the humiliated goalkeeper angrily said that the tournament was making him "feel like crap."[9] Whether such events offer a temporary escape from everyday problems or merely replicate them, they remind us that international competition can function at multiple levels of cultural and social meaning. They also point to blind spots in the historiography. We know a great deal about the history of mega-events such as the World Cup. We know very little about grassroots histories of international football encounters.

Notes

1 Quoted in Brian Oliver, "Before Pelé, There Was Andrade," *The Observer*, May 24, 2014, https://www.theguardian.com/football/2014/may/24/before-pele-there-was-andrade (accessed 7 August 2018).

2 Quoted in Simon Martin, *Football and Fascism: The National Game under Mussolini* (Oxford: Berg, 2004), 189.

3 Quoted in Paul Dietschy, *Histoire du football* (Paris: Perrin, 2014), 210.

4 Michael Charters, "Fans Can't Stop Talking about Real Madrid Gem," *Liverpool Echo and Evening Express*, May 26, 1960, 18.

5 Quoted in Dietschy, *Histoire du football*, 445.

6 David Winner, *Brilliant Orange: The Neurotic Genius of Dutch Soccer* (New York: Overlook Press, 2010), 1–2.

7 Pete Davies, *All Played Out: The Full Story of Italia '90* (London: Heinemann, 1990), 4.

8 Guy Debord, *The Society of the Spectacle* (1967; New York: Zone Books, 1994), 12.

9 Quoted in Jonathan Magee and Ruth Jeanes, "Football's Coming Home: A Critical Evaluation of the Homeless World Cup as an Intervention to Combat Social Exclusion," *International Review for the Sociology of Sport* 48, no. 1 (2013): 12.

5 | Gender

The history of modern football is the history of a repressed and marginalized sport. Revived and standardized in late-nineteenth-century Britain, football spread quickly beyond public schools and universities. A first official match, between teams representing the north and the south of England, took place in London in 1895. Football made inroads in continental Europe. Moscow hosted a match in 1911, to the surprise of the British ambassador to Russia. National associations were often hostile to public performances. The Dutch authorities banned a match between Sparta Rotterdam and an England team in 1896. Educationalists and administrators in the Netherlands, Germany, and elsewhere deemed the game unsuitable for the physique of its participants.

The First World War was football's first golden age. In England, a workers' team at the Dick, Kerr & Company transport and munitions factory in Preston became a national attraction. Matches drew crowds of between 10,000 and 50,000. The Dick, Kerr's team toured internationally. It played in France, where the game's popularity also soared. By 1921, there were 150 teams in England. Across the English Channel, a national league began in 1917, and two cup competitions were held in 1922.

Football's wartime popularity only increased institutional suspicions. In 1921, the English FA banned the game from its members' grounds for health reasons. It was a similar story elsewhere. For the next fifty years, football survived as an underground sport. From apartheid South Africa to communist East Germany, the game was played on the margins of society.

Access to equipment and pitches was limited. Participants could only play recreationally. There was no way of making a professional living.

Following the cultural and social upheavals of the 1960s, political opposition to football became increasingly difficult to justify. The game experienced a global resurgence. Italy hosted an unofficial World Cup in 1970, which drew crowds of up to 35,000 spectators. A year later, the ban on football was lifted in England. Across parts of Europe and Africa during the 1970s, grassroots initiatives forced the building of national structures and international partnerships.

Football took off in the 1990s. FIFA held the first World Cup in 1991, 87 years after the organization was founded and almost 100 years after the first matches in England and Scotland. A breakthrough occurred in 1999, when the United States hosted and won the third World Cup. Forty million Americans watched the tournament on television. The emergence of the United States as the world's leading football nation testified to the sport's popularity among the country's large suburban and middle-class population. Other powerhouses included China, Germany, and Norway. Professional leagues were created in many parts of the world after 1999.

By 2007 FIFA claimed that 26 million children and adults played football around the world. However reluctantly, administrators realized that the sport was here to stay. It became more central to popular culture, as shown by the international success of the film *Bend It Like Beckham* (2002). Yet, for all of its advances, football remained a sport on the margins. Physique was discussed more than skill. In 2004, FIFA President Sepp Blatter called on players to wear "tighter shorts." Professional leagues, even in the United States, struggled financially. Outside the World Cup, television coverage remained skeletal. Apart from a small transnational elite, professional football was not a sustainable career. In 2017, Ireland's national team threatened to strike over work conditions. Players accused the Irish FA of treating them like dirt. They shared tracksuits and changed for games in toilet cubicles.

If the above narrative seems unfamiliar, it should not be surprising. It describes the history of women's not men's football. How does our understanding of the sport's history change when we start from women's perspectives? How does it shift when we challenge the closed binary constructs upon which many of football's gendered narratives, and gender stereotypes, are based? Chapter 5 attempts to answer these questions, challenging the idea that football is, or ever was, "a man's game." The chapter begins with historiographical and theoretical approaches, focusing on how historians have, and often have not, written women into the game's history. The central section outlines a people's history of women's football, emphasizing the role of grassroots agency in the international game's survival and growth. The chapter closes by shifting focus to evolving notions of masculinity.

Football and Gender: Historiography and Theory

Football's gendered historiography is apparent in its terminology. The use of a gender signifier to identify "women's soccer" or "women's football" reveals how football history has, more often than not, left women on the sidelines. For the game played by men, a gender signifier is rarely required. The "real" history of football, it is implied, means the history of men's football. Man, to borrow from French philosopher Simone de Beauvoir, is the subject; woman is "the Other." In the indexes of many histories of football, the term "women" is, still, nowhere to be found.

The sense that football is a man's world has deep roots. J.B. Priestley's 1929 novel *The Good Companions* begins with a lyrical description of what drew "thirty-five thousand men and boys" to watch the local team in the fictionalized English mill town of Bruddersford: "For a shilling the Bruddersford United A.F.C. offered you Conflict and Art ... it turned you into a member of a new community, all brothers together for an hour and a half, for not only had you escaped from the clanking machinery of this lesser life, from work, wages, rent, doles, sick pay, insurance cards, nagging wives, ailing children, bad bosses, idle workmen, but you had escaped with most of your neighbours, with half the town ..."[1] Nick Hornby's account of his obsession with Arsenal, *Fever Pitch* (1992), begins with an exchange in bed between the narrator and his wife. She asks him what he is thinking about. The answer is as natural for him as it would be unthinkable for her: football.

This history as negation applies to popular and academic accounts of football, across a long period of time. It applies to playing and watching the game. In recent scholarship on spectatorship, the spirit of Priestley and Hornby lives on: male fandom is the norm. History as negation applies to many other supposedly "male" sports, such as cricket and rugby. It applies transnationally. Women are typically absent from histories of football in Africa, Europe, and South America. The Latin American historian Brenda Elsey observed in 2014 that many scholars react defensively to women's incursion into football's male-dominated world. Adopting "the rhetoric of sportswriters," they argue that women do not belong in the story, whether because of the alleged inferiority of women athletes, an alleged disinterest among women in playing and watching the game, or the "fact" that "women's football does not have a long history."[2]

Despite ongoing obstacles, women's football historiography has taken off since the 1990s, the key decade in globalizing the game. What happened in this primary phase echoed what happened in men's sports history in the 1970s and 1980s. Pioneers laid the academic groundwork. Women's football history had to be uncovered and described before it could be analyzed or theorized. Edited volumes and monographs tackled national histories or provided international overviews. Journal articles filled blank spots on the canvas.

The greater depth and breadth of research affected studies of the men's game. David Goldblatt's global history *The Ball Is Round* (2006) discussed the origins, suppression, and resurgence of women's football. Public history began to take note. An exhibition at the National Football Museum in Manchester in 2018 showcased memorabilia on the history of women's football. The museum also hosted "Upfront and Onside," a conference on women's football, as part of its Hidden History project. The "hidden histories" discussed there—including LGBT football communities, women and the 1966 World Cup, and football in Costa Rica, as well as photo essays on players and fans—revealed the scholarly ground broken since the 1990s.

On the back of this wide-ranging if still incomplete transformation, football began to feature more prominently in debates about gender. In a 1989 essay, Richard Holt credited feminism with sharpening understanding of sport's role in constructing and sustaining forms of male identity and "male sociability." The focus, however critical, in early texts was on sport as a male preserve. Marxists such as John Hargreaves, in *Sport, Power and Culture* (1986), betrayed frustration with the feminist tendency to prioritize gender over class. Hargreaves's analysis of sport as a site of "male hegemony" reproduced some of the assumptions that he critiqued. Football was one of many sports that he considered to be almost exclusively male. The preoccupation with hooliganism reinforced the male-centred nature of football studies, as sociologists advanced theories about why supporters behaved violently. In terms of researchers and subjects, this was a man's world, focused on patterns of male aggression usually found in white, working-class communities.

Since the 1990s, studies of male behaviour have moved beyond the hooligan minority. Eduardo Archetti's *Masculinities* (1999) examined hybrid, creolized forms of masculinity in three of Argentina's most popular pastimes: football, polo, and the tango. Football's popularity in Latin America, in societies where machismo often remains a dominant force, encouraged reflections on the sport's role in upholding, and occasionally subverting, patriarchy. An anthropological study of young supporters in Mexico City, for example, showed how Pumas fans performed "motherlessness," reproducing stereotypes about disorderly, aggressive, and violent masculinity in and around the stadium.

Studies now recognize that maleness in sport is constructed. It is constructed, moreover, in relation to what it claims not to be, most notably the (historically absent) female. Many researchers, primarily sociologists rather than historians, have interrogated hegemonic masculinity in sport. The term hegemony is taken from Italian Marxist Antonio Gramsci, whose ideas influenced a generation of cultural and sports studies scholars interested in how popular culture reproduced and reinforced dominant ideologies. Studies of sport as an "embodied experience" (i.e., as bodily action) have long since moved beyond physiology into philosophy. How, for example, can the phenomenology (the study of the perception of things) advocated by Maurice Merleau-Ponty explain the relationship between the body and consciousness on the field of play?

The feminist Judith Butler criticized Merleau-Ponty for negating women's bodily experiences, a reminder of the ongoing marginalization of women from the field and from popular discourse. Gender, as historian Joan Scott noted in a seminal 1986 essay, was a prime means of signifying "relations of power." Butler's idea of "gender performativity"—the construction of gender as an evolving series of performances shaped by societal values rather than individual choices—has implications for sports studies, for example in the relationship between sport and sexuality. Examples of football's heteronormativity—its belief in fixed and binary gender roles—are not difficult to find. Transgressors can pay a high price. In South Africa in 2008, the openly lesbian national team player Eudy Simelane was gang-raped and murdered, part of a spate of "corrective" acts of violence against gay women in the country's townships. In contrast to women's football, men's leagues have very few openly gay players. Yet masculinity is not a static concept. How football understands "manly" behaviour has undergone considerable historical evolution.

Few scholars dispute football's role in perpetuating gendered ideologies and assumptions about male privilege. Research can reveal the extent of this hegemony and how and why it was constructed. It can suggest alternative narratives. A persistent theme in research on women's football is agency: how ordinary actors organized games; challenged institutional opposition; and normalized the idea that women, as much as men, could play and watch football. Through archival and newspaper research, as well as oral histories, scholars have uncovered previously silenced voices. Historical gaps still need to be filled, though the historiography is not just an "add women and stir" recounting of unsung deeds. It also deals, in increasingly sophisticated ways, with concepts of gender and power.

Women's Football: A People's History

After two hours of goalless football in sweltering heat, the 1999 World Cup final between the United States and China went to penalty kicks. When China's Liu Ying missed in the third round, American defender Brandi Chastain had the chance to win the match and the tournament for the hosts. In front of 90,185 spectators at the Rose Bowl in California, she struck the ball home with her weaker left foot. The United States became world champions for the second time.

Chastain's moment in the spotlight ended a transformative tournament. An estimated worldwide television audience of 1 billion, including 40 million Americans, watched the 1999 competition, the third "official" (i.e., FIFA-sponsored) World Cup. The United States–Brazil semi-final had the highest audience rating for any soccer match in American cable TV history. Six hundred and fifty thousand people attended the tournament, with average crowds of 69,000 at the six US matches. President Bill Clinton received the US team at the White House. It appeared on David Letterman's *Late Show* and made the cover of magazines such as *Newsweek*, *Time*, and *Sports Illustrated*. Women's soccer briefly attained a crossover appeal that eclipsed men's soccer and challenged the "big three" American sports: baseball, basketball, and NFL football.

How did football arrive at this watershed? The journey was long and difficult. In Victorian Britain, the birthplace of organized sport and "muscular Christianity," middle-class women played sports such as tennis at a recreational level. Cycling, a symbol of female emancipation, gained some leeway but only grudgingly, given the bicycle's alleged threat to femininity and gynecology. The two most popular team sports, cricket and football, were zealously guarded male preserves. Women's teams were mocked and obstructed.

Yet, in Britain and elsewhere, women played football anyway. Teams from England and Scotland played a match in 1881. The British Ladies' Football Club, founded in 1895 by pseudonymous feminist Nettie Honeyball, played more than 100 matches, sometimes in front of crowds of 7,000 people. In 1902, a Danish newspaper lamented the fact that, in clubs and schools, women were wresting football away from men. Women played in mixed teams with men in India in the 1890s. Rejecting confinement to indoor games and cards, Bengali women such as Purna Ghosh discarded their saris and played in the 1920s. The sport was never an exclusively male activity.

Football crossed into the mainstream during the First World War. Men's deployment on the front lines and the suspension of professional football in 1915 created opportunities for working-class women at work and play. Itself a by-product of the Industrial Revolution, football was played in increasing numbers by women working in wartime industries. Thousands watched munitions factory teams compete in the Munitionettes' Cup. Businesses tapped into football's commercial potential. A local brewery sponsored Hey's Ladies in Bradford, Yorkshire champions in 1921. When the Dick, Kerr's Ladies team, based at a transport and munitions factory in Preston, played St. Helens Ladies at Goodison Park in Liverpool in 1920, 53,000 people were in attendance.

Football developed, albeit more modestly, in France. The first match took place in Paris in 1917. There were soon a dozen teams in and around the French capital. A series of games between England and France drew large crowds on both sides of the English Channel after the war. FIFA President Jules Rimet was among the 10,000 spectators for two matches at the Stade Pershing in 1921. The authorities could hardly fail to notice the new developments. There were 150 women's teams in England in 1921. Twenty-five of them founded the Ladies Football Association.

It took longer to gain footholds elsewhere. The first official record in the United States dates to 1924, when intramural games were played at Smith College in Massachusetts. Women played in Nigeria as early as 1943, when the *Nigerian Spokesman* reported on a game in Onitsha ("fine show but not up to the standard of boys' soccer").[3] By the 1940s, neighbourhood teams in the Brazilian cities of Rio de Janeiro and São Paulo attracted media attention. Eight thousand people watched a match in Costa Rica in 1949. In the same year, the first matches were played in South Korea, as part of the National Girls' and Women's Sport Games in the capital city, Seoul.

Gaps in the historical record, combined with scholarly disinterest, can make it tricky to assess the extent and quality of football activity. Male responses were less open to interpretation. As teams emerged in Brazil, one citizen wrote to President Getúlio Vargas in 1940: "growing, year by year, it is likely that in all of Brazil, 200 women's soccer clubs will be organized, this means 200 nucleuses destroying the health of 2000 future mothers who, besides, will be kept in a depressive mentality and open to rude and extravagant exhibitions." The sentiment was widely supported. One newspaper declared that "women's soccer needs to be controlled." A doctor described it as "contrary to the natural inclination of the feminine soul."[4]

Philosophers, medical experts, and administrators espoused the idea that women were biologically and temperamentally unsuited to football. It crossed all political and geographical boundaries. When Canada's Dominion Football Association moved to prevent teams playing against touring sides from England in 1922, it argued that "a woman was not built to stand the bruises gotten in playing football."[5] Before Deportivo Femenino Costa Rica's first match in 1950, María Elena Valverde recalled a doctor using assorted arguments to dissuade the women from playing. The ball would be too hard. There would be too much running. The pitch and goals would be too big. The match went ahead anyway, and Valverde's trailblazing team was soon touring Central and South America.

What caused such hostility? A short answer would be centuries of patriarchal superiority across different polities and cultures, all of which assumed that women lacked the physique and intelligence for many things, including football. Challenging these assumptions required the right historical moment. Football's growth in Britain, for example, accompanied the emancipatory demands now known as first-wave feminism. Focused on voting rights and boosted by wartime employment opportunities, the suffragette movement helped women to break into male-dominated leisure pursuits. In China, the New Culture Movement of the 1915–21 period—a revolt against Confucian values that embraced anti-imperialist and democratic ideas—opened doors to emancipation. Sheng Kunnan, a physical education teacher at the Lianjiang Women's Physical Education Institute in Shanghai, translated the rules of football into Chinese in 1924. With support from the institute's principal, the radical feminist Lu Lihua, the Lianjiang team, the only women's squad in the city, played matches against men's teams.

With rare exceptions, sports authorities viewed women's football as an intruder. When the head of sport in fascist Italy, Leandro Arpinati, reluctantly permitted the formation of a team in Milan in the early 1930s, it was on the condition that it never played publicly. The postwar backlash was by then in full swing. Nervous about the popularity of Dick, Kerr's Ladies and their peers, the English FA banned women's football in 1921. Shut out of grounds in Bradford and faced with vocal opposition to the "unseemly exhibition" of women's football, Hey's Ladies was forced to disband in 1925. The other home nation associations (Scotland, Wales, and Northern Ireland) followed England's lead, as did the authorities in Canada. In 1941, Decree Law 3199 banned women's football in Brazil. The DFB prohibited West German clubs from having women's teams or allowing women to play on their pitches in 1955. Even where football was not outlawed, it was driven to the margins. For half of the twentieth century, from the 1920s to the 1970s, the game was an underground activity.

During these lost years, activism kept football alive. Gender equality was enshrined in the constitution in communist East Germany. Women dominated the GDR's all-conquering Olympic "medal machine." Yet football received minimal support. Top teams such as Turbine Potsdam and Rotation Schlema were run by volunteers, who eked out money from local factories for travel and kit. Players jumped a variety of hurdles. Neubrandenburg's Silvia Mundt told her husband that she was putting up curtains at her mother's house and went to play football instead. Pressure from players and coaches forced the football association to create a national championship in 1979. Likewise, as pioneering player and coach Barbara Cox recalled, it was activism—whether fundraising for overseas tours or lobbying for team kits, decent referees, or access to facilities—that compelled the authorities to recognize women's soccer in New Zealand.

The struggle to be taken seriously required assertiveness. Sweden's football federation took no initiatives before 1971. Prior growth—there were 59 leagues and 4,901 licensed players in 1971—came from below. Öxabäck IF in central Sweden, for example, was founded in 1966 and started a league in 1968. Teams drew inspiration from peers in Czechoslovakia, Denmark, and Italy. In Africa, too, enthusiasts not federations organized the first teams. Football in Senegal began on the initiative of Eliot Khouma, a school coach who formed the Dakar Gazelles in 1974. With support from a friend in Italy, the Gazelles played a visiting team from Milan. They then toured Senegal, playing matches against boys' teams.

In the late 1960s and early 1970s, as second-wave feminism attacked patriarchal structures around the world, football came in from the cold. Players, coaches, and administrators forced change on the old boys' networks that ran the game. In England, an independent women's FA was formed in 1969. It had forty-four affiliated teams, many of whom had played for years in self-regulated competitions. Two years later, the FA overturned its 1921 ban, though it did not incorporate women's football on equal terms until 1993. The DFB ended its ban in 1970 and created a national league in 1974. By 1981 West Germany had 383,171 footballers in 2,701 teams. The wind of change blew beyond Europe too. After thirty-eight years of prohibition, Brazil overturned its ban on women's football in 1979.

There was no overnight transformation. A 1970 FIFA survey of its 139 member associations found that, among 90 responses, only 12 supported women's football. The inaugural World Cup, held in the same year in Italy, presented opportunities and obstacles. Organized by the privately financed, Italian-based Federation of Independent European Female Football and sponsored by the Martini & Rossi drinks company, the tournament featured teams from seven European countries. Denmark defeated Italy 2–0 in the final, in front of 50,000 spectators. The Danish team was, in fact, club side BK Femina. Founded in 1959, BK Femina was central to the growth of the Danish game in the 1960s, as Copenhagen-based teams formed an association and organized indoor and outdoor championships. The club toured internationally, making its first trip abroad to Czechoslovakia in 1968. To raise money, it performed at entertainment events and men's league matches.

The media rarely focused on BK Femina's talent. The journalist who accompanied the team on its 1968 tour wrote of one player, photographed relaxing in a bikini: "Let no-one say football players are masculine. [Here] she is relaxing beside one of Prague's open-air pools—sweet, feminine and charming." This anticipated international coverage of the 1970 World Cup. A West German journalist joked after one match that the prettiest team had lost. As the head of the Danish Football Association (DBU), Vilhelm Skousen, stated after BK Femina's victory in Italy, "The girls find themselves in a footballing no-man's-land, with no affiliation to any organized association. But no matter how much sympathy there might be for the lady football enthusiasts, their success is to some extent a result of their own self-promotion. We cannot and will not take this seriously in the DBU."[6] The growth of women's football, in Denmark as elsewhere, was due to tireless activism not enlightened leadership. In 1971, in front of a crowd of over 100,000 people at the Azteca Stadium in Mexico City, BK Femina retained the world title for Denmark, defeating the hosts 3–0 in the final. A year later, the DBU admitted women's clubs into its organization.

The DBU's backtracking was replicated across the world, as institutions, often reluctantly, opened their doors to women. Footballers from Hong Kong, Malaysia, Singapore, and Taiwan had founded the Asian Ladies Football Confederation (ALFC) in 1968. By 1974, the ALFC's influence had spread to Oceania. In 1975, Hong Kong hosted the ALFC's inaugural Asian Cup tournament. The regional confederation, the AFC, and FIFA viewed an independent women's organization as a threat. In a 1976 letter to FIFA, ALFC General Secretary Charlie Pereira asked, "Is there a clause in FIFA's rules which states that women's football cannot have their own body to organize competitions? ... What right has FIFA to insist that ALFC must not be allowed to function on its own?"[7] The price for entry into the world game, as it had been for women's organizations joining the Olympic movement, was a loss of autonomy. FIFA President João Havelange had no great sympathy for the women's game, but he was an astute politician, aware of Asia's importance to his control of the world governing body. His Asian strategy focused on communist China. The world's most populous country had a weak men's team and, after Mao's death in 1976, a pro-business government under Deng Xiaoping. In 1988, FIFA awarded its Women's Invitation Tournament, a testing ground for a World Cup, to the Chinese city of Guangzhou. Three years later, China hosted the inaugural FIFA Women's World Cup. Sponsored by the multinational confectionary company, Mars, Incorporated, the twelve-team tournament was won by the United States.

After 1991, women's football broke into male-dominated structures of the world game. Quadrennial World Cups became fixtures on the sporting calendar. Host countries were places where football was popular: Sweden (1995), the United States (1999, 2003), China (2007), Germany (2011), Canada (2015), and France (2019). Football became more prominent in the Olympics. Beginning in 2001, UEFA organized the Women's Champions League (originally known as the UEFA Women's Cup). Professional or semi-professional national leagues were introduced, with mixed commercial and sporting results. These included Division 1 Féminine in France (1975), the Swedish Damallsvenskan (1988), the Frauen-Bundesliga in Germany (1990), Denmark's Elitedivisionen (1994), and the Women's Super League in England (2010).

Most impressive was grassroots development. FIFA figures from 2007 showed that 26 million girls and women played the game worldwide, an increase of 4 million from 2000. A 2016 UEFA survey listed 20 member associations (out of 55) where girls and women's football was the most popular team sport. With exceptions such as Germany, the international game's best teams came from countries with modest profiles in men's football: Japan, Norway, Sweden, the United States, and China. In the latter two cases, football forged distinctive paths. One was grounded in mass participation. The other had a narrower basis in an elite sport system.

Since the 1970s, soccer has been viewed as the recreational sport of choice in the United States: safe, affordable, coeducational, multicultural, and suburban. This profile—a partial reverse of football's rough, urban, and masculine associations in much of the world—was probably not uppermost in players' minds. It certainly influenced parents, educators, and sports organizations. In 1977, 2.8 per cent of colleges offered women's soccer. In 2004, the figure was 88.4 per cent. From 1981 to 2001, there was a 700 per cent increase in girls playing varsity or junior varsity high-school soccer. Significantly more girls (348,000) than boys (317,000) registered in the American Youth Soccer Organization in 2001/02.

Soaring participation rates laid the foundation for success. No country has hitherto won more World Cups or Olympics than the United States. Since the 1990s, America's best-known soccer players have been women, from Mia Hamm and Hope Solo to Megan Rapinoe, politically outspoken star of the 2019 World Cup in France. The "girls of summer," the 1999 World Cup winning team, became so famous that surnames were unnecessary. Forward Abby Wambach, who scored a record 186 goals in 254 appearances for her country between 2001 and 2015, earned sponsorship deals with Dodge, Gatorade, and Panasonic. She appeared on chat shows with David Letterman and Jon Stewart, sang on *American Idol*, and was one of the first women to feature on FIFA's EA Sports video game series (in *FIFA 16*). Wambach even had a Barbie doll created in her likeness. Mass participation in soccer drove a cultural shift, one that reflected and reinforced the gains made by American women since Title IX of the Education Amendments of 1972 guaranteed equal rights to all federal educational programs, including sports.

Football developed differently in China. In contrast to the United States, China based its success in the 1980s and 1990s—World Cup runners-up (1999), Olympic silver medallists (1996), and seven times Asian Cup champions—on a small pool of players: 300 in 1986 and just 800 a decade later. As gender inequalities re-emerged throughout Chinese society in the Deng era, football appeared to be an exception. The men's team struggled. Despite chronic underfunding, the women's team collected trophies and respect. Players earned transfers to Japan and the United States. Team captain Sun Wen, from a working-class Shanghai family, became a national icon.

As US soccer went from strength to strength, Chinese football declined steeply in the early 2000s. After an 8–0 defeat to Germany at the 2004 Olympics, state support, never generous in the first place, was slashed. China stopped qualifying for World Cups and slid down FIFA's international rankings. Media interest waned. The national team's popularity in the 1990s had masked underlying weaknesses. None of China's six national sports universities supported a women's team, nor did many high schools. In a 2005 survey of parents of high-school students, more than 40 per cent of respondents felt that football was unsuitable for girls. In 2012, China had 10,000 registered women footballers. In Germany there were 1 million; in the United States, 3 million.

Is women's football a triumphant story of liberation, or do players still bump their heads against a "grass ceiling"? The answer, as the example of China suggests, is probably both. Football has grown rapidly since the 1990s. Compared to the men's game, though, it remains a financial minnow. The relative parity between male and female athletes in, for example, tennis does not exist except—and then only partially—in the United States. The world's first fully professional league, WUSA, folded in 2003 after three seasons with debts of more than US$100 million. Its successor, Women's Professional Soccer, collapsed in 2012, again after just three seasons.

These difficulties followed the breakthrough 1999 World Cup—in an affluent country where soccer was popular. From an economic point of view, the sport's problem remained what it was not. The commercialization of men's football since the 1990s left only crumbs on the table for women's clubs and competitions. Yet, as a live and television spectacle, football had great potential. Thirteen million Germans watched the 2003 World Cup final between Germany and Sweden—a larger audience than the one that watched the men's team's decisive qualification game for the 2004 European Championship. Four million Swedes, almost 45 per cent of the country's population, did the same. In England, where football overtook netball as the largest recreational sport in 2002, audiences grew steadily. A record 4 million people watched England's European Championship match against the Netherlands on the free-to-air broadcaster, Channel 4, in 2017. The team's semi-final loss to the United States at the 2019 World Cup attracted a peak audience of 11.7 million people, making it the most-watched television broadcast of the year. Also in 2019, the world record attendance for a club match—the 53,000 who watched Dick, Kerr's play St. Helens at Goodison Park in 1920—was broken at the Wanda Metropolitano Stadium in Madrid, as 60,079 people attended Atlético Madrid's clash with Barcelona. Such figures were encouraging but not typical. Average crowds at some of Europe's best clubs in the 2017/18 season—Chelsea, Lyon, Manchester City, and Wolfsburg—were under 2,000.

Changing football's economic landscape is tied to changing attitudes. Japan's men's football team, largely composed of under-23 players (i.e., footballers aged twenty-three years or younger), flew business class to the 2012 Olympics in London. Japan's women's team, reigning world champions, flew premium economy. As captain Homare Sawa noted, it should have been the other way around. The Japanese FA justified the decision on the grounds that the men were professionals and the women were not. In Japan, as elsewhere, men's teams, despite generally modest performances, continued to get more money, more sponsors, and more subsidized travel. Athletes began to mobilize against such discrimination. In 2019, Argentina's Macarena Sánchez sued her club, UAI Urquiza, and the national football association for failing to recognize her as a professional footballer. She was subsequently among fifteen women to sign the country's first professional contracts (at another club, San Lorenzo de Almagro). In the same year, twenty-eight members of the United States' national team filed a lawsuit against the governing body, US Soccer, accusing it of "institutionalized gender discrimination" related to pay, coaching, training conditions, travel, and medical care.

Male assumptions of superiority are embedded in many football cultures, but perhaps none more so than in Brazil's. Women's football was banned between 1941 and 1979. The game grew rapidly in the 1980s, with 3,000 teams contesting championships in eleven states. The media silence was deafening, unless the subject was players' nail polish, hairstyles, or lipstick colour. Machismo defined popular attitudes. Players were told to move to the kitchen or the laundry sink. Brazil's greatest footballer, Marta, FIFA World Player of the Year for five years from 2006 to 2010, is rarely mentioned alongside her male peers such as Pelé, Garrincha, and Ronaldo. Her short spell at Pelé's old club, Santos, ended in 2010 when the club closed its women's team to fund a contract for the rising star of the men's game, Neymar. The club president justified the decision as follows: "The goal of Santos is to have professional football that can last for hundreds of years. Other side activities are possible when possible."[8] Women's football was to be tolerated, and sometimes even encouraged, but only as a "side activity"—and never at the expense of the men's game.

Football strongholds tend to be countries where second-wave feminism gained influence in the 1960s and 1970s. Eight of the top ten teams in FIFA's world rankings in March 2018 arguably fell into this category: the United States, England, Germany, Canada, France, Australia, the Netherlands, and Sweden. Parity in football will only be achieved, it is reasonably argued, when global conditions for women improve. Jafar Panahi's 2006 film *Offside* follows six Iranian girls who disguise themselves as boys to bluff their way into Tehran's Azadi Stadium to watch the national team play a World Cup qualification match. Much of the film is set in a holding pen inside the stadium, as the arrested girls—able to hear but not see the game against Bahrain—await the vice squad's arrival. Women had been banned from attending football matches since the 1979 revolution established an Islamic Republic.

Panahi's film remained relevant long after its release. In March 2018, thirty-five women in fake beards and wigs were arrested for trying to watch the Tehran derby between Esteghlal and Persepolis. Later that year, following international protests, the ban was lifted, but only for two matches. Fearful of the political and social consequences of women's "sinful" exposure to violence, swearing, and male flesh, hardliners quickly reinstated the stadium embargo. In March 2019, an Esteghlal supporter, Sahar Khodayari, was arrested for trying to enter the Azadi Stadium in disguise. Upon learning in September that she might face up to six months in prison for this offence, Khodayari set herself on fire outside a Tehran courthouse. She subsequently died in hospital of her injuries. The case brought into shocking perspective the latest Sports Ministry announcement—made shortly before Khodayari's death—that women could attend a World Cup qualification match against Cambodia in October 2019.

Western critics warmly reviewed *Offside*, while FIFA led the football industry's (largely ineffective) condemnation of the treatment of women supporters. Iran's hard-line stance shone a favourable light on more inclusive attitudes to women in the West, but the comforting contrast only went so far. Women could attend English Premier League matches (and did so in increasing numbers), but sexist attitudes persisted. In 2011, two Sky Sports presenters were filmed making derogatory remarks about a lineswoman. As late as 2010, the FA's executive body had never had a female member. Ninety-four per cent of the country's playing fields did not have changing facilities for women.

The grass ceiling, then, is still in place. A more optimistic approach, though, might emphasize different elements in the history of women's football: the extraordinary recreational expansion since the 1980s, the incursions into the closely guarded spaces of men's football (as spectators, administrators, match officials, physiotherapists, and journalists), the mobilization against discriminatory practices, and the establishment of structures for elite-level competition. This international history is remarkable, a series of quietly heroic refusals to play male-assigned roles—from young Iranian women breaking into stadiums to the Costa Rican team that defied congressional hearings and medical reports to tour Central America in the 1950s. Footballers' gains have been hard won. They constantly need to be reasserted. A UEFA survey in 2017 listed, among other statistics, the "Year women's football began." For France, the year given was 1970; for England, 1993. The history of the (Other) people's game in these two countries, as in many others, went back much further and was far less reliant on male patronage than UEFA's selective reading of history suggested.

Masculinities

In *Masculinities* Eduardo Archetti recounts a conversation in 1988 with Carlos, a man in his early forties from Buenos Aires. "We Argentineans are of the football breed," Carlos said. "Yes, I know, women are not of the same breed, although they accompany us ... Argentineans are very individualistic, with little national feeling ... except when the national football team plays." Football, in this reading, incarnated national male virtues. Archetti's work identified tropes—most notably, the *potrero* (an empty, uneven urban space where football was played) and the *pibe* (the poor, skilled child footballer who inhabited the *potrero*)—that shaped the hybrid imagery of Argentinean football. The classic figure was the "golden boy" (*pibe de oro*), Diego Maradona, the world's best footballer in the 1980s. Maradona, in Carlos's view, "was pure *potrero* ... his victory is a victory against discipline and training."[9] He embodied myths that underpinned a masculine world. This world existed outside family, work, and parenthood. It was a place not of masculine duty but of masculine freedom.

Football's ties to masculinity have roots that spread in many directions. In the public schools and universities of Victorian Britain, organized sport was tied to "muscular Christianity." Sport was meant to impart the manly values of self-control, loyalty, and physical strength—in opposition to the unhealthy, unmanly threat of homosexuality and as a counterpoint to feminine characteristics of sensitivity and physical frailty. As the working class co-opted sports such as football, the emphasis shifted from "manliness" to "maleness." Professional football was less about elite ideals of manhood, with their belief in fair play, than it was about rough and ready male spaces, filled with a universal male language.

Football's heartlands were places where football reproduced the tough masculinity of the workplace: the industrialized areas of north-western

Europe, such as the Ruhr valley in Germany (Gelsenkirchen-Schalke 04) and the Nord-Pas-de-Calais (Lens), or the working-class districts of cities such as Moscow (Presnia, home to Spartak Moscow) and Buenos Aires (La Boca, home to Boca Juniors). For young peasants arriving in Moscow, football helped in repurposing rural masculinity—centred on family, land, and physical strength—for an industrial lifestyle focused on the factory and leisure time. Zulu communities in Durban during the 1920s likewise transplanted indigenous practices of martial masculinity through football. The sport's utility as a gendered urban space, where hybrid forms of masculinity could be made and remade, was almost universal. In colonial Zanzibar, as one participant in a popular form of women's music noted, "The men had their football clubs; we women had our *tarab*."[10]

Football's appeal as an enclave of male sociability came at a cost in times of crisis. During the 1914/15 season in England, professional football was criticized for prizing business as usual over patriotic duty. A higher code of masculinity was now in play, as the *Evening News* intoned on 2 September 1914, shortly after the First World War began: "The young men who play football and the young men who look on have better work to do ... They are summoned to leave their sport and to play their part in the great game."[11] Football mobilized quickly behind the war effort. By the end of 1914, 2,000 of the country's 5,000 professional footballers had joined the armed forces. The FA suspended league and cup competitions in 1915.

Masculinity tied football to the "great game" of war, but it took other forms. The game helped to build friendships and shared experiences. Footballers in the East German town of Wittenberg in the 1950s, for example, fondly recalled card games on the train to away matches. At post-match gatherings in the local pub, they grouped around the piano to sing, regardless of the result. Male sociability off the pitch was accompanied, or was meant to be accompanied, by uncomplaining toughness on it. The Wolverhampton striker Derek Dooley, who lost his leg after he was injured during a match in 1953, epitomized this stoic masculinity. "I've got no regrets," he told journalist Arthur Hopcraft in 1967. "It's a man's game after all."[12]

Football masculinity could be highly political. When Italy retained the World Cup in 1938, the press tied the team's success to the fascist concept of the *Italiano nuovo* (new Italian). On the field in France, as on the battlefields in Ethiopia, a new breed of "supermen" supposedly led the way. Such valorization of football's masculine values also occurred on the left. In Chile during the 1940s, communist newspaper *El Siglo* increased its sport coverage, extolling the virtues of the amateur game over the crassly commercial professional one. It was among worker-athletes, it argued, that the true form of male athleticism could be found. It was on poor neighbourhood pitches in the capital Santiago that manliness and ball skills originated. Football's fluidity as a male space meant that it was cut to various political cloths.

The cultural and social revolutions of the long 1960s did not leave football untouched. A laddish masculinity emerged among a new generation of players in England, led by Manchester United winger George Best. It combined hedonistic tropes—long hair, model girlfriends, mod-tailored suits, and nightclubs—with hard work. The two prominent symbols of modernity in West German football in the 1970s eschewed the short back and sides and the political reticence of their predecessors. Borussia Mönchengladbach midfielder Günter Netzer had long blond hair and was known as "the rebel on the ball." Bayern Munich defender Paul Breitner sported an Afro and beard and the nickname "Red Paul," a reference to his sympathy for the left-wing student movement. Neither Netzer nor Breitner was as rebellious as media portraits suggested. Visually and verbally, though, they challenged stereotypes of the modestly dressed, apolitical Bundesliga footballer.

Male appearances and behaviour changed on the terraces as well. In pre-1960s photographs of football crowds, it can be hard to discern individuals amid the recurrences of headwear (flat caps, bowlers, or boaters), suits and sports jackets, and Brylcreemed hair. By the 1970s, spectators and spectator culture looked very different. Young males—financially independent, distanced from their parents, and with increased leisure time—gathered on the terraces. They organized more aggressively and more tribally than their predecessors. They travelled in closed groups to away matches. They paid attention to their clothes and hairstyles.

Scholarly and popular attention focused on the minority of troublemakers, linking hooliganism to masculinity, territoriality, and what sociologists Norbert Elias and Eric Dunning called a "quest for excitement."[13] But rivalries and identities were likelier to be about style than fighting. In the late 1970s, Liverpool supporters began to sport effeminate wedge cuts. They wore straight jeans or cords and Adidas Samba trainers. On the club's frequent trips to Europe, style-conscious Scousers stockpiled sportswear from foreign companies such as Fila and Lacoste. They developed an original look that combined club loyalty with sartorial cosmopolitanism, and toughness with style and conspicuous consumption.

Elements within football resisted change. When ten-year-old Rudi Völler—future perm-haired star of the German national team—pinned a poster of Günter Netzer to his bedroom wall in 1970, his uncle told him to remove it. Netzer's hair, he said, was too long. Völler won the battle over the poster, but his uncle's attitude was widespread. For every George Best, there was a Bobby Charlton, Best's fellow Manchester United star, who had a straggly comb-over rather than Beatles-esque long hair. For every Günter Netzer or Paul Breitner, there was a Franz Beckenbauer or Berti Vogts, players deemed to represent a more politically and socially conservative West Germany. Long after the 1960s, football cultures remained suspicious of those who flouted codes of masculine behaviour. David Goldblatt remarked in 2014 that England's ideal footballer still resembled Bobby Moore, captain of the country's 1966 World Cup winners: "a working-class gentleman, socially aspirant but publicly humble, vigorously physical and unambiguously heterosexual."[14]

Football was a pronounced site of male virility and homo-social bonding in Latin America. In the San Miguel district of the Chilean capital Santiago, *barrio* (neighbourhood) teams such as Unión Condell incarnated working-class ideals of masculinity. Condell drew players and supporters from local meatpacking plants and butcher shops. Frequent references to tools of the trade—meat, knives, and bulls—underscored the club's physical and sexual superiority. Football archetypes in the region, such as the *pibe* (boy or kid) in Argentina and the *malandro* (rascal) in Brazil, emphasized a spontaneity and trickiness that was working class, male, and heterosexual. Those who deviated from heteronormative discourses could face difficult consequences.

At times, the fine-grain theoretical debates about the role of the body in sport can seem divorced from historical perspectives. But it is interesting to consider histories of the male body in football from four interlinked perspectives: the sportive body (i.e., the physical act of playing the game), the political body (the body as a site of resistance), the commodified body, and the sexual body. French sociologist Pierre Bourdieu's concept of *habitus*—a set of values, tastes, and behaviours that condition cultural identity as well as a set of transferable manners (*dispositions*) that shape how we act, move, speak, and think—is tied to class and power relations. Boxing and football, two working-class sports, were tied, in Bourdieu's view, to a *habitus* that emphasized bodily practices (*hexis*) and behaviours that valued unpretentiousness, physical confrontation, and the collective.

Bourdieu argued that, in order to have a long-term impact, *habitus* must be capable of adaptation. The writer Fredrik Ekelund reflected in 2014 on changes in Swedish football since the 1960s. He contrasted his childhood hero, the versatile Malmö player "King" Bosse Larsson ("the embodiment of the working class ... loyal, humble, always put the collective first") with Sweden's transnational contemporary superstar, the brilliant but egotistical striker Zlatan Ibrahimović. The son of Bosnian Muslim and Croatian immigrants, Ibrahimović too came from a working-class background. Unlike Larsson, he would never return to it. "In the difference between them," concluded Ekelund, "lies a whole social and cultural history."[15] The shift from the football *habitus* of Larsson to that of Ibrahimović, embodied in their different ways of speaking about and playing the game, was profound.

The modern game that emerged in the late nineteenth century was played on cordoned-off pitches of varying sizes, in front of spectators who may or may not have paid to watch. As football became commercialized, space became more closely demarcated. In stadiums with paying spectators, the pressure to entertain created a faster-paced game. Football became more productive and efficient. Helped by improved training methods and better diets, as well as the advent of professionalism, the body of the footballer changed too. Players got bigger and fitter. Running supplanted dribbling. Technical ability without some accompanying combination of strength, speed, and versatility was useless.

Manuel Francisco dos Santos, better known as *Garrincha* (Little Bird), is widely regarded as the greatest dribbler of all time. Born into poverty in the textile town of Pau Grande near Rio, Garrincha was short (5 feet 6 inches). He had crooked legs, a result of a childhood bout of polio. During his career with Botafogo and Brazil's national team, which he helped to win the 1958 and 1962 World Cup, Garrincha, in the words of historian José Leite Lopes, "embodied the *habitus* of a factory worker deriving the utmost pleasure from the marginal activities of a company town ... playing as a worker-player for the factory team, dribbling around the work routine, and transferring this hedonistic pleasure to the professional football context."[16] An alcoholic, who paid little attention to fitness, training, or a healthy lifestyle, Garrincha died in 1983 at the age of forty-nine.

Portuguese superstar Cristiano Ronaldo is also a brilliant winger, but the similarities with Garrincha largely end there. An exemplar of football's transnational appeal in the twenty-first century, Ronaldo has received innumerable honours during his career at three of the world's biggest clubs, Manchester United, Real Madrid, and Juventus. Ronaldo is tall (6 feet 2 inches) and keen to display his athleticism, on and off the pitch. Whereas Garrincha was a classical winger who hugged the touchline and concentrated on dribbling past his opponent, Ronaldo insists on a more central role. He ranges across the forward line, taking free kicks and penalties and scoring goals with outrageous skill and regularity. For Garrincha, as Eduardo Galeano remarked, "the field ... [was] a circus ring, the ball a tame beast, the game an invitation to a party."[17] For Ronaldo, football, and his body, is a more serious business.

How might the sportive body move beyond play (however serious) into political acts? Japan occupied the city of Dalian, in China's north-eastern province of Manchuria, between 1905 and 1945. Japanese-run schools emphasized discipline, subjugation, and control through the militarized masculinity of calisthenics. Bodily movements were predetermined and ritualistic. In contrast, football offered unpredictable bodily movements and magical moments. A free and untutored activity first played on the streets, it became hugely popular among Dalian males. Dalian's representative team defeated teams from Britain, Japan, and elsewhere. It embodied a rebellious form of masculinity, undermining the stereotype of the effeminate East Asian male, just as Mohun Bagan's success undercut the image of the physically weak Bengali *babu* in British India. Football did not overthrow colonial power, but it encouraged a collective rejection of the internalized idea of Chinese (or Indian) inferiority.

In the twenty-first century, the world's best footballers make much of their money through selling image rights and advertising products. Their bodies are commodities. In 2013, the year that he retired, David Beckham had a salary of US$5.2 million. His endorsements earned him US$42 million. Beckham personified the increased commercial value of footballers' bodies and a shift in how these bodies were presented. Underwear advertisements for H&M left little uncovered. Tattooed, muscular, and stubbled, Beckham looked every inch the hyper-modern footballer. The body on erotic commercial display was even more apparent in a 2006 underwear advertisement for Dolce & Gabbana, featuring members of Italy's World Cup squad. Glistening with sweat in the locker room, dressed in white underwear embossed with a small Italian flag, Fabio Cannavaro, Gennaro Gattuso, Andrea Pirlo, and Gianluca Zambrotta looked like models not footballers. Such images contrasted with older advertisements. A 1952 poster for Craven A cigarettes, for example, featured England winger Stanley Matthews. Matthews is pictured twice: on the field, running down the wing in baggy shorts, and smiling and smoking in his England shirt. The advertisement is text heavy and asexual. Beckham and Matthews both sold forms of masculinity, but the concept changed significantly between the early 1950s and the early 2000s.

The commodification of footballers' bodies—from Beckham and Ronaldo selling underwear to the retired Pelé selling the erectile dysfunction pill, Viagra—took place in a heterosexual framework. Male sports stars now attend fashion shows and pay attention to their appearance, but their sexuality is not meant to stray beyond accepted boundaries. David Beckham was photographed wearing a sarong during the 1998 World Cup, a tournament in which he was sent off during an elimination match against Argentina. At the height of subsequent public hostility, Beckham's "unmasculine" appearance was held against him. On the terraces and in the tabloids, Beckham was presented as feminized and emasculated. He was a man dressed by his wife, the Spice Girl and fashion designer, Victoria Beckham.

The fuss that surrounded David Beckham—a heterosexual icon with a wife and four children—suggests the uneasy relationship between football and sexuality. This relationship has a long history. Victorian public schools used sport to channel boys' sexual energies in "healthy" directions. Homosexuality and masturbation, what Uppingham headmaster Edward Thring obliquely termed "the devil work of impurity,"[18] were enemies of the rugged masculinity exemplified by football and rugby. The indecency trial of poet and playwright Oscar Wilde in 1894–95 exposed the differences between "natural" physicality—as represented by Wilde's accuser, the founder of the rules of modern boxing, the Marquess of Queensberry—and "unnatural" physicality, as represented by Wilde's effeminate and sickly aestheticism.

The distinction between acceptable and unacceptable forms of male sexuality has been resilient. Football was not just "a man's game" but a game for masculinities that were emphatically heterosexual. Homosexuality was decriminalized in Britain in 1967. In 2018, there were no openly gay footballers in England's four professional divisions. Ross Raisin's 2017 novel *A Natural* tells the story of Tom Pearman, an ex–Premier League prospect, who finds himself playing for a team in the fifth tier of English football. The novel's title plays on the tension between Tom's "natural" football abilities and his "unnatural" (in the context of banter-driven changing-room culture) sexual preferences. This tension is crystallized in Tom's relationship with the club's groundsman, Liam. *A Natural* closes with Tom cutting all ties to Liam, choosing career over public or even private recognition of his homosexuality. He scores the winning goal for Town in a cup tie against Spurs. A safely heterosexual celebration buries, at least temporarily, Tom's sexual identity.

Tom Pearman's story may be fictional, but it speaks to a long-standing homophobia in the English game. During the 1990s, opposition players and supporters taunted Chelsea and Blackburn full back Graeme Le Saux about his sexuality. Le Saux was straight, but his interests—collecting antiques and reading the liberal broadsheet, *The Guardian*—made him seem suspiciously different. The sense of difference was magnified in the case of Justin Fashanu, Britain's first million-pound black footballer. Fashanu's homosexuality was an open secret. Shortly before retiring in 1990, he became the first active British footballer to come out. In 1998 he committed suicide, after he was accused of sexually assaulting a seventeen-year-old boy while coaching in the United States.

In light of the child sexual abuse scandal that broke in English football in 2016 and the many reported cases of non-consensual sex with minors in other sports, Fashanu's case is complicated to assess. It is made doubly so by predatory stereotypes that surround gay men, in sport and elsewhere. Fashanu denied the charge, and his death prevented the case from going to trial. However his life ended, it is impossible not to empathize with Fashanu's isolated position during his career. Comments from his unsympathetic brother John, also a professional footballer, indicate how transgressive a threat Justin posed: "Football is like the mafia, we all move together and set the rules. They say your brother's gay, but you can't choose your family. I wouldn't like to play or get changed in the vicinity of one. That's how I feel, so you can imagine how other players feel."[19]

Such sentiments have long been part of the global game. Terrace chants are replete with homophobia, from "Dodgy keeper, dodgy keeper, takes it up the arse" to "Does your boyfriend know you're here?" In 2018, the first game of the expansion MLS franchise Los Angeles FC was marred by home supporters using the Spanish gay slur *puto* (male prostitute) to barrack the visiting goalkeeper. Fans are not the only or necessarily the worst culprits. The head of the Croatian Football Federation, Vlatko Marković, stated in 2010, "As long as I'm president, there will be no gay players. Thank goodness only healthy people play football."[20]

Progress has been made. Danish club FC Midtjylland fired its Polish goalkeeper Arek Onyszko in 2009 for anti-gay comments in his autobiography. In 2012, the English FA introduced an anti-homophobia campaign, "Opening Doors and Joining In." To what extent these and other initiatives—rainbow lacing on football boots, for example—are window dressing remains to be seen. Eighty-two per cent of respondents in a 2016 BBC survey claimed that they would have no problem with their team having openly gay footballers. Clubs such as Stonewall FC—Britain's first and highest-profile gay team, founded in 1991—have helped to increase visibility and reduce stigma. Stonewall FC play in straight and LGBT competitions. Paris hosted the twenty-third International Gay and Lesbian Football Association (IGLFA) World Cup in 2018. The Stonewall team has hitherto won it seven times.

For all that kit deals with Adidas and features in right-wing tabloids such as *The Sun* raised Stonewall FC's profile, LGBT communities, out of choice or necessity, remain on the margins of English football. For all that players and supporters profess greater tolerance for homosexuality, elite players, almost without exception, only feel comfortable coming out after they have retired. This was the case, for example, when ex-German international Thomas Hitzlsperger came out in 2014. On the commonly stated notion that a gay footballer is "no big deal," there remains a gap between rhetoric and reality, even in liberal societies. The waters were muddied by FIFA's decision to award the 2018 and 2022 World Cups to, respectively, Russia and Qatar, where same-sex relationships were either persecuted or illegal. LGBT supporters who travelled to Russia were advised not to hold hands in public. In large parts of Eastern Europe, Africa, South America, and the Middle East, football remains trenchantly heteronormative. IGLFA member teams in 2018 came from only ten countries: Argentina, Australia, Canada, the Czech Republic, France, Mexico, Spain, Sweden, the United Kingdom, and the United States. Homosexuality in football awaits its subaltern moment. Scholars have yet to explore fully its history of oppression, omission, and silence.

Notes

1 J.B. Priestley, *The Good Companions* (London: Heinemann, 1929), 3–4.

2 Brenda Elsey, "Marimachos: On Women's Football in Latin America," *The Football Scholars Forum*, December 6, 2014, http://footballscholars.org/uncategorized/marimachos-on-womens-football-in-latin-america/#more-1834 (accessed 26 April 2018).

3 Quoted in Alegi, *African Soccerscapes*, 120.

4 Leda Maria da Costa, "Beauty, Effort and Talent: A Brief History of Brazilian Women's Soccer in Press Discourse," *Soccer & Society* 15, no. 1 (2014): 84.

5 Quoted in M. Ann Hall, "The Game of Choice: Girls' and Women's Soccer in Canada," in Fan Hong and J.A. Mangan, eds., *Soccer, Women, Sexual Liberation: Kicking Off A New Era* (London: Routledge, 2004), 32.

6 Quoted in Anne Brus and Elke Trangbaek, "Asserting the Right to Play—Women's Football in Denmark," in Hong and Mangan, eds., *Soccer, Women, Sexual Liberation*, 107, 111.

7 Quoted in Jean Williams, *A Beautiful Game: International Perspectives on Women's Football* (Oxford: Berg, 2007), 84.

8 Quoted in Joshua Law, "The Greatness of Marta in a Still-Sexist Game," *These Football Times*, July 11, 2016, http://thesefootballtimes.co/2016/07/11/the-greatness-of -marta-in-a-still-sexist-game/ (accessed 18 May 2018).

9 Quoted in Eduardo Archetti, *Masculinities: Football, Polo and the Tango in Argentina* (Oxford: Berg, 1999), 161, 187.

10 Quoted in Fair, "Kickin' It," 228.

11 Quoted in Assaf Mond, "Chelsea Football Club and the Fight for Professional Football in First World War London," *The London Journal* 41, no. 3 (2016): 274.

12 Hopcraft, *The Football Man*, 63.

13 Norbert Elias and Eric Dunning, *Quest for Excitement: Sport and Leisure in the Civilizing Process* (Oxford: Basil Blackwell, 1986).

14 David Goldblatt, *The Game of Our Lives* (London: Penguin, 2014), 287.

15 Knausgård and Ekelund, *Home and Away*, 381–82.

16 José Leite Lopes, "Class, Ethnicity, and Color in the Making of Brazilian Football," *Daedalus* 129, no. 2 (2000): 261.

17 Galeano, *Soccer in Sun and Shadow*, 104.

18 Quoted in Holt, *Sport and the British*, 91.

19 Quoted in Goldblatt, *The Game of Our Lives*, 169.

20 Quoted in Jason Mitchell, *A Culture of Silence: The Story of Football's Battle with Homophobia* (London: Lulu, 2012), 15.

6 | Race

On 16 July 1950, the largest crowd in football history assembled in Rio de Janeiro's Maracanã Stadium to watch Brazil and Uruguay contest the World Cup final. Few among the 200,000 spectators doubted the outcome. The hosts were such heavy favourites that Rio's mayor proclaimed them world champions before kick off. Things turned out differently. With eleven minutes remaining and the score tied at 1–1, Uruguayan forward Ghiggia cut in from the right and sent a low shot past Brazilian goalkeeper, Moacir Barbosa. Uruguay became world champions. For Brazil, the shocking defeat, etched into folklore as the *Maracanaço* (the Maracanã blow), was a national tragedy. Journalists compared it to the dropping of the atomic bomb on Hiroshima. Pelé, Brazil's greatest player, remembered "sadness so great, so profound that it seemed like the end of a war with Brazil the loser and many people dead."[1]

In the search for scapegoats, attention fell on the players viewed as culpable for Uruguay's two goals: the defender Juvenal, the midfielder Bigode, and Barbosa. All three were black. During the 1920s and 1930s, black athletes had been essential to Brazil's projection of multiracial modernity. In his 1947 book *The Black Man in Brazilian Football*, journalist Mário Filho argued that Brazil's "mulattoism," or mixing of races, defined its unique football culture. Such progressive self-mythologizing was silenced in 1950. Stereotypes about the cowardice, indiscipline, and emotional weakness of blacks resurfaced with a vengeance. Barbosa was never allowed to forget his part in the defeat, and Brazil did not select another black goalkeeper until Dida in 1995. Barbosa died almost penniless in 2000. "Under Brazilian law," he observed in 1993, "the maximum sentence is thirty years. But my imprisonment has been for fifty."[2]

The case of Moacir Barbosa exemplified race's pivotal role in the history of the world's most successful football nation. In Brazil, football's development was accelerated by the sport's facility for crossing racial boundaries, as Mário Filho and sociologist Gilberto Freyre recognized. Football reflected and shaped debates about the benefits, or otherwise, of ethnic diversity to a nation's well-being. This was apparent in the scapegoating of Barbosa, Bigode, and Juvenal in 1950, a critique of miscegenation reinforced by Brazil's poor performance at the 1954 World Cup in Switzerland. It was apparent, too, when a multiracial team that included the seventeen-year-old Pelé and star winger Garrincha won the 1958 World Cup in Sweden, thereby shattering the racial stereotypes of the two previous tournaments.

Football is a sport that encourages cultural transfer and migration. It is played at every level by people from a variety of ethnic and national backgrounds. At the same time, it is fiercely tribal. Outsiders can be objects of suspicion as well as veneration. Stereotypes can endure. It was not only in Brazil that coaches distrusted black goalkeepers. In the late 1980s, there was not a single black goalkeeper in English professional football.

This duality makes football an exemplary site for studying race's role as a source of identity and exclusion in modern societies. Lively debates about race and Brazilian football, which dated back to the 1920s and 1930s, were not quickly replicated elsewhere. In the English-speaking world, race only began to figure in football historiography from the 1970s, when the influx of black players and sociological studies of hooliganism combined to push the issue into the spotlight. Since football's global revival in the 1990s and the increased migration of black footballers (primarily from Africa to Europe), the trickle of studies has become a flood. Race now features regularly in academic and popular discourses on the game. Historian Laurent Dubois was drawn to football by French captain Zinedine Zidane's infamous *coup de boule* (headbutt) of an Italian opponent during the 2006 World Cup final. Some suggested that Zidane, the son of Algerian migrants, had been provoked by racist insults. From this starting point, Dubois began research. Football, it turned out, was everywhere, an essential element in France's history of race and empire.

This chapter provides an international survey of the history of race and racism in football. It focuses first on pioneers, players and coaches who broke ethnic boundaries as part of the spread of the global game. Attention then turns to football's place in the history of racial persecution, from Jewish footballers in Nazi Germany to black players in colonial Africa. The chapter finally focuses on changes, and barriers to change, in the contemporary game. In parts of the world, racist attitudes appear impervious to the raft of (often ineffective) anti-racist measures introduced by FIFA, UEFA, and national associations. Elsewhere, signs of game-changing attitudes highlight football's influence as an agent of intercultural exchange.

Pioneers

"[I]s the darkie's pate too thick for it to dawn upon him that between the sticks is no place of skylark?"[3] So wrote the *Football News and Athletic Journal* in 1887, ahead of an English FA Cup game involving the country's top team, Preston North End. The subject of the racial slur was Preston goalkeeper Arthur Wharton. Born in 1865 in the British colony of Gold Coast (today Ghana), Wharton was the son of a local princess and a Methodist missionary from the Caribbean island of Grenada. He came to England in 1882 to train as a preacher, but turned to sport instead. Wharton was a good cricketer and cyclist. He was an outstanding sprinter, becoming in 1886 the first man to run the 100-yard dash in ten seconds at a national championship. And he became Britain's first black professional footballer, playing for seven clubs between 1886 and 1902. After Wharton retired, his fortunes declined. He worked as a coal miner in Yorkshire and became an alcoholic. When he died of cancer in 1930, he was buried in an unmarked grave.

Race and class prejudices condemned Arthur Wharton to obscurity, poverty, and anonymous death. Responses within the game to Wharton's presence ranged from affectionate if racialized praise for the "Dark 'Un" to overt racism. When Wharton joined Stalybridge Rovers in 1896, the local newspaper reported that the club had "bagged itself a real nigger."[4] Tottenham striker Walter Tull, the orphaned son of a Jamaican father and English mother, faced similar insults. In the "pigmentocracy" of Victorian Britain, a physiologically determined hierarchy of the races placed black people, and especially poor black people (as Tull was and as Wharton became), at the bottom. For decades, the duo remained outliers. It was not until the 1970s that black footballers effected a revolutionary transformation of English football. It was only in the late 1990s that a biographer rescued Wharton's name from the unmarked grave of sports history.

Arthur Wharton's celebrity was limited in his lifetime. The same could not be said of José Leandro Andrade. The Uruguay team that dominated world football after the First World War—winning the 1923, 1924, and 1926 South American Championships; the 1924 and 1928 Olympics; and the 1930 World Cup—contained only one black player. But José Leandro Andrade was the star of *La Celeste*. The first black football icon, Andrade, more than any other player, put the game on the international map.

Andrade was born in 1901 in north-west Uruguay, to an Argentine mother and an Afro-Brazilian former slave father, José Ignacio, who—according to legend—was ninety-eight at the time of his son's birth. Andrade later moved to the Uruguayan capital Montevideo, where he began playing football. He became an accomplished tango dancer and musician, and allegedly worked as a gigolo near the docks. Called up to the national team in 1923, the defensive midfielder helped Uruguay win the Copa América. This was the first of six major titles that he would win with *La Celeste*, though he only played thirty-four times. Andrade rarely trained. He missed about half of Uruguay's matches between 1923 and 1930.

Andrade starred in Uruguay's World Cup win in 1930, but the competition that made his reputation was the 1924 Olympics in Paris. Andrade was a dominant force in a dominant team. Uruguay won the gold medal without losing a game. The buzz around him was not confined to the field. Andrade was an exotic, sexually attractive figure. Like world heavyweight boxing champion Jack Johnson, he wore his blackness with confidence: he partied with the novelist Colette and was rumoured to have slept with the film star Josephine Baker. Andrade returned to Uruguay a star, dressed in the dandyish clothes of the 1920s bohemian: silk handkerchief, silver-capped cane, striped jacket, and bright yellow gloves. He remained a star until he stopped playing. Thereafter, as in the case of Arthur Wharton, Andrade's story headed down unhappier paths. Alcoholism and poverty laid him low. When a German journalist sought Andrade in Montevideo in 1956, he found a man too drunk to understand questions. A year later, Andrade died of tuberculosis, penniless, in an asylum.

Few matched Andrade's revolutionary impact on world football. Hugo Meisl, the Jewish "father" of Austrian football, was one of them. Meisl's career embodied the fluidly transnational milieus of central European football in the early twentieth century. Born to an upper-class family in Bohemia in 1881, he moved to the multinational capital of the Habsburg Empire, Vienna, in 1893. After playing as a teenager for Wiener Amateure (later FK Austria), Meisl built a career as an administrator and coach, training the Austrian national team from 1912 until his death in 1937. Writing in *Soccer Revolution* (1955), journalist Willy Meisl coined the term "the Whirl" to describe the brilliant interplay of his brother's *Wunderteam*. Like Borocotó and the *El Gráfico* team in Argentina, or Mário Filho in Brazil, Willy Meisl helped to turn a successful team into a "national" style of play.

Hugo Meisl was a pioneer in more than one sense of the word. He drove the introduction of professional football in Austria in 1924. He started Europe's first international club and national team competitions, the Mitropa Cup and the Central European International Cup, both in 1927. It was Meisl, alongside the Frenchman Henri Delaunay, who laid the organizational groundwork for the World Cup, first held in Uruguay in 1930. And it was Meisl's *Wunderteam* that developed a revolutionary playing style, the kind of fluid, close passing later associated with Hungary's "golden squad" and Dutch "total football." Meisl tirelessly proselytized football as an international sport. He was multilingual, with connections to progressive coaches across the continent, including Vittorio Pozzo in Italy and England's Herbert Chapman.

In an age of strident nationalism, Meisl's internationalism did not endear him to everyone. In Germany, critiques shaded into racial stereotypes. The editor of one football newspaper wrote of a FIFA Congress in 1928: "In the plenum is Hugo Meisl, the Viennese Jew, with the cunning of his race and the subversive ways of a big card shuffler." The journalist contrasted the shifty, money-minded Meisl with the DFB boss, the lawyer Felix Linnemann: "one a representative of the crass business of football, the other an apostle of amateurism."[5] By Meisl's death in 1937, the political climate had worsened. The *Wunderteam* was on its last legs, as was the football culture associated with Viennese coffee houses and the Jewish clubs, FK Austria and Hakoah Vienna. Hitler annexed Austria in 1938. The DFB annexed Austria's footballers for the national team of the "Greater Reich." There was no place in the new order for Austria's football revolutionary. When the magazine *kicker* published an article on the *Wunderteam* in 1941, every reference to its Jewish coach of twenty-five years was removed.

In the first half of the twentieth century, football's race pioneers, from Wharton to Andrade, were isolated figures. This began to change in the 1950s. Migration from former colonies created larger pools of ethnic minority footballers in Belgium, Britain, France, and Portugal. The style and success of Brazil's national team—which won three of the four World Cups held between 1958 and 1970—discredited racist stereotypes. Black and *mestizo* players featured prominently in each of the three triumphant squads. Pelé, Garrincha, Didi, Djalma Santos, Jairzinho, and others drove social change. Brazil's flawed multiracial society worked better in football than anywhere else.

Known as *O Rei* (the King), Pelé is widely regarded as the greatest foot-baller of all time. He dominated world football for almost twenty years, from his breakout at the 1958 World Cup to his swansong at the New York Cosmos in the mid-1970s. Unlike his contemporary Garrincha, Pelé was in step with football's global march toward professionalization, internation-alization, and commercialization. He was a touring celebrity with his club side, Santos. He was alive, albeit not always wisely, to the sport's money-making opportunities.

As the iconic modern footballer, Pelé's views on race and his impact on football's racial discourses make for fascinating consideration. His bril-liance, however unwittingly, broke down racial barriers. Pelé's astonishing longevity and discipline made it hard to argue that black footballers (and black Brazilians) were lazy and emotionally unstable. But Pelé's extraor-dinary success from humble beginnings—he grew up poor in the state of Minas Gerais—also placed him beyond the experiences of ordinary black players. Activists often criticized Pelé for his views on race. Not without justification, he was seen as a mouthpiece for the platitudes about racial democracy espoused by the military dictatorships that ruled Brazil for much of his career. Pelé emphasized class as much as race in the factors holding down Brazil's poorest people. Like many elite athletes, he internal-ized the belief that individual sacrifice—a professional work ethic, ascetic discipline—can overcome any obstacle. Structural inequalities and rac-ist institutional practices applied less readily to genius. In contrast to his contemporary, the boxer Muhammad Ali, Pelé never carried the political struggle for black rights, either locally or globally.

Black and ethnic minority players came later to Europe than to Brazil. A smattering of players from the Caribbean, North Africa, and sub-Saharan Africa played in the English and French leagues before the Second World War. That black players were still unusual in European football long after that time is shown by the story of Germany's first black professional, the Togolese Guy Acolatse. When Acolatse joined the second-tier Hamburg club St. Pauli in 1963, the *Bild* newspaper described him with a string of stereotypes: "dark as the night, quick as an antelope ... [with] a shot like a rifle designed to kill elephants."[6] Acolatse was seen as an oddity and an attraction. Some supporters, he recalled, approached him to see if they could scratch off his skin colour.

The transformation of English football began in the 1970s. In the late 1940s, Britain was a largely monoracial society. Between 1948 and the early 1960s, approximately 300,000 people from the Caribbean and 200,000 people from post-colonial India and Pakistan started new lives in the UK. In the age of decolonization and a booming global economy, Britain, like much of Western Europe, became a multiracial society. By 1975, it had 1.5 million black and ethnic minority citizens.

New arrivals congregated in large urban centres, where football was very popular. For Afro-Caribbean communities in London, the West Midlands, Liverpool, and Manchester, football sometimes offered contact with white working-class communities. It often engendered solidarity against a hostile outside world, as players from Highfield Rangers, a black club founded in 1970 in Leicester, testified. When arriving for away matches in small villages, team members encountered a combination of disbelief and insults, from competitors and spectators alike ("Mum, they haven't got tails like you said they would have.")[7] Highfield Rangers usually won, though, and raced up Leicestershire's football pyramid in the 1970s. Such clubs helped to change the professional game from below. The proportion of British black and ethnic minority players in the Premier League rose from 16.5 per cent in the 1992/93 season to 33 per cent in 2017/18. The scale of overachievement, from a small demographic base, was impressive. It also raised questions, as it did in the United States, about black athletic stereotypes and the lack of alternative career paths for young black men.

In the political climate of the 1970s and 1980s, the journey to the upper echelons of English football was difficult. Racial abuse, mostly from the terraces but sometimes from coaches or players, was habitual. Chelsea's Paul Canoville was booed by his own supporters. Some, with ties to the far-right National Front, tried to drive him out of the club, sending razor blades and death threats in the mail. During a game at Elland Road in Leeds, Wolverhampton defenders Bob Hazell and George Berry were subject to the usual abuse (monkey noises, chants of "fuck off back to Africa"). Afterwards, fifty National Front supporters blocked their entrance to the team bus.

How this stream of hatred affected individuals varied. Hazell and Berry stood up to the National Front supporters and got on the bus. Liverpool's first black player, Howard Gayle, likewise confronted racism head-on, even on the training ground. This earned him a reputation as "difficult." Apart from a cameo in a European Cup semi-final against Bayern Munich in 1981, Gayle had an unsuccessful career with Liverpool. The club's next black player, John Barnes, signed in 1987, was very different. Electric performances quickly made him a club legend. Rather than confronting racism, Barnes treated it with bemused contempt. During a game against local rivals Everton in 1988, he casually back-heeled off the pitch a banana thrown at him from the stands.

Black and ethnic minority players had a long history in French football. The Senegalese Raoul Diagne, son of a prominent politician, first played for France's national team in 1931. Black players such as Marius Trésor and Jean Tigana featured in the great French teams of the early 1980s. In the late 1990s and early 2000s, France had the world's best team. It won the World Cup as hosts in 1998, defeating Brazil in the final. Two years later, it won the European Championship after a dramatic victory against Italy in Rotterdam. The champions were fêted as representative of a new, multicultural France. The French tricolour flag of blue, white, and red was remade in the image of the *black-blanc-beur* national team (*beur* was an ambiguous term for North African immigrants). Of the seventeen players who appeared in the two finals, most were children of immigrants or immigrants themselves, including Zinedine Zidane (Algeria), Lilian Thuram (Guadeloupe), Marcel Desailly (Ghana), Christian Karembeu (New Caledonia in the South Pacific), Patrick Vieira (Senegal), and Thierry Henry (Antilles, or the French West Indies).

The team became a lightning rod for public debates. Far-right politicians like Jean-Marie Le Pen argued that there were "too many people of colour" in football and society. Liberal observers, as well as many immigrants, saw the team as a hopeful sign that intolerance could be defeated and integration encouraged. As one shopkeeper in a *cité* (housing estate) outside Lyon pronounced after the Zidane-inspired victory in 1998, "This team, it is *la France moderne!*"[8] Others were sceptical. The *black-blanc-beur* ideal, some academics argued, was merely neo-colonial accommodation to a mythical French multiculturalism.

The 1998 triumph was anchored in goals and performances from two players who embodied different elements of the pioneer narrative. Zinedine Zidane, who scored twice in the final, was a superstar with a raft of commercial endorsements. He rarely spoke publicly about political issues. He was quiet about his family history, most significantly about his membership of a Berber ethnic group, the Kabyle, which faced persecution in Algeria. Defender Lilian Thuram, who improbably scored twice in the semi-final win over Croatia, was, in contrast, an articulate, politically engaged figure. He spoke about slavery and racism in French history. He clashed with Le Pen and later French president Nicolas Sarkozy on immigration. He defended France's *banlieues* (suburbs) and their largely non-white inhabitants against stereotyping and neglect.

Yet the space from Zidane to Thuram was ultimately not as large as it seemed. For all of his political reticence, Zidane publicly warned against the dangers posed by right-wing extremism during the 2002 and 2017 presidential election campaigns. American poet Claudia Rankine's meditation on the 2006 *coup de boule* that spectacularly ended Zidane's career placed the footballer, and his dramatic and unavoidable act, in dialogue with key modern writers on race, including James Baldwin, Homi Bhabha, and Frantz Fanon. Zidane was no more capable of escaping the minefields of history, identity, and memory than Thuram, who faced criticism for confronting racist abuse during his time at Italian clubs Parma and Juventus and was patronizingly dismissed by President Sarkozy for empathizing with young *banlieue* residents during the riots in 2005. Like race pioneers throughout history, Thuram and Zidane were held to higher standards than their white counterparts—and faced a fiercer backlash when things went wrong. Zidane was a national hero in 1998. In 2006, to some at least, he was once again "the Arab." When France's largely black team, now without the retired Thuram and Zidane, suffered an embarrassing early elimination at the 2010 World Cup, amid a players' strike and bitter divisions within the camp, a racial undercurrent shaped the angry media response. Philosopher Alain Finkielkraut, critic of the "failures" of French assimilation, compared the ungrateful players to *banlieue* rioters: "We now have proof that the French team is not a team at all, but a gang of hooligans that knows only the morals of the mafia."[9] In France, as in many societies where tolerance and xenophobia uneasily coexisted, colour blindness was conditional.

Hitting the Bar? Histories of Racial Persecution and Resistance

Football came to Zambia as it came to many British colonies, via the administrators, industrialists, missionaries, and teachers who colonized the southern African territory in the late nineteenth century. Locals quickly adopted the game, particularly in the mining townships of the African Copperbelt. Football, like the rest of society, was segregated. Blacks were excluded from the Northern Rhodesia FA when it was formed in 1929. The Native Football Committee, founded in 1936 to oversee football on the Copperbelt, was also run by whites. "Natives" had a voice, but disputes were resolved by an unelected body of mine managers. Like other welfare structures, football was part of an imperial arsenal of social control.

Assumptions of racial superiority soon ran into resistance. Beginning in the 1930s, African players and administrators, with help from sympathetic

Europeans, created a governing body of their own, known from 1950 as the Copperbelt African FA. The Copperbelt FA was one of the first Zambian institutions in which Africans and Europeans were equally represented. It created a popular league competition and pressed the colonial authorities to uphold promises to provide facilities, equipment (such as nets), and clothing (such as boots) in the mine compounds. The Copperbelt FA gave black administrators experience and a taste for equality, as anti-colonial nationalism grew in influence. A racially integrated league competition began in 1962, under the leadership of a black businessman. By the time that the protectorate of Northern Rhodesia became independent Zambia in 1964, football's counter-hegemonic bona fides had long been proven. The new president, Kenneth Kaunda, like many post-independence African leaders, understood the sport's importance to the nation-building project. Unlike most post-independence African leaders, he liked the game too. Kaunda invested state resources in football and cultivated partnerships with European players, coaches, and clubs. He formed a ministerial cabinet team, occasionally refereed matches, and often displayed his ball-juggling skills to the crowd before games in the Zambian capital, Lusaka. "A country without sport," Kaunda stated in 1964, "was half-dead."[10]

Zambia's story was replicated across the colonial world, from the French Congo to Portuguese Mozambique. Football's modern history shaped and reflected a history of creating, and breaking, colour bars. Prejudice and persecution worked on a sliding scale, from the monkey chants on British terraces during the 1970s and 1980s to the charnel houses of the Holocaust. These were not always black and white, or black versus white, issues. In the Rwandan Civil War (1990–94), for example, football was one of the last points of unity between the country's Hutu and Tutsi populations. It was also a recruiting ground for the Hutu militia, the Interahamwe, chief perpetrators of the 1994 genocide that killed three-quarters of Rwanda's Tutsi population. State-led exclusion and violence could find willing supporters in football, but both could also meet individual and collective resistance. This is illustrated by football's role in South Africa's anti-apartheid struggle and the fate of Jewish footballers under Nazism.

Scholarship on football in the Third Reich has typically focused on the regime's treatment of Jewish players, clubs, and officials. The topic sparked controversy after the 2005 publication of Nils Havemann's *Football under the Swastika*. Commissioned by the DFB, Havemann's study downplayed the football association's ideological affinity with Nazism. It argued that business more than political motives drove its collaboration with the Hitler regime. The expulsion of Jews from German football was less about anti-Semitism than it was a pragmatic recognition of the direction in which the political wind was blowing.

Much of the debate, especially among Havemann's critics, seemed to miss the point. Apolitical and political motives were not mutually exclusive, and they contributed to the same racist end goal. Timeless phenomena (such as careerism, power, money, or fear) often concurred with a commitment to the Nazi remodelling of sport. The subject's resonance was reaffirmed in another controversy in 2016, around the self-proclaimed "anti-Nazi" status of Germany's leading club, Bayern Munich. Research by historian Markwart Herzog showed that Bayern behaved just as poorly as most other German clubs. It introduced anti-Jewish membership rules in 1935. It profited from the Nazi destruction of the workers' sports movement. Like Havemann, Herzog concluded that a mixture of autonomy, opportunism, and ideological sympathy motivated clubs' dealings with the Nazis.

Hitler became German chancellor on 30 January 1933. On 9 April, before the first nationwide boycott of Jewish stores, fourteen German clubs, including Bayern Munich and the country's best team FC Nuremberg, published the Stuttgart Declaration. It promised to "Aryanize" (i.e., remove Jews from) their organizations. Later that month, the DFB used the pages of *kicker* magazine, founded in 1920 by a Jew, Walther Bensemann, to expel Jews and Marxists from its regional associations. Most administrators willingly supported the racial reorganization of sport and society. Jewish players, coaches, and officials, not numerous in the first place, were quickly excluded: Bayern President Kurt Landauer, for example, and Karlsruhe's ex-international striker, Julius Hirsch. In 1938, after the nationwide pogrom Kristallnacht ("Night of the Broken Glass"), the Gestapo dissolved the two Jewish sports organizations, Schild and Makkabi.

The start of the Second World War in 1939 and Germany's invasion of the Soviet Union two years later internationalized the Nazi persecution of Jews. Holocaust survivors Tadeusz Borowski and Primo Levi recorded football's presence in the network of camps that the Nazis built in occupied Europe. Holocaust scholars have generally not displayed great interest in the subject. Recent research, though, has shown that football was played regularly and seriously. This was most famously the case in the "model" Jewish camp at Theresienstadt near Prague. Military courtyards there became football pitches. A league system with promotion and relegation thrived, as did amateur and youth competitions. A 1944 Nazi propaganda film featured highlights from one game, played on a sunny day in front of a large, smiling crowd. Though Czech players, including many ex-professionals, predominated, teams were multinational. They included deportees from Denmark, Germany, the Netherlands, and Slovakia. Teams were organized by camp jobs. "Kitchen," for example, won the 1943 league competition. Theresienstadt was unusual only in the depth and quality of its competitions, not in their existence. Football was played throughout the camp system, from Auschwitz, as Borowski chillingly documented, to the original Nazi concentration camp, Dachau. Dachau prisoners first organized Sunday afternoon football in 1936. Surviving artefacts from the camp include a wooden trophy, made on a prison lathe by a carpenter, bearing the inscription "Winner in football, Dachau 1944."

As survivor testimonies recounted, football was a rare and brief form of pleasurable escape. Playing the game meant claiming the limited autonomy available in the camps, but sporting joys were never unadulterated. They took place in what Primo Levi called "the grey zone," a collapsed moral space where the lines between victims and perpetrators, and between courage and complicity, were blurred. No heroic endings were open to Jewish footballers. Arnold Mostowicz, a doctor and survivor of the Łódź ghetto, witnessed one of the regular matches between Jewish prisoners and SS guards at the Hirschberg labour camp in Poland in 1944. He recalled the superior technique of the Jewish players. Dressed in striped prison jackets, they showed off for watching inmates, who cheered, booed, and contested the referee's decisions. As Mostowicz recognized, this was only a twisted glimpse of normality and the prison team's victory only a hollow form of revenge. For most deported players, including stars from MTK Budapest (József Braun, Henrik Nádler, Imre Taussig, Antal Vágó) and Hakoah Vienna (Otto Fischer, Max Scheuer), there was no escaping the Final Solution. Julius Hirsch was transported from Karlsruhe to Auschwitz in 1943. Neither the camp's entrance nor death records mention his name. He was probably gassed on arrival.

The story was different in South Africa, where black footballers played an important role in challenging and defeating institutionalized racism. When the Afrikaner National Party came to power in 1948, it introduced measures to entrench white-minority rule in a segregated society. The system was known by the Afrikaner word for "apartness," *apartheid*. It affected everything from travel and housing to who could enter a beach or sports ground. Apartheid social engineering enmeshed South Africa's non-white populations—whether black, coloured, or Indian—in an impoverished, bureaucratized, and Balkanized society, where race defined everything.

Outside the white minority, where cricket and rugby union held sway, football was South Africa's most popular sport. Despite appalling conditions, it grew rapidly. At the end of the 1950s, Durban alone had 5,000 registered players and 264 teams. The black South African Soccer Federation (SASF), founded in 1951, challenged the white-run Football Association of Southern Africa (FASA) as the sport's representative body, first by attempting to join FIFA and then by leading the international campaign against apartheid sport. At home, interracial tournaments such as Durban's Kajee Cup drew large crowds. In 1961 a group of black and Indian entrepreneurs founded a non-racial professional competition, the South African Soccer League (SASL). Large, racially mixed crowds attended matches. The SASL became integral to black culture in townships such as Soweto, near Johannesburg. Local team Moroka Swallows, SASL champions in 1965, had supporters' clubs that organized social events. Star player Kongo Malemane had a song recorded in his honour.

The SASL lasted only five years. The apartheid squeeze on facilities forced the league to shut down in 1966. In the same year, prisoners of the regime on Robben Island, including Nelson Mandela, formed the Makana Football Association. The league had nine teams. It played according to the rules of the FIFA handbook (one of the few books available on the island), using washed-up fishing nets as goals. The Makana league was a far cry from the first stab at professionalism in the SASL and from the later (often quite confusing) attempts to resurrect elite, non-racial competition, which culminated in the creation of the National Soccer League in 1985. These various organizations, from Robben Island to Durban, testified to football's subversive appeal. This was the sport that drove South Africa's sporting revolution. Football was prominent in the international anti-apartheid campaign, which led FIFA to expel South Africa in 1976, the year in which police killed at least 176 anti-apartheid protestors in the Soweto uprising. When apartheid collapsed in the early 1990s, desegregation occurred in football two years before the country's first free, multiracial elections in 1994. Systemic racism was ultimately no match for the power of football.

A Post-racial Era?

When the Englishman and former referee Stanley Rous became FIFA president in 1961, world football's governing body was an overwhelmingly white, male, and Eurocentric organization. South African football politics quickly enmeshed Rous, as the segregationist FASA and the multiracial

SASF sought international recognition for their leadership claims. Rous's sympathies were clear. After a 1963 fact-finding trip, he and his American colleague Joseph Maguire cleared FASA of intentionally practicing any form of discrimination. Rous's intransigence backfired. The recently formed Confederation of African Football (CAF) mobilized pan-African sentiment to press for a hard line against South Africa. Anger fed other frustrations, most notably the qualification criteria for the World Cup. FIFA gave one combined spot in the finals to the confederations of Africa, Asia, and Oceania. From 1950 to 1966, no African nation qualified. CAF boycotted the 1966 tournament in England, and was fined by FIFA for its troubles. But the veneer of European racial superiority was peeling. CAF was finally guaranteed one spot at the 1970 World Cup. In 1974, Brazilian João Havelange defeated Stanley Rous in the presidential election. Havelange ran on an anti-apartheid ticket. He promised greater support to the previously ostracized CAF and Asian Football Confederation (AFC). Football's moment of decolonization had, belatedly, arrived. African representation in FIFA organizations increased markedly after 1974. South Africa was expelled in 1976. Since 1998, Africa has had five guaranteed spots at the World Cup.

CAF's struggle to gain influence reflected a broader struggle for black and ethnic minority leadership in the global game. When Asian and African representation at the 1982 World Cup was doubled—to two among twenty-four teams, including fourteen from Europe—British journalist Brian Glanville complained that "Havelange has ruined the World Cup, has sold it down the river to the Afro-Asians and their ilk."[11] Even as the rhetoric softened, practices did not change, or they did not change quickly enough. Referees, an under-discussed area of football scholarship, provide an interesting example. Of the twenty-one World Cup final referees between 1930 and 2018, fifteen were Europeans. Only one, Morocco's Said Belqola (1998), came from Africa.

Post-1960s English football, as we have seen, was transformed by influxes of home-grown and, later, foreign black players. The transformation, though, was confined to the pitch. In leadership positions, a colour bar remained in place. As late as 2003, one of the FA's leading bodies, the FA Council, was entirely white. Between 2007 and 2011, no more than 4 per cent of managers at England's ninety-two league clubs were black. It was only in 2008 that former England international Paul Ince became, briefly, the first black British manager of a Premier League club. Accounts of retired black players displayed depressing similarities. Former England striker Luther Blissett applied for twenty-two jobs in the 1990s. He did not get one interview.

Neither England nor football is unique in this skewed racial demography. Black bosses are rare in many areas of British industry. In 2019, the Institute for Diversity and Ethics in Sport reported that 74.8 per cent of the players in the NBA, the most racially progressive of the "big four" North American sports, were black, but only 26.7 per cent of the head coaches were black. To combat institutionalized racism, the NFL introduced the Rooney Rule in 2003. It required all teams to interview ethnic minority candidates for senior coaching and leadership positions. Campaigners in English football, where 19 (3.4 per cent) of the 552 coaches at league clubs were black or from ethnic minorities in 2014, have pressed for something similar. In Europe's top five leagues in 2016, there was not a single black head coach. As Florent Ibenge, national team coach for the Democratic Republic of Congo, remarked, "We can play, but not lead."[12]

In England since the 1990s, overt discrimination—the monkey chants and banana throwing, the offhand remarks from coaches and commentators about laziness and indiscipline—has become less common. The cultural shift, though, was hardly universal. Private views, as many studies of race have recognized, proved harder to change than public ones, bringing into question self-congratulatory ideas about a "post-racial" era. In 2004 the ex-manager and commentator Ron Atkinson was caught off air describing Chelsea's black French defender Marcel Desailly as "a lazy, fucking thick nigger."[13] Nor has this cultural shift reached the country's large Asian population. In 2017, only 10 of the UK's 3,000 professional footballers were British Asians. The perception that "Asians can't play football"—the title of a mid-1990s study of Asians in British sport—remained in place.

As the world's top leagues became more multiracial, race became more central to football narratives. This was certainly the case in Italy's Serie A. Supporters of the Rome club Lazio, known for its far-right sympathies, welcomed Dutch midfielder Aron Winter in 1992 with graffiti calling him a "black Jew." During a pre-season friendly with fourth division club Pro Patria in 2013, AC Milan's players walked off the pitch in protest against racial abuse of Ghanaian midfielder Kevin-Prince Boateng. Four years later, another Ghanaian, Pescara's Sulley Muntari, mobilized the players' union to get a sending off overturned. Muntari had received two yellow cards in a game at Cagliari for, first, protesting to the referee about monkey chants from the stands and then walking off the pitch when nothing was done about it.

Such experiences were not uncommon. Cameroon's Samuel Eto'o celebrated a goal for Barcelona against Real Zaragoza in 2005 with a monkey dance ("I danced like a monkey because they treated me like a monkey").[14] Black players in England's under-21 team were subject to abuse from opposition players and supporters during a game in Serbia in 2013—and then to denials from the Serbian FA that anything racist had happened. This was not only a European problem. Japan's best-supported club Urawa Reds was caught up in several racist incidents. The anonymity of social media fuelled extreme views. A 2015 tweet from an Urawa fan to Gamba Osaka's Brazilian striker Patric read "Die, black man."[15]

Race's role in fan culture has always been complex. Tribal identities at certain clubs, such as Lazio, developed around explicitly racist discourses. In 2012, Landscrona, a supporters' group at Zenit St. Petersburg, wrote an open letter rejecting the Russian club's employment of black or gay footballers. In its confused mix of localism, xenophobia, and anti-commercialism, the Zenit letter encapsulated many of the contradictory elements of the "people's game" in the twenty-first century. Landscrona subsequently backtracked on some of its offensive positions. The supporters' club did not want the perception that it was racist. This in itself reflected a shift, however halting, toward a more tolerant landscape.

Football is an arena where racism has been clearly expressed and effectively challenged. The paradoxes are rich in the case of clubs such as Ajax (the Netherlands), Atlanta (Argentina), and Spurs (England) that have adopted Jewish identities. Raanan Rein's study of Atlanta, a club from the Jewish neighbourhood of Buenos Aires, Villa Crespo, charts the complexities and contradictions in the image of the Jew in modern Argentina. He notes the anti-Semitic chants of rival teams ("Here comes Hitler down the street / Killing Jews to make soap"), similar to those sung by Spurs' London rivals such as Chelsea ("Spurs are on their way to Auschwitz / Hitler's gonna gas 'em again"), and the use in both countries of hissing sounds to denote gas chambers. One Jewish fan of Atlanta's local rivals, Chacarita Juniors, confessed to joining in with anti-Semitic chants during games.[16] Some supporters' groups distanced themselves from the club's Jewish roots, even posting swastikas in sections of the ground. Spurs supporters took pride in their reputation as an anti-racist club, but their rhetorical "code-switching"—the flags, chants, and T-shirts proclaiming "Yiddo Army" or "Yid 4 Life"—did not sit comfortably with everyone. In both cases, club identity was bound to a racial Other, even though Jews formed only a small part of the support base.

By the early twenty-first century, football had a plethora of regulations, institutions, and PR campaigns to fight racism. Article 55 of FIFA's constitution promised sanctions against offending officials, players, or spectators. UEFA organized conferences and policies around the slogan "Unite against Racism" and partnered with the anti-racism organization Football Against Racism in Europe. National associations, unevenly, followed suit. Some, mostly in Western Europe, were ahead of the game. Kick It Out, the major anti-racist organization in British football, was founded in 1993. DFB campaigns in the 1990s centred on slogans such as "My friend is a foreigner" and "Show racism the red card."

The impact of anti-racism initiatives can be difficult to qualify. Does the fact, for example, that between 2013 and 2015 clubs and associations were fined for the racist behaviour of supporters in Costa Rica, Hong Kong, Peru, Poland, and Uruguay matter more than the fact that such incidents occurred in the first place? Financial penalties were often too pitiful to act as deterrents. In 2012, UEFA fined the Russian FA 30,000 Euros for racist chants from supporters during a European Championship game against the Czech Republic. Six years later, FIFA fined the same organization less (25,000 Euros) for monkey noises heard during a Russia-France match in St. Petersburg.

High visibility campaigns for tolerance coexist with ingrained racist assumptions. In Spain, a culture of denial was evident in the fallout from two incidents in 2004, the racist booing of black England players during an international match in Madrid and national team coach Luis Aragonés's description of France's Thierry Henry as a "black shit." One journalist in the Madrid football newspaper *Marca* dismissed the racism charge with the astonishing claim that "monkey chanting does not have a racist cause. It is a way of insulting the national team … a cultural thing. It was a joke."[17] FIFA's response only encouraged such trivialization. The Spanish FA's fine for the Madrid incidents was less than half what Cameroon paid for wearing an unauthorized kit at the 2004 Africa Cup of Nations. Aragonés's comment was reduced to a training ground motivational device. Federation officials denied all charges of racism. International condemnation of these and other incidents, and of the ineffective responses to them, forced the Spanish government to act. The Law Against Violence, Racism, Xenophobia, and Intolerance in Sport (2007) promised tough measures, including heavy fines and stadium closures, against offending clubs and individuals.

Legislative change effected no overnight transformations. In 2014, Barcelona defender Dani Alves responded to a banana being thrown on the pitch in a match against Villarreal by peeling it and eating it. The incident illustrated the ongoing struggle against racism, but international support for Alves's humorous response—Brazil's Marta and Argentina's Sergio Agüero were pictured eating bananas too—suggested a parallel narrative. Football may have a long history of racism, but it has an equally long history of intercultural exchanges that subverted assumptions and categorizations based on race or ethnicity. Racism has a high profile in football, but it is more endemic in many other sports and cultural activities. An international cast of interviewees for a 2015 UNESCO report was asked to rate the scale of racism in football from zero (non-existent) to ten (out of control). The average rating was under five. In Ecuador's Chota valley, the success of local Afro-Ecuadorian footballers in the early 2000s put the poor, rural region on the international map, encouraging government investment and black civic pride. In football's transnational republic—a mobile, multicultural world—history might be moving slowly, but it is moving in the right direction. As Lilian Thuram remarked in 2006, "it's the racists who are suffering. They haven't understood that society is in perpetual motion ... and that it's not going to stop."[18]

Notes

1 Quoted in Goldblatt, *The Ball Is Round*, 293.

2 Quoted in Bellos, *Futebol*, 56.

3 Quoted in Phil Vasili, *The First Black Footballer—Arthur Wharton 1865–1930: An Absence of Memory* (London: Frank Cass, 1998), 69.

4 Quoted in Goldblatt, *The Game of Our Lives*, 159.

5 Quoted in Nils Havemann, *Fußball unterm Hakenkreuz: Der DFB zwischen Sport, Politik und Kommerz* (Frankfurt/Main: Campus Verlag, 2005), 161.

6 Quoted in Niklas Wildhagen, "Guy Acolatse—The First Black Professional Footballer in Germany," *Bundesliga Fanatic*, March 17, 2014, http://bundesligafanatic .com/20140317/guy-acolatse-the-first-black-professional-footballer-in-germany/ (accessed 24 May 2018).

7 Quoted in Andrew Ward and John Williams, *Football Nation: Sixty Years of the Beautiful Game* (London: Bloomsbury, 2009), 155.

8 Quoted in Dubois, *Soccer Empire*, 127.

9 Quoted in "Steven Erlanger, "Racial Tinge Stains World Cup Exit in France," *New York Times*, June 23, 2010, https://www.nytimes.com/2010/06/24/world/europe /24france.html (accessed 29 May 2018).

10 Quoted in Hikabwa D. Chipande, "Challenge for the Ball: Elites, Fans and the Control of Football in Zambia's One-Party State, 1973–1991," *Journal of Southern African Studies* 44, no. 6 (2018): 994.

11 Quoted in Paul Darby, *African, Football and FIFA: Politics, Colonialism and Resistance* (London: Frank Cass, 2002), 99.

12 Quoted in Agence France-Presse, "We Can Play but not Lead": Black Football Coaches Fight against Europe's Barriers," *The National*, February 19, 2016, https://www.thenational.ae/sport/we-can-play-but-not-lead-black-football-coaches-fight-against-europe-s-barriers-1.181441 (accessed 31 May 2018).

13 Quoted in Goldblatt, *The Game of Our Lives*, 188.

14 "Eto'o Responds to Racist Abuse," *BBC Sport Online*, February 13, 2005, http://news.bbc.co.uk/sport2/hi/football/africa/4261881.stm (accessed 16 September 2019).

15 Justin McCurry, "Japanese Football Chiefs Investigate Racist Tweet Targeting Black Player," *The Guardian*, November 30, 2015, https://www.theguardian.com/world/2015/nov/30/japanese-football-chiefs-investigate-racist-tweet-targeting-black-player (accessed 25 August 2019).

16 Raanan Rein, *Fútbol, Jews, and the Making of Argentina*, trans. Martha Grenzeback (Stanford, CA: Stanford University Press, 2015), 146–47.

17 Quoted in Gabriel Kuhn, *Soccer vs. the State: Tackling Football and Radical Politics* (Oakland, CA: PM Press, 2011), 94.

18 Quoted in Dubois, *Soccer Empire*, 222.

7 | Spaces

On 11 September 1973, the Chilean army launched a coup that ousted Chile's democratically elected president, Salvador Allende. Allende committed suicide as soldiers closed in on the presidential palace. A junta led by General Augusto Pinochet took over. As the new regime purged the country of "communist" elements, sports arenas became killing fields. At the Estadio Chile in Santiago, those tortured and killed included poet and songwriter Victor Jara. Across town at the Estadio Nacional—Chile's national stadium and venue for the 1962 World Cup final—12,000 people were detained between September and November 1973. Forty-one people were murdered. As late as 1985, government forces used Santiago's San Eugenio stadium as a torture centre.

The 1973 coup coincided with a playoff between Chile and the Soviet Union to decide the final qualifying spot for the 1974 World Cup in West Germany. The first leg took place in Moscow two weeks after the coup and ended in a 0–0 draw. Before the return leg at the Estadio Nacional, FIFA sent a fact-finding mission to Chile. It concluded that "everything appears to be normal." "We are not concerned with politics or what regimes are ruling a country," asserted one FIFA delegate.[1] The match went ahead, but the Soviet Union boycotted it. On 21 November 1973, Chile qualified for the World Cup with a 2–0 walkover victory, in front of 15,000 people. The surreal match lasted thirty seconds. The Chilean team scored from the kick off and then left the pitch.

In sporting terms, the Pinochet regime won the battle but lost the war. Chile did not win a game or score a goal at the 1974 World Cup. It faced international remonstrations. During the match against Australia, a protestor ran onto the pitch with a banner reading "Socialist Chile," arguably the first political pitch invasion in World Cup history. After democracy returned in 1990, Chile began to make amends for the dark history of its stadiums. The Estadio Chile was renamed in Victor Jara's honour in 2004. Behind the goal at the northern end of the Estadio Nacional, a section of wooden benches was permanently left empty, in memory of the thousands of people detained, tortured, and killed in 1973.

In his forty-six-volume *Buildings of England* (1951–74), architect Nikolaus Pevsner mentioned football stadiums just twice, and then only in passing. In his perambulations of the Liverpool district of Everton, noted Simon Inglis, Pevsner observed churches, parks, and public buildings, "but walk[ed] past the solid mass of Goodison Park [home to Everton FC] as if it did not exist."[2] Pevsner may not have noticed, but football grounds shaped urban landscapes throughout the modern world. From iconic structures such as the Maracanã in Rio de Janeiro to much-loved neighbourhood grounds, they are etched into local, national, and international histories in ways that few modern public spaces—arguably, not even churches—can match. Not just venues for athletic feats, they are often, as Chile's Estadio Nacional illustrates, highly political spaces. Like the game itself, the football stadium has multifaceted and mutable importance.

This chapter examines football spaces from various international perspectives. It begins with a history of modern stadium design, from the open fields of the late nineteenth century to the multipurpose, architecturally prestigious structures of the twenty-first century. The chapter next focuses on stadiums as contested spaces: how polities sought, often in vain, to build and control football stadiums in their image. Attention then turns to stadiums and other football spaces as *lieux de mémoire* (sites of memory). The final section examines the history of stadium disasters, disasters that shed light on casual approaches to crowd safety the world over.

Intelligent Designs? A Short History of Stadiums

Ancient Greek and Roman civilizations built sports arenas, most famously the Colosseum in Rome. So did the Aztecs and other Indigenous civilizations in what became the Americas—for ball games, no less. Apart from bull rings in Spain and elsewhere, permanent sporting structures were rarely built, in Europe at least, between the fall of Rome and the birth of modern sport almost two millennia later. Premodern "folk football" happened in open public spaces, a form of play that survived the sport's codification, especially among young people. Every football culture has its equivalent of "jumpers for goalposts": the game as an impromptu kickabout, played wherever space could be found, using whatever materials were at hand. Football's enclosure began in the home of rational recreation, Britain. Between 1889 and 1910, fifty-eight English league clubs moved into spaces that they would permanently call home. Function preceded form. London club Fulham invited supporters to dump rubbish in order to form crude terracing at Craven Cottage when it opened in 1896. The key figure in early stadium design, Scottish engineer Archibald Leitch, created a simple, repeatable, and affordable blueprint: one full-length, two-tier grandstand, where middle-class spectators sat, and three open terraces. Structures were subsequently developed in piecemeal fashion, as new stands were added and open terracing roofed. British stadiums—"corrugated iron sheds ... the usual mess of badly-shuttered concrete badly finished, the scruffy collection of huts which are the turnstiles"³—changed little for much of the twentieth century. The hands-off approach made grounds dangerous places. It was only after the worst disaster in British football history, at Hillsborough in 1989, that stadiums underwent forced modernization. All-seater stadiums made the game safer, but often at the cost of affordability and originality. Iconic structures, such as the redbrick Trinity Road stand at Villa Park in Birmingham and Arsenal's art deco–influenced Highbury Stadium, were lost to the bulldozers (in 2000 and 2006, respectively). To many critics, the new stadiums that symbolized football's economic revival were soulless, identikit "leisure boxes."

Outside Britain stadium development coincided with, and was driven by, football's arrival as a mass spectator sport. In Germany and Italy, the boom came in the 1920s and 1930s, when football became popular and authoritarian regimes sought to mobilize sport for political purposes. In post-colonial Africa, prestige projects such as Independence Stadium in Accra (Ghana), National Stadium in Lagos (Nigeria), and Abidjan's Stade Félix Houphouët-Boigny (Ivory Coast) conveyed newly claimed national authority. Stadium construction or upgrading often accompanied international tournaments. Cohosts Japan and Korea built sixteen new stadiums for the 2002 World Cup at a cost of US$7.3 billion.

The expensive and the monumental only tell part of the story. Of the sixty-nine football stadiums in "the city of stadiums," Buenos Aires, only eighteen had a capacity over 25,000 in 2009. In the Argentinean capital, as in other football cities, most grounds were, and remain, neighbourhood affairs. Photographer Hans van der Meer's 2006 collection *European Fields* revealed amateur grounds shoehorned into small spaces in postindustrial towns in northern England, in the shadow of communist-era high-rise apartment buildings in Budapest, and abutting the Mediterranean Sea in Marseille. Belying football's status as an urban game, the collection showed football's ubiquity in rural spaces, in mountainous villages in Austria and Switzerland, or amid rolling farmland in the Czech Republic or Poland.

Stadium development reflected ebbs and flows in the game's global history, as well as national and regional differences in how stadiums were designed and used. At the start of the twentieth century, three of the largest stadiums in the world—Hampden Park, Ibrox Park, and Parkhead—were located in the Scottish city of Glasgow. The next largest facilities were in England. By mid-century, the great wave of stadium building in South America, from the Estadio Centenario (Uruguay, 1930) to the Maracanã (Brazil, 1950), shifted the balance of power. In 2018, only nine of the world's thirty largest stadiums were in Europe. Most were in the developing world, led by North Korea's Rungrado May Day Stadium, built in 1989 with a seated capacity of 114,000.

Many of the stadiums on this list were prestige projects, funded by state and/or private backers. Many were multipurpose facilities. In parts of north-western Europe, in Spain and Portugal, and across much of Latin America, football stadiums were built as part of sports complexes. Community hubs for *socios* (members), they offered many activities beyond football. Facilities that Buenos Aires club Atlanta developed in the Villa Crespo neighbourhood between the 1920s and 1940s, for example, included not only the football stadium (known as *el cajoncito*, or "the little box") but also tennis courts, a children's playground, a skating rink, a café, and a new clubhouse. The biggest fundraiser was not the football team, which was often a drain on resources, but carnival dances with large tango orchestras.

When Simon Inglis visited the new ground of Dutch side Vitesse Arnhem in 1998, he described a space typical of the stadium boom of the 1990s: "shiny, glass and metallic-looking, set in the middle of newly sur-faced car parks ... The location could be pretty well anywhere in western Europe: orderly, innocuous and totally anonymous."[4] Vitesse's stadium reflected the economic and technological changes of the era. Scientific advances in everything from roof design to turf management created more flexible, more profitable, and more comfortable (though often less afford-able) spaces, where football could evade limitations imposed by the weather or the passage of time.

The GelreDome, home to the world's first retractable pitch, was part of a trend toward stadiums as expensive, technologically impressive "beautiful objects," usually with one distinctive architectural feature and corporate naming rights—for example, Bayern Munich's Allianz Arena (2005) or Arsenal's Emirates Stadium (2006). In these stadiums, many critics argued, history was replaced by a simulacrum of history. Commerce reigned supreme, with television as the incumbent monarch. Juventus Stadium in Turin opened in 2011. Following a sponsorship deal with the German financial services company already bankrolling sports arenas in Munich, Nice, São Paulo, and Vienna, it was renamed the Allianz Stadium in 2017. The new home for Italy's most successful club was designed for televisual presentation and saturated with technology, from eighty-six surveillance cameras and the "Spidercam" allowing aerial photography of a game to the 2,000 square metres devoted to media spaces, such as the press box and the mix zone. Understanding the history of football spaces requires a reckoning with commercial and technological forces that have driven such transformations. But the process means little without first understanding the myriad, shifting cultural and political meanings of the modern stadium.

Contested Spaces

On 1 February 2012, barely a year after mass protests led to the fall of President Hosni Mubarak, an Egyptian Premier League match took place at the Port Said Stadium between two of the country's biggest teams, hosts Al-Masry and Cairo's Al-Ahly. When the game finished, police locked the gates around the away end. The stadium lights were turned off. Al-Masry supporters then ambushed their visitors, attacking with knives, stones, and machetes. Al-Ahly fans were stabbed, thrown off the terraces, or crushed in stampedes. Seventy-four people were killed. More than 500 people were injured. The Premier League was suspended for two years. Seventy-three defendants, including police officers and Al-Masry officials, went on trial. Ten people were sentenced to death.

The worst incident in Egyptian football history was not a tragic accident but a politically orchestrated massacre. Rumours about state complicity in the violence abounded. Video footage showed riot police failing to intervene. Al-Ahly ultras had been prominent in the anti-government protests in Tahrir Square in January 2011. They then opposed the Supreme Council of Armed Forces, which took power after Mubarak's fall and continued the army's long-standing dominance of politics. The Al-Masry attackers, many suspected, were Mubarak supporters. The massacre, it appears, was payback for Al-Ahly's political dissidence.

Like the use of Chile's Estadio Nacional as a detention and torture centre in 1973, the Port Said Stadium massacre showed how sports fields could become state-sponsored killing fields. Following French philosopher Michel Foucault, scholars such as John Bale have described the modern stadium as a place of control and surveillance, where pleasure is policed. Under the watchful eye of closed-circuit television cameras, terrace culture has been sanitized and tribal passions commodified. In this reading, the stadium serves as a "panopticon," a place where everything and everyone is visible. Visibility was certainly a trap at the Port Said Stadium, but what happened there did not easily fit Foucauldian theory. The planned inactivity of police and the failure to use surveillance—in other words, turning a blind eye to modern methods of social control—created the preconditions for the massacre. This reflected a wider struggle between state and society for control of stadiums and other public spaces.

Football historians, particularly those studying authoritarian states, have recognized the stadium as the ultimate liminal (or "in between") space. This approach draws on the work of anthropologist Victor Turner. Turner viewed societies as dynamic entities engaged in a struggle between structure and anti-structure. At the liminal moment, Turner argued, there is *communitas*, a temporarily structureless society in which equality and solidarity are foregrounded.

The football stadium provides a testing ground for Turner's theories. It is a place that straddles the public and private spheres, a place where authority (structure) and autonomy (anti-structure) vie for the upper hand. It enables ritual and repetition, on the one hand, and the unexpected, on the other. Stadiums can be sites of community and sites of violence. Stadium representatives, in the form of the host club or the police, have power, but it can slip away easily. Supporters have power too, but it often lacks direction and unity. It is short-lived. When the match is over, the spectator returns home, and the stadium returns to silence. Stadiums are thus inherently contested places.

Turner argued that *communitas* in the stadium tended to reinforce the existing order, but this was not always true. Police and army-supported violence at the Port Said Stadium in 2012 did not shore up military control of Egyptian politics. Protests continued after the game. Al-Ahly supporters staged sit-ins, clashed with the police, and broke into the headquarters of the Egyptian FA. In presidential elections that summer, the military's preferred candidate lost to a representative of the rival Muslim Brotherhood. Though the armed forces regained power in 2013, events in Port Said complicated and delayed the process. Football in Egypt, as elsewhere, was an unreliable form of political mobilization and social control.

In Mussolini's Italy, football became a key element in the fascist desire to showcase through architecture its dual commitment to Roman tradition and cultural modernity. Ideologues initially advocated theatrical productions in vast arenas, but quickly realized that football not theatre excited popular attention. In the late 1920s, the fascist party (Partito Nazionale Fascista, PNF) invested heavily in the game, creating the basis for professional, nationwide league and cup competitions.

The PNF pushed an ambitious program of stadium design. The Littoriale in Bologna was a multi-sport arena, built in the Roman style. Its inauguration in 1926 was marred by an attempt on Mussolini's life. Home to one of Europe's best teams, Bologna FC, the stadium was the brainchild of the city's mayor, Leandro Arpinati, who was one of the PNF's leading football fixers. In contrast, the Giovanni Berta Stadium in Florence (opened in 1931) was a masterpiece of modernist architecture built in the cradle of Italian fascism. Designed by Pier Luigi Nervi—with reinforced concrete structures, a state-of-the-art roof, and an iconic tower—it earned international praise, even from the Soviet Union.

Different in architectural styles, the Littoriale and the Giovanni Berta reflected tensions between national and local interests. As venues for Italy matches during the 1934 World Cup, both successfully represented "the temporary community of fascist feeling."[5] Both witnessed the kind of *campanilismo* (regionalism) that the fascist regime at times promoted and at times condemned. The Giovanni Berta was Florentine before it was Italian, an integral part of the city's identity politics. The Littoriale, a vast and under-used complex in an outlying area of a small city, did not excite such local pride. It rarely sold out for football matches. But the flames of civic rivalry could still burn brightly. Fiorentina fans were roundly abused after their team surprisingly beat Bologna in the Apennine derby at the Littoriale in 1932. Everybody involved in football, from PNF officials and local newspapers to supporters, juggled with the same contradiction. Stadiums contributed to the fascist nation-building project, while providing alternative sources of identity and entertainment.

In fascist Italy, the stadium was not an active site of anti-regime dissent. The story was different in the communist states of Eastern Europe. Archival records and eyewitness accounts have provided rich expositions of the stadium's potential for chaos and subversion. At the height of the Stalinist terror, matches between Spartak Moscow and army club CSKA Moscow were marked by a rowdiness utterly at odds with the political climate. A newspaper report on a tumultuous title decider between the two sides at CSKA's ground in 1936, for example, observed "a general attack on the field" at halftime by spectators, who "poured out like an avalanche and surrounded the playing surface like a tight wall."[6] Another crowd surge in the second half led to a broken goalpost. Such incidents were common in the 1930s. A Spartak supporter recalled terrace chants directed against CSKA ("get the soldiers") and the capital's police team, Dynamo ("get the cops"). In East Germany during the 1980s, the hated secret police team Berliner FC Dynamo (BFC) faced similar abuse: "Down with the armed eleven," "Death to BFC," even "Zyklon B for BFC."[7] BFC players were booed when they played for the national team.

How much of this anti-authoritarian mindset was political is open to debate. In the Soviet Union and the GDR, social historians have identified "grumbling conformity" as part of the uneasy social contract between rulers and ruled. The stadium offered safety in numbers. It is hard to imagine other public spaces in East Germany, for example, where people could chant "Stasi out!" or—turning a free kick into a political statement—"The Wall must go!"[8] In Romania during the 1980s, Bucharest's immense 23 August Stadium served both as a regime-sanctioned safety valve and as a site of autonomous expression. Power and resistance were not dramatic opposites; rather, they were interlinked. The country's football spaces—not only stadiums but beer gardens and sports lottery offices—relied on the state but also functioned separately from it. The burning of newspapers to celebrate goals or victories might be interpreted as low-grade dissent in that all media were state-controlled and filled with photographs of the ruling Ceauşescu family. It was more likely a creative expression of the joy that football brought, even, or perhaps especially, in difficult political circumstances.

Stadiums have their limits as sites of protest, but they are far from insignificant. Anti-regime terrace behaviour might be seen as an example of James C. Scott's "weapons of the weak," a form of everyday resistance that occurs outside major historical events but has a quietly discernible political impact. Football stadiums in Vienna provided one of the few public outlets for anti-Nazi sentiments after the forced union of Germany and Austria in 1938. The SS reported in 1940 that no game against German opposition in the Austrian capital was trouble free. After Admira Vienna drew 1–1 with Schalke in a supposed "reconciliation match" that November, the home crowd of 52,000 responded furiously to the perceived bias of the German referee, who disallowed two Admira goals. Anti-German epithets ("Piefke") were directed at the occupiers. Seats were destroyed, windows smashed, policemen attacked, and the tires on the limousine of a leading Nazi functionary slashed. Sporting anger shaded easily into political anger. Power, in its various guises, rarely took stadium protest lightly.

Landscapes of History: Stadiums and Cultural Memory

After the 1989 Hillsborough disaster (discussed below), many British football grounds were demolished, redeveloped, or relocated. Some were left vacant and overgrown. Others were buried beneath housing estates, retail parks, or supermarkets. Ayresome Park, home to Middlesbrough FC in north-east England, fell victim to this redrawing of the landscape. Opened in 1903, Ayresome Park was Scottish engineer Archibald Leitch's first complete stadium. With a 54,000 capacity, it was a venue for three games when England hosted the World Cup in 1966. All involved North Korea, including the team's 1–0 win over Italy, one of the biggest upsets in tournament history. When Simon Inglis visited in 1983, he affectionately described Ayresome Park as "one of the last of the really big grounds to have eluded the modern era of stadium design."[9] Financial difficulties almost bankrupted Middlesbrough in 1986. Nine years later, on the day that the rejuvenated club secured promotion to the Premier League, Ayresome Park hosted its final game. In 1996, it was demolished and the land sold to a homebuilding company. Middlesbrough moved across town to the imposing but blander Riverside Stadium.

What happens to a stadium when it (almost) disappears? Thirteen hundred items from Ayresome Park, ranging from floodlights and turnstiles to clocks and goalposts, were auctioned in 1996 to smaller clubs, local businesses, and private bidders. On the site of the ground, which became a housing estate, only one physical remnant survived: the western enclosure (Holgate) wall. In 2000, artist Neville Gabie was commissioned to produce a commemorative work on Ayresome Park. His project, *The Trophy Room*, situated small-scale traces of the stadium across the housing estate, landmarks that quietly noted where parts of the ground used to be.

In 2002, Gabie showed members of the 1966 North Korean team the bronze pitch puddle with stud marks that indicated the spot from where Pak Doo-Ik scored the winning goal against Italy. Closer to home, Ayresome Park's relics struggled to register. Middlesbrough FC showed little interest.

Supporters had to intervene to stop developers from tearing down the Holgate Wall in 2011. A 2010 survey revealed that most housing estate residents either did not know or did not care about *The Trophy Room*. For some, though, Gabie's work triggered fervent memories. Ayresome Park was "like a cultural cathedral where generations worshipped every other week." "It's my spiritual home, my temple to my religion." "My husband who died last year loved it here. He always said he lived on hallowed ground."[10]

Ayresome Park's afterlife reveals football's complex relationship to *lieux de mémoire*. In this one example, we see the indifference of a club to its history, the quasi-religious evocation of the stadium as a sporting cathedral, the ambiguous place of football heritage in a town's existence, an emotional attachment to place, and football's astonishing international reach.

In his work on French "memory spaces," historian Pierre Nora developed the term to mean collective sites (including places, objects, artworks, and individuals) where "memory crystallizes and secretes itself."[11] Apart from cycling's Tour de France, sport was not central to the work of Nora and his collaborators. A 2012 collection on "European sites of memory"— over 1,000 pages long, with 120 entries written by scholars from fifteen countries—similarly contained not a single mention of a football stadium. Yet sport provides rich transnational sites of collective memory. Reflecting an increased interest in public history, scholars have begun to examine how sports history is presented to the public and how sports heritage is, or is not, preserved.

As memories of Ayresome Park suggest, the clichéd idea of the stadium as sacred space retains considerable power. In modern, secularized societies, the football ground seems a likelier place of ritual and worship than the church. At many British grounds, it is possible to get married—a commercial opportunity for clubs to cash in on supporters' romantic attachment to their team and each other. You can also have your ashes scattered. The relationship between football stadiums and religious shrines is not simply metaphorical. Consider, for example, the hierarchical organization of space in both the church and the stadium and the ritualistic patterns, such as chanting or singing, that punctuate the football match and the religious service. The comparison only goes so far. The atmosphere of awed veneration in church ultimately has more in common with rigidly ritualistic social spaces, from concert halls to military parades, than it does with the football stadium, a frequently loud, rude, unpredictable, and subversive place.

The sense of quasi-religious attachment to place reflects the central role of community in football memory. This attachment creates a sense of historical continuity rooted in various elements of the stadium experience, from the place where you watch the game (whether alone, with friends, or with family) to individual and collective memories of famous matches, incidents, players, or managers. Sports historian Alan Bairner recalled going with his father to watch their team, Dunfermline Athletic, play Celtic in the 1961 Scottish Cup final at Glasgow's Hampden Park. Aside from the vivid colours, what remained in his memory were the supporters who gave him sweets and his father nips of whiskey, and a strong if unspoken father-son connection.

What marks the stadium as a *lieu de mémoire* is its capacity to evoke emotions, both good and bad. Watching Hertha Berlin games at the Olympic Stadium in the 1990s always left me with a slightly uneasy feeling. As the centrepiece of the 1936 Olympics and one of the city's few surviving pieces of Nazi architecture, it was a place heavy with historical burdens. At the same time, it was the place, more than any other, where I felt at home in Berlin, not to mention the place where I missed Alex Alves's goal of the century while getting half-time beers during a match against Cologne in 2000. In recent decades, the study of emotions has become increasingly important to historians. The "emotional turn" has largely bypassed sport. Yet emotions—individual and collective, private and public—are essential to sport's appeal and to the appeal of the sports stadium. Writing of the opening day of the Soviet football season in the capital city of the Armenian socialist republic, sportswriter Viktor Ponedel'nik rhapsodized: "Everywhere there are smiles, flowers, songs, and posters. It seemed that all the citizens of ancient Erevan [Yerevan] were hurrying toward their beautiful stadium, Razdan [Hrazdan]."[12]

Football stadiums are not only places of attachment; they are also places of trauma. This can be seen in the difficult relationship of survivors and victims' families to sites of tragedy. On the second anniversary of the 2001 Ellis Park Stadium disaster (discussed below), Kaizer Chiefs and Orlando Pirates played a memorial match there without informing the families of the forty-three people who died. The mural remembering the dead was obscurely positioned, on a concrete pillar forty feet above Gate 4, where the fatal crush occurred. The stadium, in this example, became a site of inattentiveness to suffering. It can also evoke fear, as any supporter caught up in hooligan violence might attest. Alain Bairner recalled a game in Belfast in 1984, at the height of the sectarian conflict between Northern Ireland's Catholic and Protestant (Unionist) communities. It featured running battles between Unionist and Catholic youths. Members of the Royal

Ulster Constabulary, in full riot gear, fired plastic bullets into the crowd: "The troubles had entered our sporting space and it was a frightening experience."[13]

There can be less traumatic reasons for turning away from a stadium. Munich's multipurpose Olympic Stadium was one of Europe's sports architectural showpieces, built for the 1972 Olympics. The stadium subsequently became home to the city's two football clubs, 1860 Munich and Bayern Munich. It was Bayern's home when the club became an international force, winning three consecutive European Cups between 1974 and 1976. Yet far from being a fondly regarded site of glorious victories and collective experiences, the Olympic Stadium was largely unloved. Before the club's departure for the Allianz Arena in 2005, some Bayern supporters watched their team in away matches only. This was because the stadium, for all of its design qualities and stunning vistas, was not a purely football venue. A running track separated supporters from the pitch. The open, largely unroofed structure created a poor atmosphere and left spectators exposed to the elements. As the laments for many of Britain's lost grounds and terraces suggest, football spaces rely on intimacy more than aesthetics for enduring appeal.

Twenty-first century stadiums have become increasingly corporatized spaces. In them, community is fractured by expensive tickets, gentrified audiences, the overbearing presence of sponsors, and the prioritization of television demands—as well as by a desire to market the past. Sports museums, many of which are situated in the stadium whose stories they tell, have become a global phenomenon, as clubs and federations sell history to the sports-loving public. Football is no different, as impressive new national football museums in Manchester (opened in 2012) and Dortmund (2015) illustrate. The emergence of a heritage industry might suggest that the objects, events, and individuals that make up football's history are more visible than before. But curating the past is still low on the list of priorities. FIFA's World Football Museum in Zürich is underfunded. The museum at Liverpool's Anfield stadium is shoehorned into a small section behind the iconic Spion Kop. At clubs such as Dynamo Dresden in Germany, museums are individual labours of love, run by volunteers in cramped, off-site spaces.

Many football spaces have, either figuratively or literally, fallen off the map. In the mid-2000s, journalist Jonathan Wilson visited the Bozsik Stadium in the Budapest suburb of Kispest. It was home in the 1950s to the army team, Honvéd. Honvéd provided most of the players for the country's "golden team," which blazed a revolutionary trail across world football. Sixty years later, the Bozsik Stadium was in decay: ancient flood-lights, crumbling concrete, and a muddy training pitch surrounded by rundown sheds. Though it survived and has since been renovated, other football spaces landed on history's scrapheap, from the vast open bowls of Eastern Europe (the Walter Ulbricht Stadium in Berlin or Warsaw's Stadion Dziesięciolecia) to the inner-city grounds of industrial northern England. Yet, as we saw with Middlesbrough's Ayresome Park, even a lost stadium can have an afterlife. This is true emotionally and in a physical sense too. Peel Park in north-west England was once home to Accrington Stanley, a lower-league club that folded in 1966. A site excavation more than forty years later found an array of artefacts—including brickwork, boot laces, parts of goalposts, beer bottles, and cigarette lighters—that recovered some of the material experiences of going to the game: how a match might have looked, smelled, tasted, and felt. The wider selection of drinks found on the site of the more expensive Hotel Side stand, for example, reflected class divisions among spectators. Such football archaeology offers important and touching reminders of lost sporting spaces.

Death on the Terraces

In April 1902, wooden terracing at one of the world's largest football grounds, Ibrox Park in Glasgow, collapsed during a match between England and Scotland. Twenty-five people fell to their death. More than 500 people were injured. It was modern football's first stadium disaster. In March 2009, nineteen people were crushed to death at a World Cup qualifier between Ivory Coast and Malawi at the Stade Félix Houphouët-Boigny in Abidjan. One hundred and thirty-two people were injured.

Separated by 107 years, these two disasters fit a familiar international pattern. Death in the stadium has been a rare but persistent feature of modern football, crossing historical, geographical, and political boundaries. Lessons often went unlearned. At Ibrox in 1902 and at the Stade Félix Houphouët-Boigny in 2009, the match went ahead regardless of fatalities. The Glasgow crowd was criticized for climbing onto damaged terracing to watch from a better vantage point. The Ivory Coast's Interior Minister blamed ticketless supporters for the stampede that led to the fatal crush in Abidjan. There was no public inquiry into the Ibrox disaster. Four years after the 2009 disaster, for which FIFA fined the Ivorian Football Federation US$46,800, another stampede at the Stade Félix Houphouët-Boigny, this time after a New Year's Eve fireworks festival, killed sixty-one people.

Institutional complacency or cover-ups, lax safety regulations, and a tendency to point the finger at supporters: these were defining features of the modern stadium disaster. In 1971 a second tragedy occurred at Ibrox when sixty-six Rangers fans were crushed to death at the end of an "Old Firm" match against local rivals Celtic. Police and club officials shifted as much blame as possible to supporters, despite overwhelming evidence that institutional negligence was the prime cause of the tragedy. There had been serious incidents on the same steep terracing in 1961, 1967, and 1969. Ibrox's disaster history reflected a head-in-the-sand mentality among administrators that traversed national borders. It reflected too the sport's distinctive place in the entertainment industry. At least until the 1990s, stadiums were not meant to be about comfort or safety. Terraces were crowded places, intense but potentially dangerous—and lucrative. The more bodies that entered the stadium, the greater the profits were for stadium owners.

Since 1964, fifteen countries have experienced stadium disasters that cost at least twenty lives. Two hundred and eighteen of the 276 people killed at British grounds in the twentieth century died between 1971 and 1989. Tragedy struck not only strongholds of the world game but less heralded places on the football map. In 1988, ninety-three people were killed at the Dasarath Rangasala Stadium in the Nepalese capital Kathmandu. During a match between local team Janakpur Cigarette Factory Ltd and Bangladeshi visitors, Liberation Army, spectators sought shelter from a hailstorm. Victims were beaten back by police and trampled to death against the stadium's closed exit doors.

While some disasters have received extensive scholarly attention, most notably the 1989 Hillsborough disaster, others such as the Kathmandu tragedy are barely discussed. Little research has been done on the twentieth century's worst stadium disaster, when 328 people were killed after police intervened with tear gas and batons and caused a stampede during an Olympic qualifier between Peru and Argentina at Lima's Estadio Nacional in 1964. The same is true of the Lenin (today Luzhniki) Stadium disaster in Moscow in 1982, once rumoured to have claimed 340 lives. The secrecy imposed on the Soviet media meant that an accurate death toll was never confirmed, but at least sixty-six people died in a crush on an icy stairwell during a game between Spartak Moscow and Dutch team Haarlem. Comparative scholarship on stadium disasters remains rare. Yet the subject tells us much about the sombre interconnections in football's international history.

On 15 April 1989, Liverpool FC played Nottingham Forest in an FA Cup semi-final at the Hillsborough stadium in Sheffield in northern England.

Catastrophic errors by the police and other organizations led to the deaths of ninety-six Liverpool supporters, crushed and asphyxiated against perimeter fencing on the Leppings Lane terrace. It was the worst disaster in British football history, at the end of a decade of tragedies. In 1985, English football's *annus horribilis*, fifty-six people were killed by a fire in the wooden stands at Bradford City's Valley Parade. A few weeks later, Liverpool fans attacked Juventus supporters at the European Cup final at the Heysel Stadium in Brussels. Thirty-nine people were killed. While Heysel seemed to confirm the worst fears about English hooliganism, the Bradford and Hillsborough tragedies were part of a pattern of safety mismanagement in Margaret Thatcher's Britain. This contributed in the late 1980s to a spate of fatal incidents on ferries, oil rigs, and trains.

Hillsborough was an accident waiting happen. There had been a near-fatal crush at a 1981 FA Cup semi-final between Spurs and Wolves at the same venue. Liverpool supporters had complained of dangerous overcrowding on the Leppings Lane terrace in 1988. Graphic accounts from survivors in 1989, many of whom acted heroically to save lives, were unanimous. Most fans had behaved impeccably. The response from the South Yorkshire Police, in charge of policing the match, had been hopelessly inadequate. Far too many supporters were allowed into the central "pens" (fenced-in sections of terracing) where the fatalities occurred. There was chaos and indecision once the scale of the disaster became evident—and no emergency plan. The first public inquiry into the disaster, the Taylor Report (1990), largely exonerated Liverpool supporters and strongly criticized police operations.

What happened on 15 April 1989 was widely known, but it was buried beneath a different narrative. UEFA president Jacques Georges quickly blamed the disaster on "people's frenzy to enter the stadium ... whatever the risk to the lives of others." Liverpool supporters, he said, were "like beasts waiting to charge into the arena."[14] Georges retracted his remarks, but they were the result of a campaign of disinformation. Politicians, the police, and the press sought to blame Liverpool supporters for the Hillsborough disaster. The tabloid newspaper, *The Sun*, ran a front-page article headlined "The Truth" on 19 April. It falsely claimed that Liverpool supporters had stolen from the dead and attacked police officers.

There was nothing unusual about supporters taking the blame. Police and Rangers officials emphasized the role of alcohol consumption in the 1971 Ibrox disaster, though the subsequent inquest, like the one that followed Hillsborough, found low blood alcohol levels among the deceased. In

Kathmandu in 1988 and in Abidjan in 2009, politicians blamed fatal crushes on surging, panicking crowds, rather than on baton- and tear gas–wielding police or locked stadium doors.

What made Hillsborough unusual was the scale, depth, and length of the lies told about the disaster—and the tenacity of the campaign for justice. After the first inquest returned a verdict of accidental death on the ninety-six victims, families and survivors faced a series of legal dead ends. Ongoing misconceptions about the disaster were reinforced by the perception of Liverpool as a "self-pity city," a place that cultivated a sense of victimhood. It took many years of media mobilization, research, and activism to change the parameters of public debate. *The Report of the Hillsborough Independent Panel* (2012) confirmed that lack of police control, not fan misbehaviour, caused the tragedy. With better emergency service responses, the report argued, forty-one of the ninety-six deaths might have been prevented. The 1991 accidental death inquest verdicts were quashed. In April 2016, after the longest trial by jury in British history, a second inquest ruled that the ninety-six victims of the Hillsborough disaster were unlawfully killed.

Unlike the disasters at Ibrox in 1902 and 1971 or at Bolton's Burnden Park in 1946 (where thirty-three people died in a crush during an FA Cup game against Stoke), Hillsborough had a revolutionary impact on stadium design and safety. The Taylor Report recommended the introduction of all-seater stadiums in the top two divisions of English football. This came into effect in 1994. Scotland's Premier League followed suit in 1998. UEFA and FIFA soon required all-seater stadiums for international competitions. This placed pressure on national associations to make the expensive transition from concrete terraces to plastic seating.

The removal of terracing was touted as a health and safety measure, but interested parties had different agendas. For the Conservative government, all-seater stadiums helped to control hooliganism. For leading clubs, they meant higher ticket prices and bigger profits. Grounds became safer but more sanitized and less affordable places. Liverpool's Kop terrace was torn down in 1994. Behind the seated area that replaced it, the club opened Europe's first football stadium McDonald's. Previously a site of neglect, the stadium now became an increasingly open site of commerce. New all-seater venues, often built on the outskirts of towns, were aesthetic cousins of supermarkets and retail parks.

Hillsborough's stadium legacy was mixed. Internet forums and call-in shows regularly debated the loss of atmosphere that accompanied the bull-dozing of terraces. By 2018, campaigns to reintroduce "safe standing" had achieved significant results in England and Scotland. Terraced areas survived in stadiums in Austria, Sweden, Germany (most famously, Borussia Dortmund's "Yellow Wall," a standing area for nearly 25,000 people), and other parts of the world, including the English lower leagues. For many supporters, too invested in proceedings to enjoy them sitting down (particularly as seating was usually cramped and uncomfortable), standing remained the preferred way to watch football.

In the 1990s, as Africa made its mark on world football, the continent was struck by a spate of stadium disasters. While Cameroon and Nigeria impressed at the World Cup and players like Liberia's George Weah became superstars, the domestic game was left behind. Stadiums were often in appalling states of disrepair. Forty-one people were killed in 1991 at South Africa's biggest match, the Soweto derby between Kaizer Chiefs and Orlando Pirates. As at Heysel in 1985, the 1991 fatal stampede at the Oppenheim Stadium was triggered by weapon-wielding hooligans. More often than not, though, supporters were more sinned against than sinners. Death and serious injury through crushing on overcrowded, badly policed, and decrepit terraces occurred with alarming regularity: in Kenya (1991), Liberia (1994, 2000), Sierra Leone (1995), Zambia (1996, 1998), the Democratic Republic of Congo (1996, 1998, 2000), Nigeria (1996), Egypt (1999), and Zimbabwe (2000).

The nadir came in 2001. In four incidents in four countries (the Democratic Republic of Congo, South Africa, Ghana, and the Ivory Coast) over the course of four weeks in April and May, 179 people were killed inside the continent's football stadiums. The two deadliest incidents occurred at Ellis Park in Johannesburg and the Accra Stadium in Ghana. At Ellis Park on 11 April, 43 people were killed and 158 injured after a deadly crush in the north-east corner of the stadium before a match between Kaizer Chiefs and Orlando Pirates. It was South Africa's worst football disaster. In Accra on 9 May, two late and controversial goals gave Hearts of Oak a 2–1 victory over Asante Kotoko. Unhappy Kotoko fans threw objects onto the pitch. The police tear-gassed the stands. In the ensuing stampede, 127 people died in Africa's worst stadium disaster.

What happened in Johannesburg and Accra in 2001 followed international patterns. Peter Alegi's assessment of the causes of the Ellis Park tragedy—"fundamental organizational flaws, contempt for spectator safety, and incompetence and dereliction of duty on the part of security personnel"[15]—could have been taken directly from reports on the Hillsborough disaster. As in Accra, the stampede and crush at Ellis Park was facilitated by heavy-handed, inexperienced personnel, in this case a private security company that fired tear gas into an enclosed space. As in many previous incidents, going back to the Ibrox disaster in 1902, the Chiefs-Pirates match continued, unbelievably, for thirty-four minutes before officials and TV commentators could no longer ignore the dead bodies at the side of the pitch. As after Hillsborough, victims' families found justice hard to come by. The Ngoepe Report (2002) whitewashed the egregious security errors and endemic racism that contributed to the disaster. The public inquiry into the Accra Stadium disaster concluded that the police acted recklessly in using tear gas and plastic bullets and charged six officers with manslaughter. All six were acquitted in 2003. The disaster's abiding image was the police response to post-match protests in the poor Accra suburb where many of the Kotoko victims had lived: armoured helicopters and more tear gas. In Ghana as elsewhere, class was a central factor in turning sports fields into killing fields. Stadium disasters were the most extreme manifestation of an often wilful ignorance of spectators, and spectator cultures, found in all corners of the modern world.

Notes

1 Quoted in Brenda Elsey, *Citizens & Sportsmen: Fútbol & Politics in 20th-Century Chile* (Austin, TX: University of Texas Press, 2011), 242.

2 Simon Inglis, *The Football Grounds of England and Wales* (London: Willow Books, 1983), 10.

3 B.S. Johnson, *The Unfortunates* (1969; New York: New Directions, 2007), 5–6.

4 Inglis, *Sightlines*, 26.

5 Mabel Berezin, quoted in Martin, *Football and Fascism*, 79.

6 Mikhail Romm, quoted in Edelman, *Spartak Moscow*, 94–95.

7 Quoted in McDougall, *The People's Game*, 199, 234.

8 Quoted in Mike Dennis, "Soccer Hooliganism in the German Democratic Republic," in Alan Tomlinson and Christopher Young, eds., *German Football: History, Culture, Society* (Abingdon: Routledge, 2006), 57; McDougall, *The People's Game*, 332.

9 Inglis, *The Football Grounds of England and Wales*, 78.

10 Quoted in Jason Wood and Neville Gabie, "The Football Ground and Visual Culture: Recapturing Place, Memory and Meaning at Ayresome Park," *The International History of the Journal of Sport* 28, nos. 8–9 (2011): 1196.

11 Pierre Nora, "Between Memory and History: *Les lieux de mémoire*," *Representations* 26 (1989): 7.

12 Quoted in Robert Edelman, *Serious Fun: A History of Spectator Sports in the USSR* (Oxford: Oxford University Press, 1993), 189.

13 Alan Bairner, "Emotional Grounds: Stories of Football, Memories, and Emotions," *Emotion, Space and Society* 12 (2014): 21–22.

14 Quoted in Phil Scraton, *Hillsborough: The Truth*, 6th ed. (Edinburgh: Mainstream, 2016), 171.

15 Peter Alegi, "'Like Cows Driven to a Dip': The 2001 Ellis Park Stadium Disaster in South Africa," in Paul Darby, Martin Johnes, and Gavin Mellor, eds., *Soccer and Disaster: International Perspectives* (London: Routledge, 2005), 109.

8 | Spectators

In November 1966, a crowd of 70,000 at Moscow's Lenin Stadium watched Ukrainian side Dynamo Kiev play Torpedo Moscow in the final of the USSR Cup. A photograph shows Dynamo supporters of all ages and both sexes, smiling and waving. Most are dressed in fur caps to guard against the cold weather. One banner reads, "The frost won't save Torpedo. Dynamo are going to win the cup!!!" Such optimism was justified, as Dynamo Kiev won 2–0. Across the vast, multinational Soviet republic, people rejoiced. In his apartment in the Russian city of Leningrad (today St. Petersburg), Nikita Naselenko celebrated in front of his television set. Further west, in Estonia, Helle Rätsepp did the same. In Kiev, the Andreev brothers sent the team a poem. Anticipating Dynamo's participation in European competition, they struck the right political and sporting notes: "Our own 'Internationale' / Will glow in our native Kiev!"[1] "The Internationale" referenced both the international hymn of socialism and Dynamo's yardstick, Europe's best team in the mid-1960s, Italy's Internazionale Milano (Inter Milan).

Support for Dynamo Kiev in 1966 showcased the many layers of modern fandom. Thousands watched the cup final live in the Lenin Stadium. Many more watched on television, which promoted national consciousness and transnational loyalties. Dynamo Kiev represented the city of Kiev and the Soviet republic of Ukraine, the Union's second largest national community. At the same time, the city and team were multi-ethnic enough, and Dynamo played attractive enough football, to have supporters throughout the Soviet Union. In Georgia and Armenia, for example, Dynamo Kiev symbolized both a Soviet "friendship of the peoples" and antipathy toward the imperial centre, Moscow. The reference to Inter Milan, finally, indicates that the Iron Curtain was no barrier to football exchanges. On its European Cup debut in 1967, Dynamo Kiev eliminated defending champions Celtic before losing to Poland's Górnik Zabrze in the second round. Spectatorship effortlessly crossed, and cross-referenced, local, national, and international identities.

Little authenticates football's popularity like the number of people who watch it. More than 1 billion people, roughly every seventh person on the planet, watched the 2014 World Cup final between Germany and Argentina. From a much earlier date, football was a captivating live spectacle, a weekend ritual that shaped the lives of generations of match-goers in Europe, South America, and beyond. Football was not the main draw everywhere. Hockey was more popular in Canada, as baseball was in Cuba, Japan, and the United States. A different version of football ("Aussie Rules") enticed spectators in Australia. France's biggest crowd puller was cycling's Tour de France. These were exceptions to the rule. In sport's modern history, no activity inspired such a large, passionate, and international following as football.

Spectatorship emerged as an academic subject in the 1970s. Resurgent Marxist critiques condemned sport as a dehumanizing activity—a form of play deformed into work by capitalism—and a dehumanizing spectacle, in thrall to the capitalist leisure industry. The Gramsci-influenced works of such neo-Marxists as Richard Gruneau and John Hargreaves offered more sophisticated analyses, but spectators remained in the cross hairs of the left. Writing in 1978, amid the violent disturbances associated with the Red Brigades, novelist Umberto Eco dismissed the possibility of a Sunday revolution in Italy because this was when Serie A matches took place. His despair echoed a gentler rebuke of socialists in Yorkshire's West Riding in 1909, who preferred to attend football matches than socialist meetings. In these readings, spectatorship was an escape from politics that reinforced the social order.

Leftist critiques of spectatorship partly shaped and partly reflected wider concerns about football in the 1970s and 1980s. Across Europe, fan violence preoccupied governments, media, and public opinion. In Britain, where hooliganism, and fear of hooliganism, was deeply embedded, sociologists well versed in Marxist theory helped to shape preconceptions. Fandom, wrongly, became shorthand for right-wing extremism. Studies of fan culture focused disproportionately on the troublemaking minority. This initially Anglocentric field was gradually internationalized. Scholarship on hooliganism now takes readers around the world, from early twentieth-century Ireland to contemporary Israel.

From the 1990s, the historiography on spectatorship broadened. Nick Hornby's *Fever Pitch* (1992) captured the shifting mood. In his self-reflexive account of supporting Arsenal, Hornby insisted that "most football fans do not have a criminal record, or carry knives, or urinate in pockets, or get up to any of the things that they are all supposed to."[2] Studies of British football increasingly emphasized the variety of fan activism (on the left as much as the right), elements of terrace culture such as chants and clothing, and the rise of a literary (fanzine) culture. A sophisticated literature developed on mediated spectatorship, especially on television's role in the consumption of football. The historiography of fan culture, like fan culture itself, became increasingly internationalized.

For many people, watching football was and remains a routine activity. It is rarely subject to self-analysis, just as it is rarely an archivist's priority. Consequently, it has not always left traces in the record books. At least before the 1990s, much of what came down to us about watching football came from writers. In the early 1920s, Peruvian poet Juan Parra del Riego wrote "Ode to football" ("*Oda al fútbol*") and a seventy-two-line poem about one of Uruguay's first black players, Isabelino Gradín. English novelist (and football journalist) B.S. Johnson published an experimental novel *The Unfortunates* (1969) that took as its starting point a Saturday afternoon reporting on an awful match at Nottingham Forest's fictionalized City Ground. Without the option of oral history, understanding early forms of spectatorship, often only briefly mentioned in newspaper reports, is especially difficult.

Chapter 8 examines the rich history of the world's most popular spectator sport. It first provides a history of going to the game, looking at patterns of match-day attendance since the late nineteenth century. The following section establishes taxonomies of spectatorship before investigating how fan cultures fluidly reflect and shape cultural, social, and political identities. Attention subsequently turns to hooliganism, examined here as a significant but fringe international expression of violent masculinity. The chapter closes with the armchair fan. It examines how mediated spectatorship has changed the experience of watching football, for better and for worse.

Going to the Game

Football arrived in modernity when large numbers of people came to see it.[3] Like cinema and radio, it then became an integral part of mass culture. In 1888/89, the first season of the English Football League, average attendance was 4,600. By 1913/14, it was 23,100. The first FA Cup final in 1872 attracted 2,000 people. The 1913 final at London's Crystal Palace stadium was watched by 120,000. The cup final became a national event, attended by royalty and feverishly discussed in the press. Ten years later, it moved to the newly opened Wembley Stadium. The official (and record) attendance was 126,047, but an estimated 300,000 people gained entry. As fans swamped the pitch, horse-mounted policemen tried to regain order. One light-coloured horse, Billie, became the abiding image of a day when luck, crowd self-policing, and police animals averted disaster. The "White Horse final," in which Bolton defeated West Ham 2–0, dramatically confirmed football's mass appeal.

Mass spectatorship arrived in continental Europe and South America after the First World War. The last prewar final of the German championship between Fürth and VfB Leipzig drew a crowd of 6,000. The replay of the 1922 final between Nuremberg and Hamburg in Leipzig attracted 60,000 people to a stadium designed to hold 40,000. In neighbouring Austria, and especially in the capital Vienna, the game emerged even more forcefully as a spectacle. Big matches drew audiences of 70,000 or 80,000. Only cinema mobilized people in equal numbers.

In Argentina, football, cinema, and music were the three intertwined elements of urban culture in the 1920s and 1930s. Tango stars such as Carlos Gardel performed songs about footballers, including "Patadura" (1928), whose lyrics humorously name-checked star players such as Luis Monti and Manuel Seoane. There were rags-to-riches football movies. By 1930, sports magazine *El Gráfico*, founded in 1919, sold 100,000 copies in Buenos Aires alone. The game was as entrenched in Argentina's national psyche as it was in England's or Scotland's. Fifteen thousand Argentineans crossed the River Plate to watch the 1930 World Cup final between Argentina and Uruguay in Montevideo. After Argentina's defeat, fans in Buenos Aires rioted. The Uruguayan consulate was stoned. Two people were shot dead.

Economic depression and war slowed but did not halt the spectator boom. On 22 June 1941, the German Army launched "Operation Barbarossa" and invaded its erstwhile ally, the Soviet Union. It was, most historians agree, the decisive moment of the Second World War. On the same day in Berlin, 90,000 people attended the final of the German championship between Schalke 04 and Rapid Vienna. In an extraordinary game, Rapid, who only joined the league in 1938 after Austria's annexation to the Third Reich, overturned a 3–0 deficit to win 4–3, scoring all four goals in six minutes. Tens of thousands of supporters thronged Vienna's main railway station to welcome home the victors. Official speakers, including prominent Viennese Nazis, were booed. The regime soon took revenge. Most of the Rapid team was dispatched to the Eastern Front to fight the Soviet Union. Domestic competitions had largely been shut down in the First World War. Twenty years later, football's popularity made a blanket closure inadvisable. Mass Observation, the British social research organization, noted in 1940 that "one Saturday afternoon of League matches could probably do more to affect people's spirits than the recent £50,000 Government poster campaign urging cheerfulness."[4] Only Poland, ground zero in the Nazi war of racial annihilation, cancelled its national championship for the entire war. In 1942, at the height of the German Army's siege of Leningrad, with people dying of starvation and bread rations limited to 125 grams per day, crowds of 8,000 still attended games. Across occupied Europe, the desire to watch football, now implanted in multiple generations, was strong. The same was true, albeit sometimes for different reasons, in countries removed from the frontlines of conflict. In British-occupied Nigeria, nationwide "goodwill tours" by the African-run team from Lagos, Zik's Athletic Club, brought record attendances. Wartime matches in front of crowds numbering between 2,000 and 5,000 people were often followed by an anti-colonial speech from club founder Nnamdi ("Zik") Azikiwe, as well as a fundraising dance.

Football's continuance during the Second World War fed into the golden age of spectatorship after 1945. In peacetime conditions, even amid economic privation and Cold War tensions, watching football represented a return to normality. Affordable leisure-time options were in short supply, so the attendance boom crossed political and continental borders. In England, record crowds of 41.3 million people attended Football League matches in the 1948/49 season. One hundred thousand people watched the 1956 East German league match between Rotation Leipzig and Lokomotive Leipzig at the newly constructed Central Stadium, the record crowd for a domestic fixture in Germany.

Live football never again consistently attracted the numbers that it did between the mid-1940s and the mid-1950s. Many factors contributed to the decline, but the chief culprit, at least in Europe and South America, was television. Football, like cinema, could not escape television's cultural and social impact. From the peak year, 1954, attendances in the Argentinean league dropped by 40 per cent in the following decade. Over a similar period, television set ownership in the country rose from 5,000 (1953) to 800,000 (1960). Football authorities were suspicious, even as they tentatively embraced the new technology. When Sweden played the Soviet Union in a televised World Cup quarter-final in 1958, there were only 32,000 people in the 50,000-capacity Råsunda Stadium. Revenues from broadcasting rights did not meet the shortfall in spectator income from low attendances. Tournament organizers were not alone in doubting this brave new world. British television screened eleven live games from Sweden. An outraged individual wrote to *The Times* newspaper: "Midsummer football on television! Science has given us many horrors, including the H-bomb, but surely this is the end."⁵

Television's influence became a major talking point. Aggregate English Football League attendance dropped from 41.3 million (1948/49) to 16.5 million in the 1985/86 season. The *Liverpool Echo* newspaper canvassed its readers in 1961 about the league's "missing millions." Television was the chief menace, but there were other factors: increased spending power and leisure-time options, decrepit stadiums with bad food and no protection from the elements, hostility or indifference to women supporters, and poor standards of play. From the mid-1960s, the threat of violence in and around the stadium entered the mix.

The English decline reflected broader trends. Between 1976 and 1990, aggregate East German Oberliga attendance dropped from 2.5 million to 1.5 million. Average attendance in the Soviet Union fell from 27,000 in the 1987 season to 16,000 in 1990, as communism lurched toward its endgame. The story was similar in stable Western European polities. Aggregate crowds in West Germany shrank from 26 million in the late 1970s to 18 million in 1990. By the late 1980s, when average Swedish attendance bottomed out at 3,929 (down from 9,489 in 1971), ice hockey was close to replacing football as the country's number one sport. The introduction of a national championship in Brazil in 1971 initially boosted attendance, but this did not last. In the 1970s, 105 matches in the country recorded attendances of over 100,000. In the following decade, matches with that many spectators dropped to 57. In the 1990s, it was 23.

There were exceptions, often in places that experienced on-field success and avoided the worst excesses of hooliganism. Attendance in France, Portugal, and Romania, for example, remained steady or increased in the dark years of spectatorship. In Italy, Serie A's peak attendance years (the mid-1980s) came at European football's lowest ebb. Following the 1985 Heysel Stadium disaster, when rioting Liverpool fans caused the deaths of thirty-nine Juventus supporters, British Prime Minister Margaret Thatcher apparently asked football officials if matches required supporters. In the birthplace of modern football, the national game's reputation was so bad that the country's leader wanted it played behind closed doors.

Football's free-market turn in the 1990s was a mixed blessing for live spectatorship. The revival narrative was strongest in England, where the Hillsborough disaster led to the introduction of safer but more expensive all-seater stadiums. The Premier League's creation in 1992 expanded the global TV audience for English football. It also helped attendance figures, as better football and better marketing built a more attractive brand. In the opening Premier League season (1992/93), average attendance was 21,222. In the 2017/18 season, the figure had almost doubled to 38,310. There was a similarly impressive spike in the rebranded Championship (the second tier of English football), and more modest increases in the two lower-tier professional leagues, League One and League Two.

Attendance increased in many of Western Europe's wealthiest leagues. In France's Ligue 1, average attendance doubled from 11,493 in the 1991/92 season to 22,548 in 2017/18. In Germany's Bundesliga, Europe's poster child for affordable, "authentic" fan experiences, average attendance in the 2017/18 season was 44,511, up from 24,267 in 1991/92. Italy, as it had been in the 1980s, was the exception. From a peak of 38,872 in 1985, average Serie A attendance dropped to a low of 18,473 in the 2006/07 season, the year after the *Calciopoli* scandal (see Chapter 3). In the 2017/18 season, average attendance was 24,706.

Italy's post-1980s experience was more globally representative than England's. Increased disparities of wealth in and between national leagues and increased televised options made it harder for clubs to draw crowds— and, in some cases, less important, as TV revenues replaced gate receipts as the main source of income. Television did not kill football as a live sport, but it did not always help. In Africa, the marginalization of local competition in favour of televised products such as the English Premier League did little to encourage attendance. Outside the strongest leagues in Algeria and South Africa, five-figure crowds were rare. Average attendance for Nigerian Premier League matches in the 2015/16 season was 5,000; in England's third tier (League One), it was 7,163. Average attendance in Serie A of the Brazilian Championship in 2018 was 18,080, less than half of that year's average attendance in the English Premier League. Most of Brazil's best footballers played abroad, as did most of Chile's, and no wonder: average attendance in Chile in 2016/17 was 6,938, less than the average gate at English League One matches.

The narrative of disparity and decline can be misleading. In 2018, two of the world's ten best-attended leagues were in what were once considered untapped markets, the MLS (North America) and the Chinese Super League. In the same year, the European Professional Football Leagues reported a drop in attendance figures since the 2010/11 season. Decline was most dramatic in countries that faced economic or political crises, such as Greece, Turkey, and Ukraine. But 120 million people, roughly one-sixth of the continent's population, watched a live match in the 2016/17 season. Attendance was up in nine domestic competitions, with the biggest improvements in Sweden, where ice hockey's advances had been held off, and Israel, where the Ligat ha'Al saw a 13.7 per cent increase. Even UEFA's worst-attended top-tier competition, Azerbaijan's premier league, had a cumulative audience of almost 400,000, a 7 per cent increase on 2010/11 numbers. Reports of football's death as live entertainment were exaggerated.

Terrace Cultures

So much for statistics: what lay behind them? Who went to the game and why? No short history can do justice to the motivations that have sent people to the stadium over the past 150 years or to the complex layers of identity formed as a result of these experiences. Many individual and collective histories of match-going have been left unrecorded. This is especially true of lower-league professional and amateur matches. Spectatorship was never confined to large stadiums or elite competition. It often took place in the front of the proverbial "one man and his dog." Who were the 500 spectators who gathered in 1955 to watch the final of the steelworkers' tournament in the East German town of Eisenhüttenstadt? What drives an average crowd of 368 to attend matches in the third tier of Denmark's Divisionsforeningen, Europe's worst-attended professional league? There may be as many reasons for watching a game as there are supporters.

In *Fever Pitch*, Nick Hornby remarked, "I fell in love with football as I was later to fall in love with women: suddenly, inexplicably, uncritically, giving no thought to the pain or disruption it would bring with it."[6] Many people recall the first, youthful sights and sounds of the stadium (the crowd noise, the greenness of the grass) as what hooked them. Others come to football less directly. Atlanta's centrality to community life in the Buenos Aires neighbourhood of Villa Crespo—organizing dances, barbecues, and athletic events—was often the starting point for lifelong support of its football team. Not everyone caught the football bug. Writer Roberto

Arlt watched his first game, Argentina's 2–0 win over Uruguay in 1929, at the age of twenty-nine. It was a journalistic assignment, and Arlt was not impressed. He left the packed stadium before Argentina's second goal, appalled by the supporters' behaviour and glad to be back in more pleasant surroundings on Buenos Aires's Avenida la Plata.

Using a pair of opposites (hot-cool and traditional-consumer), Richard Giulianotti (2002) identified four categories of spectator identity. Supporters (traditional/hot) have a long-term commitment to their team, a "thick solidarity" that values community, family, and the ground as an emotional place. Followers (traditional/cool) value authenticity, but from a greater distance. Their choices may be, for example, "second teams" that reflect their values, such as St. Pauli, Hamburg's radical left-wing club. Fans (hot/consumer) are deeply committed to their club but through a more market-oriented set of relationships. Finally, *flâneurs* (cool/consumer) incarnate a postmodern world in motion. The term denotes a detached, cosmopolitan (virtual) "stroller," whose loyalties are transferrable: a fan of Portuguese star Cristiano Ronaldo, for example, who follows the player from Manchester United to Real Madrid to Juventus.

When it emerged in late Victorian Britain, football's supreme virtue was its appeal to civic pride. Clubs, as journalist Arthur Hopcraft noted, "raised the banner of town chauvinism and prospered under it."[7] Such tribalism was not confined to Britain. From the *campanilismo* (regionalism) that complicated the fascist takeover of Italian football to the regional resistance to Kwame Nkrumah's reorganization of Ghanaian football in the 1960s, football's role as a lightning rod for local identities caused constant political headaches. The head of East German sport, Manfred Ewald, could not hold back the tides of "local patriotism," even in the highest ranks of the communist party: "Earlier in Germany ... every little prince kept his own ballet. Today they support football teams."[8] Eric Hobsbawm's remark that "the imagined community of millions seems more real as a team of eleven named people" referenced football's role in symbolizing nationhood.[9] Football as a symbol of unity applied on a local scale too, especially in urban centres otherwise characterized by dispersal and segregation.

From Boca Juniors in the Buenos Aires neighbourhood of La Boca to Liverpool FC in that city's L4 district, football clubs have always been anchored in neighbourhoods. The rarity of North American–style franchise relocation—moving the Dodgers from Brooklyn to Los Angeles—testifies to the power of this idea. In the working-class Moscow district of Krasnaia Presnia, the founding in 1922 of Spartak Moscow came from the streets. Young men wanted somewhere to watch and especially play football. Players such as striker Pavel Kanunnikov, whose left leg was inscribed with a tattoo that read "I shoot, I kill," inspired local kids such as Anatoly Akimov, a Krasnaia Presnia resident who became Spartak's goalkeeper in the 1930s.

The club's ambitions soon expanded beyond neighbourhood horizons. Spartak developed a cross-city rivalry with Dynamo Moscow, founded in 1923 and supported by the Soviet Union's police state. During the 1930s, as Stalin's program of forced industrialization almost doubled Moscow's population, Spartak became known as the *narodnaia komanda* (people's team). This was partly for political and partly for sporting reasons. Spartak was the only Soviet side to defeat the all-star Basque team that toured the country in 1937. The club was less closely tied to repressive state structures than Dynamo (police) or CSKA (army). After the Second World War, Spartak's fan base, like that of Dynamo Kiev, extended across the Soviet Union. The club had many Armenian players and coaches. Many supporters in the Armenian republic, when they were not rooting for local side Ararat Yerevan, thus gave Spartak their backing. At the same time, Spartak kept its local appeal, as young supporters played out the rivalry with Dynamo Moscow not only in the stadium but in kickabouts in the courtyards of apartment buildings.

In the Congolese capital Brazzaville after the Second World War, as in Moscow during the 1930s, there was a wave of migration. Many of the newcomers were young men. They built an urban football culture that thrived at every level, from *mwana-foot* (street football) in neighbourhood leagues to well-supported clubs from Poto-Poto (L'Étoile du Congo) and Bacongo (Diables Noirs). Far from passive consumers, those who watched football were likelier to play it. In Brazzaville, as in the *musseques* (slums) of Luanda, capital city of the Portuguese colony of Angola, football, like cinema and music, drove the creation of autonomous leisure spaces.

Brazzaville's top two teams were breakaway organizations. They rejected colonial control and expressed neighbourhood solidarity. The "Black Devils" (Diables Noirs) in Bacongo arose from a merger of local teams, with the aim of challenging Poto-Poto teams for supremacy. From the 1950s onwards, supporters of Diables Noirs, L'Étoile, and Renaissance (Poto-Poto's other leading team) made raucous trips across town to support their team against local rivals, bringing with them bands, dances, and home-made flags. Players became cult heroes. Matches were discussed in cafés and bars. Being part of the crowd was an essential urban experience.

Neighbourhood was in part tied to ethnicity. Diables Noirs was the team of the Lari people, many of whom lived in Bacongo. The team was regarded as the "manioc of mother," the sporting equivalent of the manioc bread that children took from their mothers. The bread was eaten regardless of the taste, just as Diables Noirs was supported whether it won or lost.

In Brazzaville, Moscow, and elsewhere, football's local appeal was often rooted in shared male experiences. This was a game of male sociability, a tool for friendship and cultural continuity in a rapidly moving world. Male bonding drew many people to the Buenos Aires club, Atlanta. One supporter, born in 1947, remembered mornings when he met his uncle to go to home games. They first went to his uncle's regular café and then strolled to the stadium with a large group of older men: "I walked holding my uncle's hand, listening without talking, but very excited and happy and eager to get to the stands. Entering the field and settling in the stands made my heart beat faster and fill with joy."[10]

Such male rites of passage were almost universal. Peter was five when he first went with his uncle to watch Bournemouth, a club on the south coast of England. When Peter's father stopped working on Saturday afternoons, Peter started going with him. Later he went with a group of friends. Until he left for university in Leeds, Peter watched football almost exclusively in male company. In Soviet-era Armenia, stadiums were overwhelmingly male spaces, where terrace abuse combined anti-communist politics and crude misogyny: "Referee, fuck your wife in front of the Lenin Mausoleum!" Armenian artist and Yerevan Ararat fan Levon Abramian concluded that "to be a fan is to be gathered with others and to be free."[11] For many people watching football, and for many of those writing about watching football, this was understood as a male freedom, an escape through the turnstiles from work and domestic drudgery into J.B. Priestley's "altogether more splendid kind of life."[12]

This, though, was never the whole story. For as long as men have watched football, women have watched too. Reporting on the aftermath of a match involving Preston North End in 1884, the referee observed, "I was tackled by a flock of infuriated beings in petticoats supposed to be women, who were without doubt in some cases mothers, if I may judge from the innocent babes suckling at their breasts. They brandished their umbrellas and shook their fists in my face."[13] A year later, the same club abandoned its "Ladies Free" concession because so many women turned up for games.

Though evidence is patchy and often takes the form of patronizing newspaper reports, it appears that women attended football matches after the First World War in significant numbers. Reporting on a cup tie between Leicester City and Clapton in 1922, the *Leicester Mercury* noted "a good sprinkling of women in the crowd." Quite a number of them "faced the Cup-tie crush without a male escort. If Leicester is any criterion, then the lure of the English Cup is rapidly infecting the female mind."[14] When Adrian Killen attended his first Liverpool game, the 1950 FA Cup final loss to Arsenal at Wembley, he accompanied his grandmother (on whose knees he sat) and his mother, who was in tears at the final whistle. Tradition was not handed down exclusively through the male line.

It is commonly suggested that spectator violence, especially in the 1970s and 1980s, drove women away from football. In contrast to the relatively safe environment of the interwar period, stadiums became narrower sites of aggressive masculinity. In *The Football Man* (1968), Arthur Hopcraft gave a menacing description of Liverpool's Kop terrace. This was a place of pickpockets and knives, as well as humorous chants and sporting applause for visiting teams. Yet women still inhabited this apparently male space. During a Boxing Day game in the early 1970s, one supporter even went into labour on the Kop. She gave birth in the club's first aid room.

Before the 1978 World Cup in Argentina, one newspaper noted a "surprise mutation": "the women ... have fallen into the trap of the eleven against eleven. And this is not mere tolerance, condescension or kindness, but rather something summarily similar to the passion of the masses, until now almost exclusively masculine."[15] Such comments revealed more about the source than the subject. In Argentina, as elsewhere, the "surprise mutation" was not that surprising. Many women supported Atlanta, where players used to come on to the field and throw flowers to the crowd. Victor Zamenfeld's grandmother prayed for the team and for all of her relatives, men and women, who went to the match. Novelist Manuela Fingueret, born near the club's stadium, was an Atlanta supporter, while Brazilian poet Anna Amélia de Queiroz was a regular at matches in Rio de Janeiro (she married Fluminense's goalkeeper Marcos de Mendonça in 1922). Despite the ban on women's football in Brazil between 1941 and 1979, women became accepted, even fêted parts of the match-day experience. Dulce Rosalina, for example, was the first female leader of a supporters' club (at Vasco da Gama in 1956) and won the 1961 fan of the year award from the magazine *Revista do Esporte*.

The invisibility of women in terrace histories, like the invisibility of women in the game's history, is not necessarily because they were not there. Anton Kuznetsov, a CSKA Moscow supporter, only discovered after he got married in 1968 that his wife was a Spartak Moscow fan. Previously, he had not thought to ask her about that quintessentially "male" subject, football. Industry narratives trumpet the fact that more women have followed football since the 1990s, when the game became safer, more family friendly, and more widely available on television. Evidence in fact shows marginal increases in female spectatorship in such competitions as the English Premier League. Women's allegedly increased visibility in spectator culture sometimes appeared to be a Trojan horse for critiques of football's gentrification, with women representing the game's new middle-class audience. There is underlying hostility toward incursions into what were once regarded, however inaccurately, as male spaces.

Female spectators have long been a common sight in Italian football. Yet zones of exclusion remain. First appearing in the late 1960s and 1970s, *ultrà* (ultras) were self-organized, often politicized supporters' movements intent on creating a dramatic spectacle in the stadium. Ultra groups on both left and right were typically seen as male preserves, where macho personas were cultivated. One 1994 study of the *ultrà* mentioned women only once, in connection with the sale of promotional material and the sewing of banners and flags. Women *ultrà* groups, though, were present in significant numbers at many clubs, and not only as ancillaries to men. Of 264 people interviewed for a 1990 study of Bologna ultras, 45 were women. In 2002, there were thirty-five women-only *ultrà* groups across the country, including the Irriducibili Girls at Lazio, All Girls at Parma (where women constituted 40 per cent of the match-day crowd), and Reggio's Carmen Borghi. Women played leading roles in many cross-gender ultra groups. The mainstream media ignored this activism.

During the 2002 World Cup in Japan and South Korea, media coverage of "feminized spectatorship" was often unflattering. Women supporters in Japan were dismissed as *mi-ha*, a derogatory term for those, like Giulianotti's cool/consumer *flâneurs*, deemed unreliable and superficial in their affections. The assumption that women supporters were less important and thus less worthy of serious consideration persisted, even as progress was made. In 2018, Lazio ultras were widely condemned for distributing leaflets requesting that women be banned from "sacred" parts of the Curva Nord (north stand) in Rome's Olympic Stadium.

Like female spectatorship, transnational fandom has deeper roots than is sometimes assumed. On the island of Malta, the first Manchester United supporters' club was founded in 1959. Founder member John Calleja had previously contacted staff at Old Trafford and travelled to Manchester for games. He now sought like-minded locals to share his passion. Eighty people attended the first meeting. The club still exists, and is recognized as the world's oldest continuous Manchester United supporters' club. Supporters' groups for other teams soon followed. A lawyer and MP founded a Juventus Malta fan club in the 1960s. By the 1970s, small numbers of Maltese fans journeyed regularly to England or Italy to watch their favourite team.

The cross-pollination of fan cultures increased in the 1950s, as television and travel opened up the football world to spectators as well as players. Cultural transfer often elided the political divisions of the Cold War. In socialist Yugoslavia, the first supporters' club was formed as early as 1950. Adopting trends from the recent World Cup in Brazil, Zagreb-based supporters of Croatian side Hajduk Split named their organization Torcida, the Portuguese word for supporters. Torcida's leaders were well-connected students. Many were communist party members. The team that they supported had represented Tito's Partisans during the Second World War and had toured Italy, Malta, and the Middle East as the Football Group of the National Liberation Army. Yet these establishment credentials were not incompatible with new forms of spectatorship, drawn from the non-communist world. For a key match between Hajduk and rivals Red Star Belgrade in Split in 1950, Torcida equipped supporters with bells, whistles, trumpets, and rattles. The choreography contributed to an intense atmosphere, full of chants and music. There were two pitch invasions and later joyous celebrations in the city centre, as Hajduk won the game and all but clinched the league title. Party officials in Belgrade, the Serbian capital of the federal republic, were suspicious, but more because of Torcida's links to Croatian nationalism than because of its imitation of foreign practices. Torcida was banned and only re-emerged after Tito's death in 1980, when Yugoslavia's political system, and football culture, became increasingly fragmented and nationalistic.

As spectator culture internationalized, cross-border influences grew, in Eastern Europe and elsewhere. When Polish champions Legia Warsaw played Dutch side Feyenoord in the semi-final of the 1970 European Cup, Legia's supporters encountered a new fan culture: loud and colourful, with flags everywhere. In neighbouring East Germany, closed off from the West by the Berlin Wall, football constantly breached the Iron Curtain. Citizens travelled to Czechoslovakia, Hungary, and Poland to watch West Germany or Bayern Munich play. The secret police struggled to infiltrate supporters' clubs, many of which paid open tribute to Western culture. Of twenty-eight Berliner FC Dynamo supporters' clubs on the Stasi's radar in 1986, nine had

English names. These names referenced everything from politics (Black Panther) to pop culture (Beatles BFC Club).

Football Anglophilia was more pronounced, and less risky, in Scandinavia. Norwegian television screened English matches from 1969. A 2006 survey of supporters found that *Tippekampen* (the slang term for the live Saturday game broadcast from England) was the most important factor in adopting an English team, ahead of liking the club kit or a player. Supporters' clubs existed across the region by the 1970s. Liverpool, then England's best side, led the way. The Liverpool Scandinavian Supporters' Club, founded in 1980, counted 10,000 members in 1994 and 21,634 members in 1998.

As international air travel became cheaper (especially in Europe) and televised football options almost endless, transnational fandom moved to another level. From the 1990s, Scandinavian supporters of Liverpool or Manchester United regularly visited Anfield or Old Trafford, often in large numbers. The English Premier League conquered new television markets, most notably in East Asia (Indonesia, Singapore, and Thailand) and, to a lesser extent, in North America. The advent of social media made spectatorship more remote and more accessible, as fans became at once engaged with and detached from events in an often distant stadium. Before the 2014 World Cup in Brazil, journalist Simon Kuper suggested that football might be entering a post-nationalist era, in which supporters simply chose to cheer on the team that they liked best.

It would be an exaggeration to argue that football lost touch with its local or national roots, just as it would be misleading to posit Richard Giulianotti's "post-fan"—the middle class, reflexive, and critically engaged cousin of the "post-tourist"—as the new face of spectatorship. Football has always housed different types of fandom. Spectator identities can encompass different class and gender backgrounds. They can evoke local, national, and transnational loyalties. They can provoke varied levels of engagement. A spectator might be irredeemably partisan or a neutral observer who hopes, usually in vain, for the match that he or she will never forget. Spectatorship, however practiced, is a routine source of unpredictability.

Histories of Violence

On 29 May 1985, the Heysel Stadium in Brussels hosted the European Cup final between Juventus and Liverpool. The stadium was not fit for purpose. Grass sprouted from crumbling terraces. Ticketless fans entered through holes in the perimeter wall. Turnstiles were absent or unstaffed. The police lacked numbers, a clear operational strategy, and, in some cases, batteries for their walkie-talkies. Fans threw missiles at each other. At 7:20 p.m., Liverpool supporters broke through flimsy fencing and charged Juventus fans on the supposedly neutral terrace, Block Z. Fans rushed to escape, and a wall collapsed. Thirty-nine people were killed. Graphic images of death in the stadium were broadcast to a global audience. Juventus's subsequent 1–0 victory was meaningless. Liverpool supporters' good reputation was destroyed. English clubs were banned from European competition for five years. "If this is football," claimed an editorial in *L'Équipe*, the French newspaper that founded the European Cup, "let it die."[16]

In England, the Heysel disaster confirmed every prejudice about football supporters. The Thatcher government's anti-hooligan campaign went into overdrive. A *Times* editorial on 31 May predicted that "British football may eventually have to be played in fortified amphitheatres with iron cages where there used to be terraces, and a breathalyser machine at every turnstile."[17] Heysel was a European tragedy, a multinational disaster in which everyone from UEFA to English hooligans was culpable. It was, arguably, the lowest point in the continent's football history. As experts, politicians, and newspapers weighed in on the subject, Heysel only reinforced public fascination with hooliganism.

No aspect of terrace culture has produced more scholarship than hooliganism. In the 1970s and 1980s, a sociological cottage industry developed around the subject in Britain. Researchers at Leicester University were especially influential. Violence, the Leicester school argued, was part of "a quest for excitement" common to working-class, male leisure pursuits in modern industrial societies. Research on hooligan demographics in other West European countries, including Belgium, Italy, and West Germany, reached similar conclusions. Communist states in Eastern Europe claimed to have overcome class conflict, leaving no reason for spectator violence. It was the sickness of capitalism, they argued, that caused disasters like Heysel. Yet, to communist bewilderment, spectator violence reared its ugly head throughout the Soviet bloc. If football was a vehicle for Cold War cultural transfer, hooliganism was part of the crossover.

Research on hooliganism produced valuable findings, though it gave a misleadingly narrow impression of the motivations and experiences of supporters. The imbalance played well with research bodies, governments, and much of public opinion. Hooliganism was a pop cultural obsession. In Britain, memoirs and novels—with such titles as *Armed for the Match*,

Eurotrashed, and *March of the Hooligans*—did brisk sales. Undercover documentaries took viewers inside the "firms" and "crews" that organized trouble. Movies such as *I.D.* (1995) and *Green Street* (2005) fetishized football violence even as they critiqued it. The imagined world of fighting, drinking, and sex was a commercial goldmine. Sensationalist media coverage made the "hooligan problem" seem larger than it was. The drift to violence became a self-fulfilling prophecy.

Even at the peak of hooligan hysteria in the mid-1980s, violence was not part of most people's match-going experiences. At Liverpool's Anfield stadium in the three seasons from 1985/86 to 1987/88, for example, there were 531 arrests and ejections among an aggregate crowd of almost 2.87 million. This was an average of slightly more than two people per match. On a typical weekend of action in the East German Oberliga in 1987, twenty-five people were arrested for public order offences out of an aggregate crowd of 62,000.

Sports violence, the Leicester school argued, was not confined to football. Spectator unrest, moreover, was a feature of the global, not merely the British game—and long predated the 1960s. Research of the international press between 1908 and 1983 uncovered 101 incidents of football-related violence in thirty-seven countries. Problems typically began in the 1920s and 1930s, as football became popular across Europe and South America. More people attended games, especially more young, working-class men. Fierce local and national rivalries developed. The Swedish FA was not alone in struggling to cope with the upsurge in disorder. When placards requesting good behaviour did not work, it closed the grounds of clubs with the rowdiest spectators in 1933.

One country prominent on the Leicester list was Ireland. Derived from a late nineteenth-century music hall song about an unruly Irish family, the term "hooligan" was soon applied to football. Sectarian tensions between Catholic supporters of Belfast Celtic and Protestant supporters of Linfield led to violent clashes at a match in Belfast in 1912. Sixty people went to hospital, one with a gunshot wound. There was more fighting and gunfire at a game between Belfast Celtic and Glentoran in 1920. Unrest took place against a backdrop of political violence and civil war, as the Catholic majority sought independence from British rule. Ireland was partitioned in 1922. The Protestant north remained part of the United Kingdom. The twenty-six counties of the largely Catholic south formed the Irish Free State. Hooligan incidents, though, continued. There were frequent pitch invasions. Referees were assaulted. A match in Ardee was abandoned in

1931 after spectators, both men and women, fought on the streets with hurling sticks and fire irons. The causes of unruliness matched Europe-wide trends: bigger crowds, local partisanship, and heavy drinking. High levels of youth unemployment also played a role.

For much of the first century of modern football, match-day disorder was largely spontaneous. It was directed at players and referees (in the form of missile throwing or pitch invasions), rather than at fellow supporters. From the Irish Free State to Weimar Germany, events on the pitch triggered violence. The same was true in South Africa. The emotional intensity of the game, often combined with the liberal consumption of home-brewed alcohol, caused occasional fights and riots. An angry crowd killed a referee in Johannesburg in 1940.

Spectator violence developed new characteristics in the 1960s. As crowds shrank across Europe and South America, groups of young males colonized the terraces. They organized more aggressively and more tribally than had the audiences of the 1930s and 1940s, claiming "ends" or *curva* for themselves. With more money in their pockets (a consequence of the postwar economic boom) and more leisure time, they travelled regularly to away matches. Confrontation with rival fans was sought, or at least not avoided. In England, gangs ("firms") developed a mobile, violent, and internationally imitated hooligan culture. In South Africa, crowd trouble increased for the reasons that it increased elsewhere: heavy drinking, local rivalries, contempt for an older generation of "softer" fans, and the emergence of a youthful "rowdy masculinity." A letter writer to black newspaper *Soweto* in 1966 lamented that disorder now kept him and his wife away from the stadium: "Don't these people who throw stones, use sticks and swear at people realize that in the excitement of a soccer game it takes very little to start big trouble?"[18]

The line between hooligan and fanatic was often blurred. Italian ultras created intimidating spectacles in the stadium. Their South America cousins, the *barras bravas*, offered an equally combustible mixture of political engagement, pyrotechnical displays, and violence. The "carnival armies" of the Scots and the Danes cultivated a more celebratory image. Denmark's traveling fans, first sighted in large numbers at the 1984 European Championship in France, were generally more affluent and more inclusive to women than Danish domestic crowds. They called themselves *Roligans* (Funsters), a Danish pun on the much-feared "hooligan." The English, Italian, and South American models, though, were youthful, masculine, autonomous, and hostile to authority. The combination caused sleepless nights among politicians in democracies and dictatorships. It encouraged heavy-handedness. The police sometimes behaved more violently than the spectators. "Hooliganism" was often in the eye of the beholder.

Hooliganism encouraged transnational connections. During unrest at a match in communist Czechoslovakia between Dukla Banská Bystrica and Sparta Prague in June 1985, Sparta fans chanted "Liverpool, Liverpool," in morbid tribute to the perpetrators of the Heysel disaster a few weeks earlier. An inspiration for Spartak Moscow *fanaty* (fanatics) was the raucous behaviour of Rangers fans during and after the Scottish side's 1972 European Cup Winners' Cup final victory over Dynamo Moscow in Barcelona. They twice invaded the pitch and clashed with Franco's police, as post-match celebrations turned ugly. The unruliness was exciting, recalled young Spartak fan Yuri Slezkine. So was the fact that many Rangers fans, and players, had long hair. In post-Tito Yugoslavia, supporters' groups paid homage to West European pioneers. FK Vojvodina's Red Firm, founded in 1989, derived its name from West Ham's notorious hooligan group, the Inter City Firm. Other supporters' groups adopted English names, as they did in East Germany. Yugoslavia's proximity to Italy meant that the *ultrà* model was also influential. *Supertifo*, an Italian supporters' magazine, was read throughout the country. Supporters thus combined elements of English fan culture (heavy drinking, fighting) and Italian fan culture (stadium choreography) to create home-grown subcultures. Hooliganism, like punk music, was everywhere subject to "creolization." Local traditions and identities reshaped foreign role models.

Many football histories, particularly those focused on Western Europe, see the 1990s as the beginning of the end for hooliganism. In safer, family-friendly stadiums, with better football and tighter security measures on display, violence had fewer places to hide. Fighting fans increasingly staged confrontations far from the stadium, in prearranged meeting places. This "appointment hooliganism" suggested that violence had been displaced, not eradicated. An important shift, at least in England, was that hooliganism was depoliticized. Previously regarded as a major social problem, hooliganism now became a spoiler in the feel-good story of football's revival. As the game gentrified, violent incidents—never that common in the first place—significantly decreased, but they did continue to inhabit the margins of spectatorship. There were twenty-seven hooligan incidents in the 1992/93 season. A minority of England fans caused trouble at the 1996 European Championship in England and at the World Cup in France two years later.

In places on the wrong end of football's political and economic transformation, things got worse not better. Simon Kuper attended a BFC game in East Berlin in 1991, shortly after German reunification. So many of the crowd of 1,000 were hooligans, he observed, that "it was possible to speak of a lunatic majority."[19] In East Germany, as elsewhere in Eastern Europe, the collapse of communism and "shock therapy" transition to free-market economics had unhappy consequences. Players left for the West. Attendances plummeted. Troublemakers were often the last men standing. In the 1980s, BFC was the GDR's best team, competing regularly in the European Cup. The same club opened the 1992/93 season in German football's third tier, playing in front of seventy-six people. Media coverage only came BFC's way when supporters attacked an asylum shelter in Greifswald. At many clubs in post-communist Europe, nationalist and racist elements became more visible and audible in often half-empty stadiums. Spartak Moscow, once the Soviet Union's "people's team," became a magnet for Russian nationalists, including skinheads. During the Yugoslav wars (1991–95), supporters' groups were fertile recruitment grounds for the national armies that contested the territories of the socialist federation. Members of Red Star Belgrade's Delije ("Heroes") supporters' club, closely tied to Serb warlord Arkan, took part in ethnic cleansing in Bosnia and Herzegovina, Croatia, and Kosovo.

Football violence was linked to broader upheavals. The worst year of violence in Argentinean football history (2002) came after the country's economic meltdown a year earlier. The Jewish-Arab conflict in Israel manifested itself in football, as it did in every aspect of daily life. In 2012, hundreds of supporters of Beitar Jerusalem, a club associated with the right-wing, anti-Arab Likud party, assaulted Arab workers in a mall near Beitar's Teddy Stadium. So long as violence remains part of modern societies, it will remain part of football. Crossing the street, though, is far more dangerous than going to the match.

The Armchair Fan

In May 1949, Wolverhampton Wanderers and Leicester City contested the sixty-eighth final of England's showpiece competition, the FA Cup. Valerie Gisborn, from Leicester, listened to the match on the radio at home with her mother. Valerie's father did not go to Wembley Stadium either. He watched Leicester's 3–1 defeat at a friend's house, on a brand-new, black-and-white television set. Valerie's diary recounts her father's sense of wonder at the viewing experience: "He was so thrilled he could hardly wait to get indoors to tell us about it. What a weird and wonderful thing it was ... [Dad] reckoned it was better than actually being at Wembley."[20]

Television brought revolutionary changes to armchair spectatorship, but football's media story did not begin there. Newspapers and radio first built national, and even international, communities of supporters. Publications such as *El Gráfico* (Argentina), *kicker* (Germany), *Corriere dello Sport* (Italy), and *Marca* (Spain) made the game visible and discussable in millions of households and workplaces from the 1920s and 1930s onwards. Football dominated the ever-expanding sports sections of daily newspapers. The *Manchester Evening Chronicle* first published the "Football Pink," a Saturday sports edition printed on pink paper, in 1904. This began a tradition of local "Pinks" and "Greens," which provided match-going fans in Britain with cherished, near-live reports on just-completed matches.

Radio was no less important. Historian Eric Hobsbawm recalled listening to Austria play England at a friend's house in Vienna in 1930, the only English boy in a room full of Austrian supporters. Though some West Germans watched the 1954 World Cup final victory over Hungary on television, the technology was in its infancy. The iconic memory of the game, shared by millions of people, was Herbert Zimmermann's ecstatic, disbelieving radio commentary.

Television posed a challenge to live spectatorship in ways that newspapers and radio, however thrillingly presented, could not. Football's entry into the screen age enlarged and privatized the viewing experience. The transformation was not immediate. From the 1950s to the 1980s, televised football was limited. Live coverage in Norway in the 1970s was restricted to the weekly Saturday *Tippekampen* game from England, the English FA Cup final, finals of UEFA competitions, and select matches from the Norwegian league. State-owned television in apartheid South Africa first screened live matches in 1981. The BBC, the world's oldest broadcasting institution, did not show a live Football League match until 1983.

In this period, highlights shows, such as the BBC's *Match of the Day*, first broadcast in 1964, and West Germany's *Sportschau* (1961), were popular. Television, though, was at best first among equals. In England in the late 1960s, a big game could attract between 7 and 10 million television viewers. Each weekend, up to 1 million people played football and more than 1 million people attended matches. Many millions more played the football "pools" (lottery). Radio, arguably, still mattered more than television.

Generations of Italians grew up listening to Sunday afternoon Serie A commentaries on *Tutto il calcio minuto per minuto* (All the football minute by minute). In East Germany on Saturday afternoons, listeners enjoyed live second-half updates from the day's Oberliga matches, as well as coverage of the West German Bundesliga. Transistor radios allowed people to keep up with other matches as they watched their team in action. Print media was also still influential. Until the end of the twentieth century, millions of supporters leaving grounds on Saturday afternoons picked up a "Pink" to discover results of games around Britain. In Japan, the phenomenal success of Yōichi Takahashi's *manga* (comic book) series about a soccer-loving youth, *Captain Tsubasa*—first published in 1981—is often credited with football's transformation into a national sport on a par with baseball. By 2008, the series had a circulation of 70 million at home. An additional 10 million copies were sold abroad in ten countries.

Despite the resilience of older media forms, television's cultural and political influence steadily increased. There were close relations between Globo, the Brazilian station that broadcast the iconic colour broadcasts of the 1970 World Cup, and the country's military dictatorship. The 1986 World Cup in Mexico was a closed partnership between the ruling Institutional Revolutionary Party (Partido Revolucionario Institucional) and its media ally, Televisa. When Guillermo Cañedo, head of the organizing committee and former Televisa boss, heard criticisms of high ticket prices and empty seats, he curtly responded that people could watch on TV.

Saturation coverage began in the 1990s. In previous decades, live or recorded broadcasts were usually free-to-air, often on state-run or state-supported networks. Private companies now entered the field and transformed it. English football's conversion from run-down domestic product to lucrative global spectacle was bankrolled by Rupert Murdoch's satellite TV company, BSkyB (later Sky Television), which in 1992 paid the then vast sum of £304 million for a three-year deal to show the new Premier League competition. Less than a decade later, the company happily paid four times as much for the same product. TV deals skyrocketed, as deregulation opened up markets. Not everyone was as successful as Sky or the French company Canal+, which dominated the television market and owned one of the country's largest clubs, Paris Saint-Germain, from 1991 to 2006. KirchMedia, which paid 3 billion Euros for a four-year deal to broadcast Bundesliga matches in 2000, was declared bankrupt in 2002, triggering a financial crisis in German football. Its pay-TV service made too little profit for it to survive.

A central figure in football's transformation into soap-operatic television spectacle was the Italian media tycoon and politician Silvio Berlusconi. Berlusconi's Fininvest (later Mediaset) company first dabbled in televised football in the 1980s. In 1986, Berlusconi purchased one of Italy's biggest clubs, AC Milan. Helped by a revolutionary coach, Arrigo Sacchi, and three brilliant Dutch players, Ruud Gullit, Marco van Basten, and Frank Rijkaard, Berlusconi's Milan became Europe's best football team. As his football and media empire grew, so did his political ambitions. In 1994, Berlusconi began the first of four stints as Italian prime minister. Boundaries between football, television, and politics all but collapsed. Berlusconi's centre-right political party, Forza Italia (Let's Go Italy), was named after a football chant. Its leader combined football rhetoric and televisual dramatics to appeal to an electorate composed, after all, of millions of football fans. Despite his later fall from grace—he was convicted of tax fraud in 2013, given a suspended prison sentence, and banned from public office—Berlusconi remained popular in many quarters. He was AC Milan chairman until Fininvest sold the club to Chinese investors in 2017.

On the back of such deals, companies, and characters, football—or at least football's biggest events and wealthiest leagues—became a transnational television colossus. The sale of international broadcasting rights became as important as the sale of domestic rights. Sky's three-year purchase of domestic broadcasting rights for the English Premier League in 2009 was worth £1.8 billion. The international deal over a similar period was worth £1.4 billion. The three-year broadcasting deals struck in 2019 were worth, respectively, £5 billion (domestic) and £4.2 billion (international). The EPL currently sells regional rights to 212 countries. Games in the 2015/16 season were shown in 643 million households worldwide.

With vast audiences for the English game in East Asia, clubs such as Manchester United have cultivated local markets through tours, television, and merchandise. The result is a transnational fan base, which includes many people who have never set foot in Old Trafford. In 2010, Muslim clerics in Malaysia warned supporters to repent of their love for Manchester United because the club's "Red Devil" badge was a symbol of evil. Few took the injunction against devil worship seriously. In 2016, the Astro company paid an undisclosed amount to broadcast every EPL match live in Malaysia for three seasons: a total of 1140 games. Another three-year deal was signed in 2019.

How has television changed the way that football is seen? In the stadium, each spectator has their own view of the game, limited but autonomous.

Each person is directly part of a collective experience. In front of the television, the armchair viewer has multiple views of the game, including replays, but no control, or limited control, over what they are shown. The viewer can still share in a communal experience (for example, by watching a game in a bar or public viewing area), but the screen creates a buffer from the spectacle. Part of that spectacle for the armchair fan is the spectator. Despite Margaret Thatcher's musings, football has no television appeal without the crowd, as anyone who has watched a behind-closed-doors match could testify.

Many theorists of spectacle, such as the Marxist Guy Debord, have little time for "the endless series of trivial confrontations" set up by television and sport. But the relationship cannot be easily dismissed. Writing in the mid-1980s, when technology was less advanced than it is today, John Hargreaves noted that television cameras reproduced a football match from the perspective of a middle-class spectator, who typically sat in the main stand on the halfway line, and emphasized the individual over the collective. Television, in other words, was no neutral arbiter. How football was presented to an armchair audience mattered, from the "phantom crowd effect" piped into living rooms to the spatial and temporal interruptions created by action replays or the intrusion of graphics. By the second decade of the twenty-first century, television productions of major matches were not unlike feature films, shot with an array of high-tech cameras and monitors and edited with a fine eye for dramatic spectacle (the inevitable cut, for example, to fans weeping in the stands after their team is defeated).

In the present age of electronic distraction, live attendance at games has become a form of hybrid spectatorship. Video screens showing line-ups and replays, LED perimeter advertising, and the addictive pull of smartphones can all detract from the direct experience of watching the game. This is to say nothing of the Video Assistant Referee (VAR) system introduced by FIFA at the 2018 World Cup in Russia. Designed to help match officials with borderline decisions (relating to, for example, offsides, penalties, and red cards), VAR provided split-screen drama for the tournament's television audience. In-stadium video screens replayed incidents and decisions too, as the boundaries between live and mediated spectatorship became ever more blurred.

It is too reductive to argue that television has been the gravedigger of "traditional" football. The medium has played a vital if contested role in football's international history. Writing in 2013, Albrecht Sonntag called 8:45 p.m., the kick-off time for midweek Champions League games,

"European hour." UEFA introduced split kick-off times (6 p.m. and 9 p.m.) in 2018, undermining—for predictable, profit-driven reasons—the idea of a "sacred time" for the playing and watching of European football. Yet the shared televisual experience of UEFA's flagship competition has fostered what journalist Peter Berlin termed "European familiarity" far more effectively than the European Parliament or the European Central Bank.

The history of armchair fandom suggests how television built multilayered spectator identities from the local, national, and transnational loyalties inspired by Dynamo Kiev in the Soviet Union to the international support today for Barcelona, a club rooted in Catalan nationalism, or Brazil, one of the few shared passions of Israelis and Palestinians and a cultural beacon across the Global South. For a Honduran immigrant watching soccer in a sport bar in the United States in 2009, the game on the screen could affirm "home" national loyalties. It could encourage pan-ethnic Latino solidarity, a sense of football's role in separating Latin Americans from their US cousins. And it could encourage transnational links to distant teams: support for Italy's Inter Milan, for example, because Honduras's star striker, David Suazo, played there. Television, for all of its faults, has made football a more global game and its spectators more global citizens.

Notes

1 Manfred Zeller, *Sport and Society in the Soviet Union: The Politics of Football after Stalin* (London: IB Tauris, 2018), 168, 176.

2 Nick Hornby, *Fever Pitch* (London: Victor Gollancz, 1992), 96.

3 Attendance figures in this section draw on many sources listed in the bibliography, as well as the following web-based resources: http://www.european-football-statistics.co.uk/attn.htm; https://www.worldfootball.net/; and European Leagues Fan Attendance Report (2018), https://europeanleagues.com/wp-content/uploads/FINAL-EPFL_FA_18-VERSION-2018.01.12.pdf (all accessed 23 September 2019).

4 Quoted in Walvin, *The People's Game*, 151.

5 Quoted in Simon Tyers, "How World Cup TV Coverage Has Changed Since the 1950s," *The Guardian*, July 7, 2014, https://www.theguardian.com/football/when-saturday-comes-blog/2014/jul/07/world-cup-tv-television-coverage-changed-1954-1958 (accessed 23 March 2018).

6 Hornby, *Fever Pitch*, 15.

7 Hopcraft, *The Football Man*, 186.

8 Quoted in McDougall, *The People's Game*, 52.

9 Eric Hobsbawm, *Nations and Nationalism Since 1870: Programme, Myth, Reality* (Cambridge: Cambridge University Press, 1990), 143.

10 Quoted in Rein, *Fútbol, Jews, and the Making of Argentina*, 152–53.

11 Quoted in Simon Kuper, *Football against the Enemy* (London: Orion Books, 1994), 46–47.

12 Priestley, *The Good Companions*, 4.

13 Quoted in Rogan Taylor, *Football and Its Fans: Supporters and Their Relations with the Game, 1885–1985* (Leicester: Leicester University Press, 1992), 7.

14 Quoted in Eric Dunning, Patrick Murphy, and John Williams, *Football on Trial: Spectator Violence and Development in the Football World* (London: Routledge, 1990), 77–78.

15 Quoted in Rein, *Fútbol, Jews, and the Making of Argentina*, 155.

16 Quoted in Goldblatt, *The Ball Is Round*, 543.

17 "After Brussels," *The Times*, May 31, 1985, 11.

18 Quoted in Alegi, *Laduma!*, 132.

19 Kuper, *Football against the Enemy*, 18.

20 Quoted in David Kynaston, *Austerity Britain, 1945–1951* (London: Bloomsbury, 2008), 336.

9 | Confrontations

When Italy played Haiti at the 1974 World Cup, there was only one expected outcome. Haiti, a small, poor Caribbean island nation, was making its World Cup debut. Italy was twice world champions, and one of the game's superpowers. Goalkeeper Dino Zoff had not conceded a goal in international football since 1972, a world record span of twelve matches. This was all forgotten in the forty-sixth minute. Haitian striker Emmanuel "Manno" Sanon received a pass from midfielder Philippe Vorbe, ran through the Italian defence, and gave Haiti a 1–0 lead. Zoff's record was broken at 1,143 minutes, by a twenty-two-year-old who earned US$200 per month playing for Don Bosco FC in Pétion-Ville, a suburb of the Haitian capital, Port-au-Prince.

Haiti's fairy tale did not last long. Italy recovered from Sanon's strike and won the opening game 3–1. Haiti then lost heavily to Poland (7–0) and more respectably to Argentina (3–1). Between the Italy and Poland games, defender Ernst Jean-Joseph failed a FIFA drug test. Politics, never far from the surface in Haitian football, now sprang into ugly view. During the 1960s, Haitian President François "Papa Doc" Duvalier—mindful, like many dictators, of sport's potential to distract citizens from less pleasant aspects of their lives—had lavished money on football. The national team narrowly missed qualification for the 1970 World Cup. When Duvalier died in 1971, he was succeeded by his son Jean-Claude ("Baby Doc"), a football fanatic who closely followed the game in Italy and South America. Haiti qualified for the 1974 tournament in West Germany, amid complaints from CONCACAF rivals about intimidation and voodoo.

The Haitian team, like fellow 1974 debutants, Zaire, was kept on a short political leash. After his failed drug test, Jean-Joseph was abducted from the team hotel by enforcers from the notorious death squad, the Tonton Macoutes, established by Papa Doc in 1959. Back in Haiti, he telephoned to reassure the squad in West Germany that he was alive. A favourite of Baby Doc's, Jean-Joseph recovered from his disgrace to play for the national team again. He thus avoided the fate of Haiti's first football hero, Joe Gaetjens. A Haitian native who played football in New York after the Second World War, Gaetjens scored the winning goal for the United States in its shock win over England at the 1950 World Cup. He returned to the island in 1954. His family opposed the Duvalier dictatorship. In 1964, shortly after Papa Doc declared himself president for life and the rest of Gaetjens's family fled into exile, the Tonton Macoutes arrested Gaetjens. He was never seen again.

Writing of Mussolini's use of sport as a political pacifier, Italian anti-fascist Carlo Levi despaired of citizens "reduced to interesting themselves, like babies, in the gratuitous bounce of a ball."[1] Yet, in Italy as in Haiti under the Duvaliers, it was not quite that simple. The Haitian team's success in the early 1970s was undoubtedly an escape from hardship and oppression, a limited substitute for political action against a fearsome regime. But it was also a source of national pride. Football gave credence to the black nationalism cynically, and otherwise unsuccessfully, peddled by Duvalier *père et fils*. From the team's distinctive tangerine shirts to the Bob Lemoine song "Toup Pou Yo" ("Kick for Goal"), the sporting narrative of the period is remembered fondly, even if the political one is not. Before it was destroyed in the 2010 earthquake, a mural in Port-au-Prince depicted the four nationalist heroes of Caribbean liberation. They were Toussaint Louverture (leader of the Haitian Revolution), Fidel Castro, Che Guevara, and Manno Sanon. It was the football player, not the dictators, who stayed the political course.

For the philosopher and sociologist Theodor Adorno, sport was "the colourless reflection of a hardened callous life." Its practitioners were "no longer capable of helping themselves." Its audience was composed of the "howling devotees of the stadium." Both were alienated by a leisure pursuit that was "nothing other than a shadowy continuation of labour" and the capitalist system represented by this labour.[2] In such "opiate of the masses" reflections—repeated by Marxist theorists from Karl Kautsky to Terry Eagleton—there is an unsmiling, and elitist, dismissal of a vital form of popular culture. This was parodied in a sketch from the 1970s British comedy, *Monty Python's Flying Circus*. In it, Karl Marx appears on a television game show with Mao, Lenin, and Che Guevara. He effortlessly answers questions about the class struggle but has no idea that West Ham's nickname is the Hammers. Marx eventually misses out on the big prize, a "beautiful lounge suite," because he does not know who won the 1949 FA Cup. Critiques of football's allegedly dangerous apoliticism are often based on narrow definitions of politics. They ignore, or underestimate, football's historical and contemporary role as a site of tensions and even confrontations. Even when we think of such monomaniacs as Sepp Herberger, the German national team coach whose 361 Second World War notebooks referenced nothing but football, or Liverpool manager Bill Shankly, who gave his home address as Liverpool's Anfield stadium when staying in hotels, we cannot consider them outside the politics of their eras. Herberger was a Nazi fellow traveller and the protégé of staunch anti-Semite Otto Nerz. Like many in the DFB, he acquiesced to Hitler's regime for sporting and political reasons. Shankly was a socialist who saw football, like politics, as a collective endeavour. Addressing massed ranks of supporters in Liverpool city centre after a 1971 FA Cup final loss to Arsenal, he boasted that "Chairman Mao has never seen the greatest show of red strength."[3]

Football, then, is a fluid political entity. The sport might offer a means of propaganda and tool for depoliticizing the masses, but it rarely does so reliably. Football can also encourage resistance to authority, what anthropologist and Spartak Moscow supporter Vladimir Shinkaryov called "a small way of saying 'No.'"[4] Many journalists and ex-players have suggested that Zaire's poor performance at the 1974 World Cup—the Leopards lost their three matches to Brazil, Scotland, and Yugoslavia by a combined score of fourteen to nil—was a form of protest against the broken financial promises of the kleptocratic dictatorship of Mobutu Sese Seko.

Chapter 9 interrogates the complex relationship between power and resistance on and around the contested fields of modern football. Borrowing from George Orwell's famous description of sport—"war minus the shooting"—the next section looks at football's place in military conflicts and armed uprisings. Ranging from Stalin's gulags to Franco's Spain, the chapter then examines autonomy versus conformity when football meets dictatorship. The concluding section analyzes political mobilization, from cult Hamburg club St. Pauli to protests about past and present at Liverpool FC.

"War Minus the Shooting"?

In December 1945, the novelist George Orwell wrote an essay for the socialist magazine *Tribune*, titled "The Sporting Spirit." He pulled no punches. "Serious sport," argued Orwell, "has nothing to do with fair play. It is bound up with hatred, jealousy, boastfulness, disregard of all rules and sadistic pleasure in witnessing violence: in other words it is war minus the shooting." "If you wanted to add to the vast fund of ill-will existing in the world at this moment," he continued, "you could hardly do it better than by a series of football matches between Jews and Arabs, Germans and Czechs, Indians and British, Russians and Poles, and Italians and Jugoslavs, each match to be watched by a mixed audience of 100,000 spectators."[5]

Orwell wrote his essay shortly after Dynamo Moscow's four-match tour of Britain in November 1945. Designed as a goodwill exchange between wartime allies, the Soviet team's polished play ruffled a few sporting and political feathers. Tensions in what came to be known as the Cold War also complicated Anglo-Soviet relations. Yet, in many quarters, the Soviet team received a warm welcome. Enlightened voices in the FA, mindful of insularity, recognized that the Soviet game, with its emphasis on passing, technique, and the collective, had lessons to impart. The Soviets, in turn, took much from their immersion in British football culture.

Orwell's conclusions matched the dismissal of sport elsewhere in his work—football is prominent among the cheap, trashy diversions offered to the oppressed "proles" in *1984*—and, unsurprisingly, ignored the tour's role in cultural and political exchange. Football can foster cross-border connections, even in times of war. This was exemplified by the match, or series of matches, that happened in the no man's land between British and German soldiers on Christmas Day 1914. The truce on the Western Front was an act of defiance against authority, initiated by soldiers against the wishes of their commanding officers. *The Times* published a letter from a doctor attached to the Rifle Brigade on 1 January 1915, confirming that a "them and us" match had been played in front of the British trench. The brigade's official history denied that it happened. On the German side, soldiers from the 133rd Royal Saxon Regiment wrote of a "Tommy and Fritz" match against Scottish troops, played on frozen ground with caps laid down for goalposts. The poet and First World War veteran Robert Graves fictionalized the encounter in a 1962 short story, allowing the Germans to keep their 3–2 victory but suggesting that the winning goal was offside.

Football, as Russian novelist Vladimir Nabokov suggested in 1926, was hardly an equivalent "substitute for the goose march." "To search in [sport] for signs of barbarity is pointless," he argued, "if only because a real barbarian is always a truly awful sportsman."[6] Nonetheless Orwell's scepticism about sport's martial tendencies was not wholly misplaced. Football has on occasion played an important role in symbolizing conflict, and sometimes even in starting it. In August 1942, a match between Ukrainian side FC Start and a German Flakelf (air defence team) in German-occupied Kiev came to represent the "war of annihilation" between Germany and the Soviet Union that began in 1941. Seeking revenge for an earlier loss to Start, the German team was defeated 4–2. Within a week, half of the Start team had been sent to labour camps. Four players were eventually murdered. The so-called "death match" was much mythologized, first in the Soviet Union and later in the West, inspiring movies (notably John Huston's *Escape to Victory* in 1981), books, and controversies. The initial Stalinist story—that a ragtag team of Ukrainian footballers had all paid the ultimate price for defying Nazi savagery—was exaggerated. It elided the role played by Ukrainian collaborators—most notably Georgi Shvetsov, the anti-Semitic coach of nationalist team Rukh—in the arrest of the Start team. Not all of the Start players died. Nor were they, in playing terms at least, underdogs: most were drawn from Dynamo Kiev, one of the Soviet Union's strongest prewar teams. But the "death match" was an undoubtedly heroic act. Start players refused to give the Nazi salute and then outplayed their opponents in a hostile environment, knowing that reprisals were inevitable. Their rebellion was a local inspiration for further acts of resistance, from restoring icons to churches to hiding Jews.

Football conflicts were not always so well known. In 1962, Gabon played Congo-Brazzaville in two qualification matches for the Coupe des Tropiques. Tensions between the two former colonies of French Equatorial Africa found expression on the field. There was chaos at the first match in Brazzaville, as 30,000 Congolese supporters attacked the referee and threatened the Gabonese team. Anti-Congolese violence followed the return match in the Gabonese capital, Libreville. Nine people were killed in two days of rioting. The homes of hundreds of Congolese migrants in the Akébé neighbourhood were burned to the ground. Gabon's government expelled 2,700 Congolese. Reciprocal violence ensued against the small Gabonese populations in the Congolese cities of Brazzaville and Pointe-Noire, many of whom fled the country. The two countries broke off diplomatic relations. Reconciliation required outside mediation, led by Cameroon after France refused to intervene.

Sometimes football shades from militaristic metaphor into combat zones. It becomes, to rephrase Orwell, "war with the shooting." In June 1969, the Central American nations of El Salvador and Honduras played each other for a place at the 1970 World Cup. "Nobody in the world paid any attention," Polish journalist Ryszard Kapuściński wryly noted.[7] Honduras won the first leg 1–0, after locals ensured that the visiting El Salvador team had a sleepless night at its hotel in the capital, Tegucigalpa. After watching the defeat on television, an eighteen-year-old Salvadoran woman, Amelia Bolanios, shot herself in the heart. Tensions were high for the second leg. This time the Honduran team got the sleepless night treatment, as El Salvador supporters threw rotten eggs and dead rats inside its hotel rooms. The visitors arrived at the Flor Blanca Stadium in San Salvador exhausted and under armed guard. Instead of the Honduran flag, a dirty rag was hoisted up the flagpole during pre-match anthem ceremonies. El Salvador, unsurprisingly, won 3–0. Honduras players, their coach admitted, were happy to leave the ground alive. A third, tiebreaking match was required. It took place in Mexico on 27 June and El Salvador won 3–2. On the same day, El Salvador broke off diplomatic relations with Honduras, claiming that the Honduran government had failed to punish crimes against expatriate Salvadorans that amounted to genocide. On 14 July, Salvadoran military forces bombed targets inside Honduras and then launched a ground invasion. To the disbelief of officials in Washington, who struggled to grasp how soccer could produce so much vitriol and violence in two Central American "banana republics," the Football War had begun.

The Football War lasted only four days and ended in stalemate. In that time, 6,000 people were killed, 12,000 were wounded, and 50,000 displaced from their homes. Land, rather than football, was the conflict's underlying cause. Tensions had grown during the 1960s between poor, landless Salvadorans and poor, landless Hondurans over the former's large (and sometimes illegal) presence in Honduras, the poorer but bigger of the two countries. Hostilities around the World Cup qualifying matches actuated a deeper dispute, as Hondurans were encouraged to "pick up a stick and kill a Salvadoran," mobs in San Salvador beat and shot Hondurans, and Salvadorans fled Honduras in fear of their lives.

As Ryszard Kapuściński learned, the line between football and politics in Latin America was vague. Stadiums served a dual purpose. They were sites of entertainment during peacetime and concentration camps during war. When Brazil brilliantly won the 1970 World Cup in Mexico, an exiled Brazilian colleague of Kapuściński's was heartbroken. This would delay the fall of the country's military dictatorship by at least five years, he said. In fact civilian rule did not return to Brazil until 1985. The long-awaited change was prompted in part by a democracy movement promoted by footballers at the Corinthians club in São Paulo (see below).

It was not only in Latin America that football met politics and violence. The sport had a central role in the bloody dissolution of Yugoslavia.

A plaque at the Maksimir Stadium, home to Dinamo Zagreb, marks 13 May 1990 as the start of Croatia's war for independence from the Serb-led Yugoslav state. On that day, Dinamo Zagreb hosted rivals Red Star Belgrade in a vital league match. Before the game, Red Star supporters' groups, most notably Delije ("Heroes"), chanted Serb nationalist slogans and damaged Croat- and Slovene-owned businesses. Inside the stadium, tensions spilled into a full-scale riot. There were pitched battles between Delije and its Zagreb counterpart, the Bad Blue Boys. The Bad Blue Boys set parts of the stadium on fire and clashed with the police, widely seen in Croatia as a Serb-dominated institution. In the riot's iconic moment, Dinamo Zagreb captain Zvonimir Boban used a flying drop kick to stop a policeman from beating a Zagreb fan. The spectacular image flashed across television screens around the world. The match was cancelled. The Bad Blue Boys rioted late into the night, targeting Serb-owned businesses and waving Croatian flags.

The media response to the match partly reflected nationalist positions. The Serbian press condemned Boban's clash with the policeman. Red Star captain Dragan Stojković even called for him to be imprisoned. The Croatian media were, predictably, more sympathetic. Many in the Yugoslav press, though, blamed both sides. As one sports newspaper lamented, "Everything has gone to the dogs—football fans from two cities have destroyed everything the socialist government built over the past 45 years."[8]

Was the Maksimir riot the spark that lit the Yugoslav wars? Recent research suggests that the "Maksimir myth" reflected what happened subsequently in the region, rather than what happened on the day. The war between Serbia and Croatia did not begin until May 1991, a year after the riot and following a full season in the Yugoslav First Federal League. Nationalist-fuelled hooligan clashes were common at Yugoslav stadiums in the late 1980s and early 1990s. Contrary to later Serb nationalist legend, paramilitary leader Arkan—involved with Red Star's security in 1990— was a peripheral figure on 13 May. Many of the Delije leadership, who joined Arkan's notorious paramilitary unit during the war, were not even in Zagreb that day.

On the Croatian side, the match's symbolism centred on Boban's defence of a Zagreb supporter from police violence. Boban did not initially present his actions in a Croatian nationalist light. The fan he defended was in fact a relative from their native Herzegovina. However, once the war began, myth outdistanced fact. The actions of Boban and the Bad Blue Boys became foundational moments in the creation of an independent Croatia. As in the 1969 war between El Salvador and Honduras, football was a powerful catalyst for conflict in Yugoslavia, feeding nationalist legends on both sides. But it was not the root cause.

Hardcore supporters, or ultras, were prominent in the Yugoslav wars. The same was true in the Egyptian revolution of 2011. When mass protests against the army-backed regime of Hosni Mubarak began on 25 January, supporters of Cairo's two biggest clubs, Al-Ahly and Zamalek, were on the frontlines of the fighting in Tahrir Square. This was not surprising. Ultra groups had a long history of confronting riot police. They knew how to organize mass protests, withstand tear-gas attacks, and signal when to retreat or move forward. Some observers felt that, without ultra leadership, the Tahrir Square protests—crucial in toppling the Mubarak government— might have failed. The pro-Mubarak Supreme Council of the Armed Forces did not forget the defeat. It was complicit in the 2012 Port Said Stadium disaster, in which seventy-four Al-Ahly ultras were killed (see Chapter 7).

Egyptian ultras made national protests, but there was a strong element of internationalism in their organization and ideology. Repurposing a model of fandom that originated in Italy, Al-Ahly and Zamalek fans tied anti-Mubarak protests to attacks on modern football. Criticism of Egyptian football's neo-liberalization—increased ticket prices, securitized stadiums, and television's dominance—echoed anti-corporate supporters' protests throughout Europe. Scholars are still debating football's importance to the revolutionary upheavals in Egypt. Some suggest that the sport was only a substitute for "real" politics, until real politics returned in 2011. Others argue, perhaps more convincingly, that ultras consistently played a leading role at the radical edge of protest, challenging in turn the Mubarak regime, the army-led government that followed it, and the Muslim Brotherhood that ruled the country from 2012 to 2013.

Football and the Dictators

When a junta took power in Argentina in 1976, it suspended regular programming on all radio stations and television channels. As military marches and communiqués filled the airwaves, there was one exception to the rule. The new government allowed the broadcast of Argentina's match against Poland to go ahead. Removing football from the schedule was too big a political risk. Under the leadership of Jorge Rafael Videla, the junta ploughed vast sums into Argentina's hosting of the 1978 World Cup. The US$700 million investment, 10 per cent of the national budget, paid off, at least in the short term. Argentina became world champions for the first time. The perpetrators and victims of Argentina's "dirty war" were briefly united in a moment of national celebration. Prisoner Graciela Daleo recalled how she rejoiced with the man who had tortured her with electric drills at the detention centre in the Navy School of Mechanics (Escuela Superior de Mecánica de la Armada), just a few hundred metres from the River Plate stadium where the final was played. This was a false sense of unity, as Daleo and exiled Argentinean leftists recognized. Journalist Shlomo Slutzky called the World Cup "nothing but a show mounted by the military junta in order to continue murdering Argentine citizens."[9]

Some dictators liked football more than others. General Franco listened to Real Madrid games on his transistor radio while out shooting partridges. Libyan leader Muammar Gaddafi bought shares in Juventus in 2002. He encouraged the professional career of his third son, Al-Saadi, who had short, unsuccessful spells at two other Italian clubs, Udinese and Perugia, in the mid-2000s. Hitler, famously, watched only one football match in his life—Germany's loss to Norway at the 1936 Olympics—and left before the end. Stalin evinced no interest in the game either, though some of his henchmen, such as secret police chief Lavrentiy Beria, were fanatics. Family members of authoritarian leaders sometimes received football portfolios. Nicolae Ceauşescu's son, Valentin, was president of Romania's top club, Steaua Bucharest, in the 1980s. Saddam Hussein's murderous eldest son, Uday, ran Iraqi sport. He regularly ordered the torture and imprisonment of underperforming footballers.

Wherever football built mass appeal, political figures recognized the game's importance as a means of exerting authority and winning popularity. This was true in Europe, where Real Madrid served as international ambassadors for Franco's dictatorship, just as Steaua Bucharest did for Ceauşescu's communist tyranny. It was true in Latin America, where any number of caudillos (military dictators), from Médici in Brazil and Videla in Argentina to Stroessner in Paraguay and Pinochet in Chile, used football to shore up their regimes. It was true in Africa, where football served as a vehicle for anti-colonial, authoritarian nation building, from Kwame Nkrumah's Ghana to Mobutu Sese Seko's Zaire.

Football, though, proved to be a slippery customer for authoritarian regimes. A broad-based force under nobody's direct or permanent control, the game allowed for many, often overlapping, forms of conformity and resistance. It provided liminal spaces where officials, players, and supporters expressed a variety of attitudes to the political system under which they lived. These grey zones were very much apparent in Spanish football during the long rule of General Francisco Franco (1939–75).

In historian Raymond Carr's assessment, football—like bullfighting, cinema, and soap operas—formed part of a "culture of evasion" in Francoist Spain.[10] It provided the opportunity to talk about something other than taboo subjects such as the civil war, the police state, or poverty. From the state's perspective, football was the ultimate soporific. Broadcaster RTVE transmitted a regular flow of matches. It screened 714 Spanish and international games between 1960 and 1976, as well as extensive highlights on the Sunday night *Estudio Estadio* program. Atlético Madrid president Vicente Calderón was asked in 1969 whether he thought that football was making Spain stupid. His response revealed how the supposedly antipolitical presentation of sport was itself political to the core: "I wish that football would make the country stupid, and I wish that the people would think about football for three days before and three days after the match. In this way, they would not think about other, more dangerous things."[11] By this point, the European supremacy of Atlético's cross-town rivals, Real Madrid, had passed. Franco's favourite team, though, remained Spain's best ambassador. The club, unlike the regime, was held in high regard. Lucrative tours of Europe, the United States, the Middle East, and North Africa served as diplomatic calling cards, normalizing the presence of Francoist Spain on the international stage.

There were many cracks in football's façade of apolitical conformity. The biggest challenges to Madrid's political and sporting primacy came from the regions. Clubs such as Barcelona (Catalonia) and Athletic Bilbao (the Basque country) appeared to be natural homes for anti-Francoist activities and activists. Catalonia and the Basque country had been centres of Republican resistance to Franco's Nationalists during the civil war (1936–39); it was a Basque football team, as we saw in Chapter 2, that toured to rally international support for the fight against Franco. The postwar suppression of the Basque and Catalan languages and cultures left the region's football clubs as arguably the last remaining symbols of alternative identities in a remorselessly unitary state.

Compromises were made, especially in Barcelona's case. The club's actions during the Franco era have been scrutinized, as scholars and journalists attempt to disentangle Barcelona's heroic post-1975 self-image from a more complex reality. Barcelona survived the civil war but fell into the hands of Francoist sympathizers, including members of the blue-shirted fascist organization, the Falange. Presidents such as Francesc Miró-Sans, elected in 1953, publically ingratiated themselves with the Franco regime even as they pressed Barcelona's cause behind the scenes (for example, in complaints about referees) and gradually reintroduced Catalan symbols and the Catalan language to the Camp Nou stadium. Like Barcelona, Athletic Bilbao survived the civil war, though it was ordered to change its name, from the English "Athletic" to the Castilian "Atlético." Francoist loyalists staffed a new board. The excellent Bilbao team of the mid-1940s was held up as a representative of the "Spanish fury," a physically imposing, attacking style of play that supposedly embodied the martial qualities of nationalist Spain.

Concessions notwithstanding, anti-Francoism at Athletic Bilbao and Barcelona was genuine. Approximately 9,500 of Barcelona's 16,000 *socios* (members) at the outbreak of the civil war died fighting the Nationalists or were purged, imprisoned, or forced into exile. Casualties included Barcelona president Josep Sunyol, who was killed in 1936. Attempts to depoliticize Barcelona after 1939 did not really work. There was crowd unrest in both legs of the 1943 cup semi-final between Barcelona and Real Madrid. Tensions only increased when Real Madrid, with the football federation's help, snatched Argentinean Alfredo Di Stéfano from under Barcelona's noses in 1953. This catalyzed Real's domination of Spanish and European football and mounting Catalan complaints about injustices on and off the field.

In Bilbao the catalyst arrived five years later, when Athletic defeated Real Madrid in the Spanish cup final. Much to Bilbao's anger, the match took place in Real's Santiago Bernabéu stadium, rather than at a neutral venue. With the club's support, 30,000 Basques attended the final, creating a hostile atmosphere that weakened Real's home advantage. Bilbao's successes, combined with its anti-Francoist reputation, meant that it had 293 nationwide supporters' clubs by 1968.

The resurgence of Basque and Catalan nationalism in the final decade of Franco's rule encouraged open displays of defiance. In 1971, a group of Athletic fans—supporters of the violent Basque separatist organization ETA—smuggled the outlawed Basque flag, the *ikurriña*, onto the terraces for the first time, prompting scuffles with the police. A year earlier, Barcelona's controversial loss to Real Madrid in the cup quarter-final prompted a pitch invasion from angry Barcelona supporters. The match was briefly suspended. The political significance of such incidents was unmistakable. A handbill distributed at the Camp Nou before the 1970 cup final, in which Real Madrid played Valencia, called on supporters to protest against the Francoist state. The charge sheet included sporting complaints (most notably corrupt refereeing), but these were linked to political griev-ances: the lack of public investment, the ban on the Catalan language, and the attempted erasure of the Catalan people.

For authoritarian regimes, football *campanilismo* (regionalism) was a continual headache. The history of Spanish football under Franco fit an international narrative. Civic loyalties complicated attempts to centralize and nationalize football in Mussolini's Italy and Nkrumah's Ghana. In the federal socialist republic of Yugoslavia, as in Spain, regional loyalties were grounded in claims to national self-determination against the claims of dictatorial state power. The ruling authorities in Belgrade had less suc-cess than their Spanish counterparts in keeping a lid on tensions, especially after Tito's death in 1980. Football, as we saw, played an important role in the escalation of hostilities that led to civil war and the disintegration of Yugoslavia in the 1990s. Less dramatically, clubs in other communist states served as rallying points against centralized power: for example, Dynamo Dresden in East Germany, Dynamo Kiev in the Soviet Union, and Slovan Bratislava in Czechoslovakia.

Football had a habit of upsetting what political scientist James C. Scott called "the public transcript."[12] How politically significant was this? Much depends on definitions of "politics" and "resistance." Even where they were the spark for unrest, as in Yugoslavia in 1990 or Egypt in 2011, football protests did not bring down regimes. They often did not achieve more modest goals. The handbill calling for Franco to be whistled at during the 1970 Spanish cup final led nowhere. There was no whistling, as the regime gave free tickets to those willing to applaud Franco. The flurry of protest letters from angry citizens about the corrupt dominance of BFC did not stop "the Stasi team" from winning ten straight East German league titles between 1979 and 1988.

Such examples might suggest that football was an unproductive form of dissent. That would be misleading. Football's popularity and its fram-ing as a harmless, apolitical activity paradoxically made it political. In this catch-22 situation, political targets could be attacked indirectly under the guise of club partisanship: the Francoist state via criticisms of Real Madrid, for example, or the GDR's surveillance state via anti-BFC complaints. The fact that dictatorships around the world tried, often with limited success, to mould the game in their image—and fretted over any blemishes to that image—only reiterated football's political power.

Football under dictatorship was not only a story of power versus resist-ance and centre versus periphery, played out among rival supporters at big clubs in large stadiums. The sport touched everyday life, even in unlikely places. The vast Soviet prison camp (gulag) system built under Stalin is traditionally depicted as a place of unimaginable horrors. Recent research, though, has shown that football and other sports were played regularly in the gulag, as they were in Nazi concentration camps and in the apartheid prison on Robben Island. Prisoners played pick-up games in open spaces. Camp teams played against guard teams on proper pitches, often in front of large crowds. They sometimes played outside the camp, against local opposition. Talented players got increased food rations. Winning teams gave camp commandants bragging rights over their peers. Nikolai Starostin, one of the founders of Spartak Moscow, was sent to the gulag in 1942. In his memoirs he wrote, "Over the years, I ceased to be amazed by the fact that camp chiefs ... the embodiment of the brutality and horrors of the gulag related to everything concerning football so sympathetically. Their immense power over people was nothing compared to the power of football over them."[13] The structures of the outside world were replicated in the camps, which ran their own Spartakiads, the mass, multi-sport competitions held throughout the Soviet Union. The team from the Medgora camp won the 1935 football Spartakiad at the White Sea-Baltic Combine, showcasing excellent defence and skilled attack to defeat Kem 2–0. Two weeks later, Medgora earned a credible 2–2 draw against a local secret police (NKVD) team.

Football's promotion in the camps reflected the Soviet regime's desire for a physically robust, healthy society—and the kind of workforce, free and unfree, needed for Stalin's ambitious program of industrialization. Sport was the rehabilitative counterpoint to the gulag's repressive features. As in many prison systems, it served as a tool of re-education. But football was also promoted because it was popular. Gulag football offered a break from monotonous routines. The timeless experience of play provided moments of respite, even freedom. For skilled players, it meant better food and opportunities to travel beyond the camp perimeter. Gulag football broke down barriers, however temporarily, between prisoners, guards, camp officers, and, on occasion, the outside world. Such interactions were closely monitored. But football allowed connections to be made, and borders to be crossed, even in horrendous circumstances.

The People's Game

In April 1982, elections took place for a new president of Corinthians, a football club in the large industrial city of São Paulo in southern Brazil. Running on an "Order and Truth" ticket, ex-president Vicente Matheus represented the *cartolas* (top hats), the business and political elites who supported Brazil's military dictatorship, in power since 1964. Matheus's opponent was Waldemar Pires, who ran on the Democracia Corinthiana (Corinthian Democracy) ticket. Corinthian Democracy represented the supporters, players, and officials who sought to democratize not only their football club but Brazil itself. The charismatic midfielder and doctor, Sócrates, became the movement's spokesperson. Alongside fellow players Walter Casagrande and Wladimir, he campaigned to loosen the reigns of authority, both within the club (from beer in the changing rooms to an end to players' pre-match confinement in training camps) and nationally. The trio thus followed in the footsteps of such footballers as Botafogo midfielder Afonsinho, who was banned by club management in 1970 for wearing his hair and beard too long and subsequently took his struggle against authoritarian regulations through the legal system. Afonsinho's victory symbolized the ongoing struggle against Brazil's military dictatorship, a rebel stance praised by singer and activist Gilberto Gil in his 1973 song "Meio de Campo" ("Midfielder"): "Scoring a goal in this match is not easy, my brother."[14]

At Corinthians, everyone had the same right to vote on club affairs, from the president to the kit man. The creation of a more open club culture had political implications, but it was also grounded, as Sócrates noted, in the simple thrill of playing football, "preserving the lucid, joyous, and pleasurable nature of this activity."[15] Democratization found a willing audience. *Torcidas* (supporters' groups) paraded a banner that read: "Win or lose but always with democracy." Corinthians won the 1982 São Paulo state championship with "Corinthian Democracy" on their shirts instead of a corporate sponsor. In March 1983, Pires won the club's presidential election. The following year, Sócrates spoke before a crowd of 1.5 million in São Paulo. He promised not to depart for Italian team Fiorentina if a constitutional amendment was passed granting the country free elections. The amendment was defeated. Sócrates left for Italy. A year later, though, Brazil's twenty-one-year military dictatorship ended.

Corinthian Democracy did not last long. Most of the club's democratic reforms did not survive Sócrates. Corporate sponsorship returned, as did authoritarian coaches. But the movement played an important part in Brazil's transition to civilian government and democracy in the 1980s. Football, in this case, was neither the clichéd "opiate of the masses" nor a top-down tool for unthinking national unity. Instead it was a forum for activism. This was not as uncommon as might seem, in Brazil or elsewhere.

During the mass student and workers' protests in Paris in May 1968, the Footballers' Action Committee, a group representing players in the Paris region, tried to occupy the headquarters of the French Football Federation. Its manifesto demanded football's liberation from enslavement to money. In San Miguel, a working-class district of the Chilean capital, Santiago, amateur clubs served as testing grounds for radical politics and union activism in the 1950s and 1960s. In England in 1985, the creation of the Football Supporters' Association in a Liverpool pub gave voice to supporters when their stock was at an historic low. Football's multifaceted role in political mobilization forms the subject of the final part of Chapter 9.

In recent years, supporters of St. Pauli have begun wearing T-shirts displaying (in English) the slogan, "FC St. Pauli: Non established since 1910." The T-shirts and the supporters can be found in unlikely places. The Hamburg-based club claims 11 million worldwide fans. It has supporters' clubs as far away as Calcutta. The distinctive Jolly Roger (skull and crossbones) insignia has become a global symbol of discerning football taste. Yet St. Pauli is, by most estimates, a small club. It is not even the biggest club in Hamburg, a title that belongs to 1983 European Cup champions Hamburger SV. St. Pauli has spent eight seasons in the Bundesliga and never won a major honour.

Why does a club with such a modest record attract a global following? The short answer is politics. Perhaps more than any club in world football, St. Pauli is tied to a leftist, nonconformist identity that has little to do with on-field performances. The wealthy seaport of Hamburg did not incorporate the St. Pauli district until 1894. It subsequently retained a distance from authority, even in the Nazi era. In the 1960s, St. Pauli was the centre of a youth culture based on music, sex, and drugs. It was on the Reeperbahn, the heart of St. Pauli's famous red-light district, that the Beatles forged their sound and identity. When a St. Pauli player scored a goal, he was allegedly rewarded with a trip to a local brothel.

By the 1970s and 1980s, the area was in economic decline. Commercial and municipal forces wanted redevelopment and gentrification. Community groups opposed such changes. It was in this context that St. Pauli terrace culture became actively leftist. One of Germany's first fanzines, *Millerntor Roar!* (1989), grew out of an anti-racist supporters' group. The club's *Fanladen* (fan shop) was less a place for selling merchandise than a meeting point and social education centre. St. Pauli's progressive reputation gradually won it an international following. Since the turn of the century, it has hosted anti-fascist memorials and anti-racism tournaments and supported local and international humanitarian causes. In 2006, St. Pauli ran an alternative World Cup alongside the main event then running with great fanfare in Germany. It was open to political entities not recognized by FIFA: Gibraltar, Greenland, Northern Cyprus, Tibet, and Zanzibar. Scholars and supporters have sometimes viewed St. Pauli's romantic self-image with scepticism. Just as the St. Pauli district has been gentrified since the late 1980s, so the club's fan base has grappled with the contradictions of being an increasingly successful global "brand." The high-wire act of modern football, which pits authenticity and tradition against commercialization and globalization, has played out with particular intensity in this corner of Hamburg. It poses dilemmas common to supporters of all clubs with left-wing identities, from Livorno in Italy to Hapoel Tel Aviv in Israel. Many of these dilemmas, moreover, override divisions between left and right.

Liverpool FC is based in a working-class port city, dominated since the 1980s by the Labour Party. Its most famous manager, Bill Shankly, was a socialist. For much of its history, the club was a conservative (and Conservative) institution. When supporters mobilized against George Gillett and Tom Hicks, during the American businessmen's disastrous tenure as club owners (2007–10), protest negotiated complex political fields. The supporters' union Spirit of Shankly was formed in 2008 at the Sandon pub where Liverpool FC was founded in 1892. Its name paid tribute to the city's favourite socialist son and to militant political traditions. Spirit of Shankly and other protest groups honoured local identities in ways that, often unwittingly, excluded Liverpool's community of international supporters. The anti-Americanism in a prominent protest slogan, "Yanks out," did not sit comfortably with some of the club's many US-based supporters' groups. Who belonged or who was allowed to belong here?

Spirit of Shankly quickly acknowledged the club's global fan base and the city's transnational history, opening international branches in 2010. But tensions between locals and "out-of-towners" were present at many big football clubs in the twenty-first century. Debates about ticket access and prices, corporate ownership, commercialism, and the balance between local and global interests had no easy answers. In 2016, around 10,000 Liverpool supporters walked out of a game against Sunderland in protest against high ticket prices at Anfield. Liverpool led 2–0 when the exodus occurred in the seventy-seventh minute. The game ended 2–2. Fenway Sports Group, the American investment company that purchased the club in 2010, got the message. It immediately scrapped plans for top-price tickets of £77.

At Liverpool the politics of the present was tied to the politics of the (still-living) past. Groups such as Spirit of Shankly acknowledged their affiliation to older groups that challenged the injustices that followed the 1989 Hillsborough disaster (see Chapter 7). Founded in 1998, the Hillsborough Justice Campaign provided counselling advice for survivors, organized match-day protests, and sold fundraising merchandise at a small shop outside Anfield. Some of the major breakthroughs in the "Justice for the 96" campaign occurred during the Hicks and Gillett era. In 2016, a few months after the walkout over ticket prices, a second inquest concluded that the ninety-six victims of the Hillsborough disaster had been unlawfully killed. The relationship was not always direct, but Hillsborough activism galvanized protest on a range of smaller, football-related issues. It embedded fierce civic loyalties in a club with vast international appeal.

James C. Scott's *Weapons of the Weak* (1985) examined "everyday resistance" to authority among Malayan peasants. He argued that ordinary confrontations between the peasantry and its oppressors were more important than heroic, but isolated and usually doomed, political uprisings. During his studies, Scott played in goal for a team from the Malaysian village that he called "Sedaka." Helping his teammates to a modest record in the 1979 dry season (two wins, five draws, and one defeat), Scott learned through game-related travel and socializing about the subversion of class hierarchies through language.

Football's role in providing a space for grassroots agency is often a subtle and fluid one. Harry Walker's 2013 study of the Urarina people of Amazonian Peru noted the ubiquity of football's presence and the multiplicity of its meanings. Public events often centred on a football tournament, giving opportunities to outsiders (whether from the neighbouring village or the London School of Economics) to bond with a local community. Football was a form of play, a means of expressing joy in one's body and surroundings. It also took more organized forms. In cross-community festivals, rules were strictly followed. Teams played to win. This transition from play to game, Walker argued, reflected the desire of many Urarina to integrate more closely into the Peruvian (i.e., non-Indigenous) state. In this example, football is both an autonomous space for recreation and a form of sociality that benefits the development of the Peruvian nation, perhaps—though certainly not always—at the expense of Urarina identity. On the Chambira River where the Urarina people live, as in so many other parts of the world, it is sport and football in particular, not religion, that drives the modernizing project.

Notes

1 Quoted in Macon Benoit, "The Politicization of Football: The European Game and the Approach to the Second World War," *Soccer & Society* 9, no. 4 (2008): 544.

2 Quoted in David Inglis, "Theodor Adorno on Sport: The *Jeu D'Esprit* of Despair," in Richard Giulianotti, ed., *Sport and Modern Social Theorists* (Basingstoke: Palgrave Macmillan, 2004), 85.

3 Quoted in Mark Broomy, "No. 67—Chairman Mao Has Never Seen the Greatest Show of Red Strength," *This is Anfield*, July 18, 2009, https://www.thisisanfield.com/2009/07/no-67-chairman-mao-has-never-seen-the-greatest-show-of-red-strength/ (accessed 20 June 2019).

4 Quoted in Kuper, *Football against the Enemy*, 40.

5 George Orwell, "The Sporting Spirit," *Tribune*, December 14, 1945, 10–11. Available at https://www.orwellfoundation.com/the-orwell-foundation/orwell/essays-and-other-works/the-sporting-spirit/ (accessed 24 September 2019).

6 Quoted in Thomas Karshan, *Vladimir Nabokov and the Art of Play* (Oxford: Oxford University Press, 2011), 64.

7 Ryszard Kapuściński, *The Soccer War*, trans. William Brand (New York: Vintage, 1992), 157.

8 Quoted in Richard Mills, *The Politics of Football in Yugoslavia: Sport, Nationalism and the State* (London: IB Tauris, 2018), 209.

9 Quoted in Raanan Rein, "Football, Politics and Protest: The International Campaign against the 1978 World Cup in Argentina," in Stefan Rinke and Kay Schiller, eds., *The FIFA World Cup, 1930–2010: Politics, Commerce, Spectacle and Identities* (Wallstein: Göttingen, 2014), 255.

10 Raymond Carr and Juan Pablo Fusi, *Spain: Dictatorship to Democracy*, 2nd ed. (London: George Allen & Unwin, 1981), 122.

11 Quoted in Duncan Shaw, "The Political Instrumentalisation of Professional Football in Francoist Spain, 1939–1975" (PhD diss., University of London, 1988), 147.

12 James C. Scott, *Domination and the Arts of Resistance: Hidden Transcripts* (New Haven: Yale University Press, 1990), 3–4.

13 Quoted in Steve Maddox, "Gulag Football: Competitive and Recreational Sport in Stalin's System of Forced Labour," *Kritika* 19, no. 3 (2018): 525.

14 Quoted in Euclides de Freitas Couto, "Football, Control and Resistance in the Brazilian Military Dictatorship in the 1970s," *The International Journal of the History of Sport* 31, no. 10 (2014): 1270.

15 Quoted in Kuhn, *Soccer vs. the State*, 112.

10 | Conclusion

In November 2015, a coordinated series of terrorist attacks by the jihadist Islamic State organization struck Paris. Gunmen and suicide bombers targeted crowded and popular places in the French capital: cafés, restaurants, a rock concert at the Bataclan theatre (where 89 of the 130 victims died), and a football match. The attacks began at a friendly between France and Germany at the Stade de France in northern Paris. Among the 79,000 spectators was French President François Hollande. One of three suicide bombers tried to enter the stadium, but security guards turned him away. He and the other bombers then detonated their devices near the stadium, killing themselves and one bystander. Amid nervous scenes—two of the detonations were heard on the live television broadcast—and Hollande's half-time evacuation from the stadium, the match was played to a finish. Afterwards, fans waited on the pitch before getting security clearance to go home. The German team was advised not to return to its hotel and spent the night at the stadium. The French team stayed behind too, in an act of solidarity.

The botched Stade de France attacks indicated football's vulnerability in the post-9/11 world. With their transnational popularity and internationally known stars, big matches, like big concerts, were attractive targets for extremists. Despite tight security, terrorist violence was a constant threat and an occasional reality. The sport's vulnerability was reinforced in April 2017, when three home-made pipe bombs struck the Borussia Dortmund team bus en route to the club's stadium for a Champions League quarter-final against Monaco. Nobody was seriously injured. Initial suspicion fell on the Islamic State. Investigations, though, revealed the culprit to be a lone German-Russian terrorist. Prosecutors accused him of seeking to profit from a fall in the club's share prices that would follow the explosions. He forged letters that would lead police to suspect that the culprits were radical Islamists.

Just a month after the Paris attacks, FIFA's Ethics Committee suspended from the sport for eight years the two most powerful men in world football. Sepp Blatter had resigned as FIFA president in June 2015 amid corruption allegations (see Chapter 3). UEFA President Michel Platini, long touted as Blatter's successor, now joined him on the political scrapheap. Neither man was found guilty of corruption. Rather, they had presided over a "culture of expectation and entitlement" from FIFA headquarters in Zürich, as American lawyer Michael Garcia's 2017 report into the bidding processes for the 2018 and 2022 World Cups concluded.[1]

More than half of the FIFA Executive Committee members who voted on the 2018 and 2022 bids were subsequently removed from office or indicted on criminal charges. Public cynicism was not easily assuaged, particularly regarding FIFA's decision to award the 2022 World Cup to the small, desert-covered, and oil-rich Middle Eastern state of Qatar, a decision in which Platini (as deputy FIFA president) played a contentious role. Despite claims that the country's intense heat would not be an issue, the tournament was shifted from its traditional June-July slot to November-December 2022, in the middle of many domestic seasons. Organizations such as Amnesty International highlighted human rights abuses of foreign workers building World Cup venues. When the tournament is finally played—"with the players bused from air-conditioned compounds to guarded training sessions to sealed stadiums, all the undesirables kept out along with the heat, everything looking sharp and shimmery in next-next-gen 4D Ultra HD, the matches continuously streamed and permanently rewatchable in a multitude of formats, and all the contentious refereeing decisions replayed in real time by machines that finally get them right"[2]—it will be an eye-popping spectacle. But how much will it resemble the sport that spread across the globe more than a century earlier?

From terrorism to corruption, international football seemed to mirror the dangers, divisions, and inequalities of the twenty-first century world. Viewing football as a modern morality tale, many observers felt that it had made a Faustian bargain with money and power, the price of which was the game's soul. With saturation TV coverage, corrupt organizational bodies, priced-out fans, securitized and corporate mega-events, and absurdly paid players, football looked like a game that had eaten itself. In his study of play, *Homo Ludens* (1938), Dutch historian Johan Huizinga warned that "with the increasing systematization and regimentation of sport, something of the pure play-quality is inevitably lost."[3] Eight decades later, events in Paris, Zürich, and Qatar suggested that profit and violence had long overwhelmed football's "play-element."

Yet such gloomy prognoses do not tell the whole story. Modern football cannot be reduced to a cautionary tale about greed and disenfranchisement, not least because the hyper-commercial spectacle criticized by many observers is immensely, and indeed increasingly, popular. Why has football retained global appeal? Few activities allow for such varied local, national, and international dialogues or provide such consistent means of connecting people at so many levels. Few activities, and certainly no other sports, have adapted so successfully to the screen age. Recent research suggests that younger generations of viewers, rather than prizing evenly matched contests and surprise results, in fact prefer "quality of product" and stacked-deck predictability, the same big clubs and the same superstars showcasing their brilliance on the world's media stage.

Away from headlines about corruption and violence or TV deals and megastars, there are as many stories as there are individuals, clubs, and countries that play the game. The World Cup, for example, looked very different from the perspective of the footballers of American Samoa than it did from FIFA headquarters. The 2014 documentary *Next Goal Wins* charted the national team's recovery from a record 31–0 loss to Australia in 2001 and its attempts, with a squad featuring international football's first transgender player, to win a match in the Oceania Football Confederation qualification tournament for the 2014 World Cup. In a similar vein, the 2006 documentary *Goal Dreams* recounted the unique difficulties facing Palestine's national team, as it sought to establish a presence in world football.

Palestinian football history, like the history of the nation it represents, has been shaped by the communal violence that characterized the Arab-Jewish conflict after the founding of Israel in 1948, and by the second-class status that Arab citizens of Israel have endured since then. The national team, as *Goal Dreams* revealed, faced the same logistical challenges as ordinary Palestinians in moving around Israel, let alone in gaining authorization to play abroad. The Palestinian FA joined FIFA in 1998 (as of 2018 it was still not a full member of the UN). Without statehood, though, developing a viable football culture was difficult. In the Israeli league, Arab-Israeli tensions sometimes spilled onto the playing field. Supporters of Bnei Sakhnin, a club with cross-communal traditions, clashed with supporters of Beitar Jerusalem, a club with links to the right-wing Likud party. Maya Zinshtein's 2016 documentary *Forever Pure* recounted Beitar's 2012/13 season, when supporters' group La Familia— guardians of the club's "pure" Jewish identity—organized protests after the signing of two Muslim players from Chechnya, the first non-Jews to play for the club. The film's climax focused on a relegation decider between Bnei and Beitar, as communal hostilities reached boiling point. Wearing facemasks, Bnei supporters wished Beitar fans dead from swine flu. The visitors responded with chants of "death to the Arabs." The two Chechens, bewildered by the racist maelstrom around them, left Israel after the game, never to return. Beitar's goalkeeper and chairman, both accused of besmirching Jewish honour, were hounded out of the self-proclaimed "most racist club in the country."

As in many parts of the world, football in Palestine can foment ethnic tensions, but it can also promote cultural exchange. Like Daniel Barenboim and Edward Said's West-Eastern Divan Orchestra, various organizations have used football to encourage reconciliation between Arabs and Jews. In doing so, they draw on football's popular appeal and its long history in the region. From the British Mandate period (1918–48), Christians, Jews, and Arabs played the game in schools. Aspiring players in Jerusalem, Haifa, and Jaffa filled leather balls with old clothing to play on the streets. There are currently professional men's leagues in the Gaza Strip and Jerusalem's West Bank. A women's league with six teams was founded in 2011. The opening match drew 8,000 people to the Faisal al-Husseini International Stadium in the West Bank. Players faced local problems, including pitches made inaccessible by Israeli military checkpoints. They also faced universal obstacles, most notably patriarchal resistance to the idea of women playing "a man's sport."

Far below the American Samoan and Palestinian national teams (ranked, respectively, 192nd and 99th in FIFA's world rankings in June 2018), Huizinga's play-element remains alive and well. FIFA listed 265 million football players worldwide in 2007, as well as 5 million referees. This was roughly 4 per cent of the world's population. A far greater number regularly watch the game, either live or on television. FIFA claimed that television coverage of the 2018 World Cup in Russia reached 3.572 billion people, or 51.3 per cent of the world's population.

Much of football's enduring popularity lies in its quotidian pleasures. In the films of German director Rainer Werner Fassbinder or the novels of Russian writer Vladimir Nabokov, football is never the central element of the story but rather a thrumming in the background of the lives of the characters. Football features at important moments in each film in Fassbinder's *BRD Trilogy*, his ambitious chronicle of the postwar history of West Germany. In the second of the films, *Veronika Voss* (1982), a sports journalist is drawn to a drug-addicted actress who had been a star in the Nazi era. When his attempts to help her run into powerful opposition, and she dies, the journalist wearily tells a taxi driver to return him to the football stadium, a place of sad but safe retreat from the harsh realities of a politically engaged life. In Nabokov's *Glory* (1932), the novel's hero, Martin—like Nabokov, a student and goalkeeper at Cambridge University—dreams of a clandestine expedition to his native Russia, currently in the throes of the Bolshevik Revolution. His youthful belief that this will happen is tied to his dreams about football. In these dreams, Martin dwells lovingly and soothingly on pre-match preparations ("pulling on the stockings with the colored tops, putting on the black shorts, tying the laces of the robust boots") in anticipation of great deeds to come.[4]

In these examples, football functions as it does for many people around the world: as the backdrop to more important events in their lives, a form of escape that is significant precisely because it appears trivial. The appearance is misleading. Football, as this book has shown, is far from trivial in its political, economic, and sociocultural implications. The game was integral to the identity of perhaps the twentieth century's biggest global music star. A ball was rarely far from the feet of Bob Marley, who idolized Pelé and chose his tour manager for much of the 1970s, Allan "Skill" Cole, because of his football talents (Cole played three times for Jamaica's national team) rather than his music business experience. He once remarked, "If you want to get to know me, you will have to play football against me and the Wailers." It was examination of a foot injury sustained during a match that led to Marley's cancer diagnosis and death at the age of thirty-six in 1981. At his funeral, he was buried with his red Gibson guitar, a bud of marijuana, a Bible—and a football. "Football," Bob Marley once told French television, "is freedom."[5]

Today's football historians are in a stronger position than previous generations. There is in 2019 an ever-expanding literature that takes in anthropologists, economists, historians, kinesiologists, and sociologists. There are specialist journals, collaborative research projects, and conferences and workshops. Some areas of the game have established complex historiographies, most notably hooliganism. Others have grown in force and diversity over the past three decades: gender, migration, and space. Football histories and football historians have from time to time exerted public influence. The sport's potential for academic-popular crossover is immense.

Yet, as a branch of the discipline of history, football remains threadbare in many places. Like other areas of sport studies, it has the benefits and drawbacks of being spread across many disciplines, not all of which speak the same language. While some observers argue that sports history is on the rise, others bemoan the limited, even declining place of sport in university history courses. Due to its global popularity, football may be less vulnerable in this regard than more niche sports. Hitherto a growing but still modest number of historians has taken up the challenge of giving football a sophisticated historical footing. The sport is not yet an integral part of cultural history in the way that, for example, cinema is. Nor is it an integral part of social history in the way that, for example, the labour movement is.

What is the future of football historiography? The potential is vast. The literature on fan culture, for example, has grown exponentially since the 1990s, but it remains disproportionately focused on spectator violence and male supporters. We know relatively little, still, about how ordinary people watched and especially played football from the 1860s to today. Recreational or amateur football is, arguably, the great, untapped resource of football history. This is particularly the case for women. As we saw in Chapter 5, the gender imbalance in the historiography is as pronounced as the gender imbalance in the game. This is beginning to change—witness, for example, a recent oral history project that has rescued from obscurity the early history of Manchester City Ladies (founded in 1988)—but only slowly. By piecing together (often patchy) archival resources and conducting interviews, historians can recreate everyday histories of football cultures around the world, focusing on previously marginalized stories and voices.

Many of the future developments in football historiography will no doubt be local and national histories. This makes sense for a sport rooted in, and today marketed around, local and national rivalries. But football scholarship, like football itself, is linked by transnational networks. Increasingly, football historians are thinking in transnational ways. This is only to be encouraged because the game is entrenched, like few other human activities, in global popular culture. The contested fields of football's history are resolutely international. They outline, to return to Nabokov, a "portable world," one that has contributed profoundly to the imagining and making of modern societies.

Notes

1 FIFA Ethics Committee, *Report on the Inquiry into the 2018/2022 FIFA World Cup Bidding Process*, report prepared by Chairman Michael J. Garcia and Deputy Chairman Cornel Borbély and released in full in 2017 (after being held by FIFA for three years), https://img.fifa.com/image/upload/wnr43dgn3yysafypuq8r.pdf (accessed 27 July 2018): 331.

2 David Runciman, "The Last World Cup," *London Review of Books* 40, no. 12 (2018): 7.

3 Johan Huizinga, *Homo Ludens: A Study of the Play-Element in Culture* (London: Routledge, 1949), 197.

4 Vladimir Nabokov, *Glory*, trans. Dimitri Nabokov (New York: McGraw-Hill, 1971), 109.

5 Quoted in Edd Norval, "How Bob Marley's Love of Football Made the Game Beautiful," *These Football Times*, February 19, 2019, https://thesefootballtimes.co /2019/02/19/how-bob-marleys-love-of-football-made-the-game-beautiful/ (accessed 14 May 2019).

Appendix
FIFA Member Associations

Country	National Association Founded	Joined FIFA
Afghanistan	1922	1948
Albania	1930	1932
Algeria	1962	1964
American Samoa**	1984	1998
Andorra	1994	1996
Angola	1979	1980
Anguilla**	1988	1996
Antigua and Barbuda	1928	1972
Argentina	1893	1912
Armenia[1]	1992	1992
Aruba**	1932	1988
Australia	1961	1963
Austria	1904	1905
Azerbaijan[2]	1992	1994
Bahamas	1967	1968
Bahrain	1957	1968
Bangladesh	1972	1976
Barbados	1910	1968
Belarus[3]	1989	1992

(Continued)

Country	National Association Founded	Joined FIFA
Belgium*	1895	1904
Belize	1980	1986
Benin	1962	1964
Bermuda**	1928	1962
Bhutan	1983	2000
Bolivia	1925	1926
Bosnia and Herzegovina[4]	1992	1996
Botswana	1970	1978
Brazil	1914	1923
British Virgin Islands**	1974	1996
Brunei Darussalam	1959	1972
Bulgaria	1923	1924
Burkina Faso	1960	1964
Burundi	1948	1972
Cambodia	1933	1954
Cameroon	1959	1962
Canada	1912	1913
Cape Verde Islands	1982	1986
Cayman Islands**	1966	1992
Central African Republic	1961	1964
Chad	1962	1964
Chile	1895	1913
China	1924	1931
Chinese Taipei**	1924	1954
Colombia	1924	1936
Comoros	1979	2005
Congo	1962	1964
Congo DR	1919	1964
Cook Islands**	1971	1994
Costa Rica	1921	1927
Côte d'Ivoire	1960	1964
Croatia[5]	1912	1992
Cuba	1929	1929
Curaçao**	1921	1932

Country	National Association Founded	Joined FIFA
Cyprus	1934	1948
Czech Republic[6]	1901	1907
Denmark*	1889	1904
Djibouti	1979	1994
Dominica	1970	1994
Dominican Republic	1953	1958
Ecuador	1925	1926
Egypt	1921	1923
El Salvador	1935	1938
England**[7]	1863	1905
Equatorial Guinea	1957	1986
Eritrea	1996	1998
Estonia[8]	1921	1923
Eswatini	1968	1978
Ethiopia	1943	1952
Faroe Islands**	1979	1988
Fiji	1938	1964
Finland	1907	1908
France*[9]	1919	1904
Gabon	1962	1966
Gambia	1952	1968
Georgia[10]	1990	1992
Germany[11]	1900	1904
Ghana	1957	1958
Gibraltar**	1895	2016
Greece	1926	1927
Grenada	1924	1978
Guam**	1975	1996
Guatemala	1919	1946
Guinea	1960	1962
Guinea-Bissau	1974	1986
Guyana	1902	1970
Haiti	1904	1934
Honduras	1935	1946

(Continued)

Country	National Association Founded	Joined FIFA
Hong Kong**	1914	1954
Hungary	1901	1907
Iceland	1947	1947
India	1937	1948
Indonesia	1943	1952
Iran	1920	1948
Iraq	1948	1950
Israel[12]	1928	1929
Italy	1898	1905
Jamaica	1910	1962
Japan	1921	1921
Jordan	1949	1956
Kazakhstan[13]	1914	1994
Kenya	1960	1960
Korea DPR	1945	1958
Korea Republic	1933	1948
Kosovo**[14]	1946	2016
Kuwait	1952	1964
Kyrgyz Republic[15]	1992	1994
Laos	1951	1952
Latvia[16]	1921	1923
Lebanon	1933	1936
Lesotho	1932	1964
Liberia	1936	1964
Libya	1962	1964
Liechtenstein	1934	1976
Lithuania[17]	1922	1923
Luxembourg	1908	1910
Macau**	1939	1978
Madagascar	1961	1964
Malawi	1966	1968
Malaysia	1933	1954
Maldives	1982	1986
Mali	1960	1964

Country	National Association Founded	Joined FIFA
Malta	1900	1960
Mauritania	1961	1970
Mauritius	1952	1964
Mexico	1927	1929
Moldova[18]	1990	1994
Mongolia	1959	1998
Montenegro[19]	1931	2007
Montserrat**	1994	1996
Morocco	1955	1960
Mozambique	1976	1980
Myanmar	1947	1948
Namibia	1990	1992
Nepal	1951	1972
Netherlands*	1889	1904
New Caledonia**	1928	2004
New Zealand	1891	1948
Nicaragua	1931	1950
Niger	1964	1964
Nigeria	1945	1960
North Macedonia[20]	1926	1994
Northern Ireland**[21]	1880	1911
Norway	1902	1908
Oman	1978	1980
Pakistan	1947	1948
Palestine**	1928	1998
Panama	1937	1938
Papua New Guinea	1962	1966
Paraguay	1906	1925
Peru	1922	1924
Philippines	1907	1930
Poland	1919	1923
Portugal	1914	1923
Puerto Rico**	1940	1960
Qatar	1960	1972

(Continued)

Country	National Association Founded	Joined FIFA
Republic of Ireland	1921	1923
Romania	1909	1923
Russia[22]	1912	1912
Rwanda	1972	1978
Samoa	1968	1986
San Marino	1931	1988
São Tomé and Príncipe	1975	1986
Saudi Arabia	1956	1956
Scotland**[23]	1873	1910
Senegal	1960	1964
Serbia[24]	1919	1923
Seychelles	1979	1986
Sierra Leone	1960	1960
Singapore	1892	1952
Slovakia[25]	1938	1994
Slovenia[26]	1920	1992
Solomon Islands	1978	1988
Somalia	1951	1962
South Africa[27]	1991	1992
South Sudan	2012	2012
Spain*[28]	1913	1904
Sri Lanka	1939	1952
St. Kitts and Nevis	1932	1992
St. Lucia	1979	1988
St. Vincent and the Grenadines	1979	1988
Sudan	1936	1948
Suriname	1920	1929
Sweden*	1904	1904
Switzerland*	1895	1904
Syria	1936	1937
Tahiti**	1989	1990
Tajikistan[29]	1936	1994
Tanzania	1930	1964

Country	National Association Founded	Joined FIFA
Thailand	1916	1925
Timor-Leste	2002	2005
Togo	1960	1964
Tonga	1965	1994
Trinidad and Tobago	1908	1964
Tunisia	1957	1960
Turkey	1923	1923
Turkmenistan[30]	1992	1994
Turks and Caicos Islands**	1988	1998
Uganda	1924	1960
Ukraine[31]	1991	1992
United Arab Emirates	1971	1974
Uruguay	1900	1923
US Virgin Islands**	1989	1998
USA	1913	1914
Uzbekistan[32]	1946	1994
Vanuatu	1934	1998
Venezuela	1926	1952
Vietnam[33]	1960	1964
Wales**[34]	1876	1910
Yemen	1962	1980
Zambia	1929	1964
Zimbabwe	1965	1965

Source: Adapted from https://www.fifa.com/associations/.

* FIFA founder member.
** Non-UN member state.

Notes

1 Sub-association of the Football Federation of the USSR, 1934–91; the USSR federation joined FIFA in 1946.

2 Sub-association of the Football Federation of the USSR, 1934–91.

3 Sub-association of the Football Federation of the USSR, 1934–91.

4 Sub-association of the Football Association of Yugoslavia (FSJ), 1920–96; the FSJ joined FIFA in 1923.

5 Sub-association of the FSJ, 1919–92.

6 Bohemian Football Union, 1901–22; Czechoslovak Football Association, 1922–93.

7 Non-member of FIFA, 1920–24 and 1928–46.

8 Sub-association of the Football Federation of the USSR, 1940–91.

9 Original FIFA membership was through the Union des Sociétés Françaises de Sports Athlétiques.

10 Sub-association of the Football Federation of the USSR, 1934–90.

11 Aside from the DFB (1904–present), other German member associations were the Saarland FA (1952–56) and the Football Association of the GDR (DFV), 1952–90.

12 Palestine Football Federation, 1928–48.

13 Sub-association of the Football Federation of the USSR, 1934–91.

14 Sub-association of the FSJ, 1946–2003; sub-association of the Football Association of Serbia and Montenegro, 2003–08.

15 Sub-association of the Football Federation of the USSR, 1934–91.

16 Sub-association of the Football Federation of the USSR, 1940–91.

17 Sub-association of the Football Federation of the USSR, 1940–91.

18 Sub-association of the Football Federation of the USSR, 1940–91.

19 Sub-association of the FSJ, 1931–2003; sub-association of the Football Association of Serbia and Montenegro, 2003–07.

20 Sub-association of the FSJ, 1926–94.

21 Non-member of FIFA, 1920–24 and 1928–46.

22 Sub-association of the Football Federation of the USSR, 1934–91.

23 Non-member of FIFA, 1920–24 and 1928–46.

24 Sub-association of the FSJ, 1919–2003; sub-association of the Football Association of Serbia and Montenegro, 2003–07.

25 Sub-association of the Czechoslovak Football Association, 1922–93.

26 Sub-association of the FSJ, 1920–92.

27 Original, white-run South African FA was a FIFA member 1910–24 and 1952–76.

28 Original FIFA membership was through the Madrid Football Club (Real Madrid).

29 Sub-association of the Football Federation of the USSR, 1934–91.

30 Sub-association of the Football Federation of the USSR, 1934–91.

31 Sub-association of the Football Federation of the USSR, 1934–91.

32 Sub-association of the Football Federation of the USSR, 1934–91.

33 Original FIFA membership was through South Vietnam (joined 1952); unified Socialist Republic of Vietnam joined in 1976.

34 Non-member of FIFA, 1920–24 and 1928–46.

Select Bibliography

The bibliography represents the historiography that has been consulted and synthesized for this book. Works in the general section were used in multiple chapters.

General

Alegi, Peter. *African Soccerscapes: How a Continent Changed the World's Game*. Athens, OH: Ohio University Press, 2010.

———. *Laduma! Soccer, Politics and Society in South Africa, from Its Origins to 2010*. 2nd ed. Scottsville: University of Kwa-Zulu Natal Press, 2010.

Alegi, Peter, and Chris Bolsmann, eds. *South Africa and the Global Game: Football, Apartheid and Beyond*. Abingdon: Routledge, 2010.

Bellos, Alex. *Futebol: The Brazilian Way of Life*. London: Bloomsbury, 2002.

Darby, Paul. *Africa, Football and FIFA: Politics, Colonialism and Resistance*. London: Routledge, 2002.

Dietschy, Paul, *Histoire du football*. Paris: Perrin, 2014.

Dubois, Laurent. *Soccer Empire: The World Cup and the Future of France*. Berkeley, CA: University of California Press, 2010.

Edelman, Robert. *Spartak Moscow: A History of the People's Team in the Workers' State*. Ithaca, NY: Cornell University Press, 2009.

Edelman, Robert, and Wayne Wilson, eds. *The Oxford Handbook of Sport Studies*. Oxford: Oxford University, Press, 2017.

Elsey, Brenda. *Citizens and Sportsmen: Fútbol and Politics in Twentieth-Century Chile*. Austin, TX: University of Texas Press, 2011.

Fair, Laura. "Kickin' It: Leisure, Politics and Football in Colonial Zanzibar, 1900s–1950s." *Africa* 76, no. 2 (1997): 224–51.

Finn, Gerry, and Richard Giulianotti, eds. *Football Culture: Local Contests, Global Visions.* London: Frank Cass, 2000.

Foot, John. *Calcio: A History of Italian Football.* London: Harper Perennial, 2007.

Giulianotti, Richard. *Football: A Sociology of the Game.* Cambridge: Polity Press, 1999.

———. ed. *Sport and Modern Social Theorists.* Basingstoke: Palgrave Macmillan, 2004.

Goldblatt, David. *The Ball Is Round: A Global History of Football.* London: Penguin, 2006.

———. *The Game of Our Lives: The Meaning and Making of English Football.* London: Penguin, 2014

Gray, Daniel. *Saturday 3 PM: 50 Eternal Delights of Modern Football.* London: Bloomsbury, 2016.

Hamzeh, Manal, and Heather Sykes. "Egyptian Football Ultras and the January 25th Revolution: Anti-corporate, Anti-militarist and Martyrdom Masculinities." *Anthropology of the Middle East* 9, no. 2 (2014): 91–107.

Hargreaves, John. *Sport, Power and Culture.* Cambridge: Polity Press, 1986.

Havemann, Nils. *Fußball unterm Hakenkreuz: Der DFB zwischen Sport, Politik und Kommerz.* Frankfurt/Main: Campus Verlag, 2005.

———. *Samstags um halb 4: Die Geschichte der Fußballbundesliga.* Munich: Seidel, 2013.

Herzog, Markwart, and Fabian Brändle. *European Football during the Second World War: Training and Entertainment, Ideology and Propaganda.* Bern: Peter Lang, 2018.

Hesse-Lichtenberger, Ulrich. *Tor! The Story of German Football.* London: WSC Books, 2002.

Holt, Richard. *Sport and the British: A Modern History.* Oxford: Oxford University Press, 1989.

Hopcraft, Arthur. *The Football Man.* London: Aurum Press, 2006. First published 1968 by Collins (London).

Hornby, Nick. *Fever Pitch.* London: Victor Gollancz, 1992.

Hughson, John, David Inglis, and Marcus Free. *The Uses of Sport.* London: Routledge, 2005.

Hughson, John, Kevin Moore, Ramón Spaaij, and Joseph Maguire, eds. *Routledge Handbook of Football Studies.* London: Routledge, 2017.

Keys, Barbara. *Globalizing Sport: National Rivalry and International Community in the 1930s.* Cambridge, MA: Harvard University Press, 2006.

Knausgård, Karl Ove, and Fredrik Ekelund. *Home and Away: Writing the Beautiful Game.* Translated by Don Bartlett and Séan Kinsella. Toronto: Knopf Canada, 2017.

Kuhn, Gabriel. *Soccer vs. the State: Tackling Football and Radical Politics.* Oakland, CA: PM Press, 2011.

Kuper, Simon. *Football against the Enemy.* London: Orion Books, 1994.

Marschik, Matthias. "Between Manipulation and Resistance: Viennese Football in the Nazi Era." *Journal of Contemporary History* 34, no. 2 (1999): 215–29.

———. "Mitteleuropa: Politische Konzepte—Sportliche Praxis." *Historical Social Research* 31, no. 1 (2006): 88–108.

Martin, Phyllis. *Leisure and Society in Colonial Brazzaville.* Cambridge: Cambridge University Press, 1995.

Martin, Simon. *Football and Fascism: The National Game under Mussolini*. Oxford: Berg, 2004.

McDougall, Alan. *The People's Game: Football, State and Society in East Germany*. Cambridge: Cambridge University Press, 2014.

Mills, Richard. *The Politics of Football in Yugoslavia: Sport, Nationalism and the State*. London: I.B. Tauris, 2018.

Millward, Peter. *The Global Football League: Transnational Networks, Social Movements and Sport in the New Media Age*. Basingstoke: Palgrave Macmillan, 2011.

Rein, Raanan. *Fútbol, Jews, and the Making of Argentina*. Translated by Martha Grenzeback. Stanford, CA: Stanford University Press, 2015.

Rinke, Stefan, and Kay Schiller, eds. *The FIFA World Cup, 1930–2010: Politics, Commerce, Spectacle and Identities*. Wallstein: Göttingen, 2014.

Riordan, James. "Amateurism, Sport and the Left: Amateurism for All versus Amateur Elitism." *Sport in History* 26, no. 3 (2006): 468–83.

Simpson, Kevin. *Soccer under the Swastika: Stories of Survival and Resistance during the Holocaust*. Lanham, MD: Rowman & Littlefield, 2016.

Tomlinson, Alan, and Christopher Young, eds. *German Football: History, Culture, Society*. London: Routledge, 2006.

Tomlinson, Alan, Christopher Young, and Richard Holt, eds. *Sport and the Transformation of Modern Europe: States, Media, and Markets, 1950–2010*. Abingdon: Routledge, 2011.

Tuastad, Dag. "From Football Riot to Revolution: The Political Role of Football in the Arab World." *Soccer & Society* 15, no. 3 (2014): 376–88.

Vamplew, Wray. "Creating the English Premier Football League: A Brief Economic History with Some Possible Lessons for Asian Soccer." *The International Journal of the History of Sport* 34, nos. 17–18 (2017): 1807–18.

Walvin, James. *The People's Game: The History of Football Revisited*. Edinburgh: Mainstream, 1994.

Ward, Andrew, and John Williams. *Football Nation: Sixty Years of the Beautiful Game*. London: Bloomsbury, 2009.

Williams, John. *Red Men: Liverpool Football Club—The Biography*. Edinburgh: Mainstream, 2011.

Wilson, Jonathan. *Angels with Dirty Faces: The Footballing History of Argentina*. London: Orion, 2016.

———. *Behind the Curtain: Football in Eastern Europe*. London: Orion, 2006.

Winner, David. *Brilliant Orange: The Neurotic Genius of Dutch Soccer*. New York: Overlook Press, 2010.

Wood, David. *Football and Literature in South America*. Abingdon: Routledge, 2017.

Zeller, Manfred. *Sport and Society in the Soviet Union: The Politics of Football after Stalin*. London: I.B. Tauris, 2018.

Chapter 1

Abizaid, Christian, Oliver T. Coomes, Yoshito Takasaki, and J. Pablo Arroyo-Mora. "Rural Social Networks along Amazonian Rivers: Seeds, Labor and Soccer among Communities on the Napo River, Peru." *Geographical Review* 108, no. 1 (2018): 92–119.

Brown, Matthew. "British Informal Empire and the Origins of Association Football in South America." *Soccer & Society* 16, nos. 2–3 (2014): 169–82.

Collins, Tony. "Early Football and the Emergence of Modern Soccer, c. 1840–1880." *The International Journal of the History of Sport* 32, no. 9 (2015): 1127–42.

Dimeo, Paul. "Football and Politics in Bengal: Colonialism, Nationalism, Communalism." *Soccer & Society* 2, no. 2 (2001): 57–74.

Hilbrenner, Anke, and Britta Lenz. "Looking at European Sports from an Eastern European Perspective: Football in the Multi-ethnic Polish Territories," *European Review* 19, no. 4 (2011): 595–610.

Larcher-Goscha, Agathe. "Du football au Vietnam (1905–1949): Colonialisme, culture sportive et sociabilités en jeux." *Outre-Mers* 96, nos. 364–365 (2009): 61–89.

Maranhão, Tiago. "Apollonians and Dionysians: The Role of Football in Gilberto Freyre's Vision of Brazilian people." *Soccer & Society* 8, no. 4 (2007): 510–23.

Markovits, Andrei, and Steven Hellerman. *Offside: Soccer and American Exceptionalism.* Princeton, NJ: Princeton University Press, 2001.

McKibbin, Ross. "Sports History: Status, Definitions and Meanings." *Sport in History* 31 no. 2 (2011): 167–74.

Schiller, Kay, and Christopher Young. "The History and Historiography of Sport in Germany: Social, Cultural and Political Perspectives." *German History* 27, no. 3 (2009): 313–30.

Taylor, Matthew. "Sport, Transnationalism, and Global History." *Journal of Global History* 8, no. 2 (2013): 199–208.

Tomlinson, Alan, and Christopher Young. "Towards a New History of European Sport." *European Review* 19 (2011): 287–307.

Chapter 2

Agergaard, Sine, and Nina Clara Tiesler, eds. *Women, Soccer and Transnational Migration.* London: Routledge, 2014.

Bale, John, and Joseph Maguire, eds. *The Global Sports Arena: Athletic Talent Migration in an Interdependent World.* London: Frank Cass, 1994.

Bolchover, David. *The Greatest Comeback: From Genocide to Football Glory.* London: Biteback, 2017.

Botelho, Vera, and Bente Ovedie Skogvang. "Moving for the Love of the Game? International Migration of Female Footballers into Scandinavian Countries." *Soccer & Society* 12, no. 6 (2011): 806–19.

———. "The Pioneers—Early Years of the Scandinavian Emigration of Women Footballers." *Soccer & Society* 14, no. 6 (2011): 799–815.

Clay, Catrine. *Trautmann's Journey: From Hitler Youth to FA Cup Legend.* London: Yellow Jersey, 2011.

Cleveland, Todd. "Following the Ball: African Soccer Players, Labor Strategies and Emigration across the Portuguese Colonial Empire, 1949–1975." *Cadernos de Estudos Africanos* 26 (2013): 15–41.

Darby, Paul. "Moving Players, Traversing Perspectives: Global Value Chains, Production Networks and Ghanaian Football Labour Migration." *Geoforum* 50 (2013): 43–53.

Darby, Paul, Gerard Akindes, and Matthew Kirwin. "Football Academies and the Migration of Labour to Europe." *Journal of Sport & Social Issues* 31, no. 2 (2007): 143–61.

Foer, Franklin. *How Soccer Explains the World: An Unlikely Theory of Globalization.* New York: First Harper Perennial, 2005.

Fontaine, Marion. "Football, Migration, and Coalmining in Northern France, 1920s–1980s." *International Review of Social History* 60 (2015): 253–73.

Fox, Norman. *Prophet or Traitor? The Jimmy Hogan Story.* Manchester: Parrs Wood, 2003.

Frenkiel, Stanislas. "Migratory Networks Used by Algerian Professional Footballers in France: From Colonial Times to the Postcolonial Era, 1932–1991." *The International Journal of the History of Sport* 32, no. 7 (2015): 952–64.

Hawkey, Ian. *Di Stéfano.* London: Penguin, 2017.

Hay, Roy, and Nick Guoth. "No Single Pattern: Australian Migrant Minorities and the Round Ball Code in Victoria." *Soccer & Society* 10, no. 6 (2009): 823–42.

Kainz, Martin. *Red Bull Ghana: Eine Akademie auf verlorenem Boden.* Vienna and Berlin: LIT Verlag, 2014.

Lanfranchi, Pierre, and Matthew Taylor. *Moving with the Ball: The Migration of Professional Footballers.* Oxford: Berg, 2001.

McDowell, Matthew. "Scottish Football and Colonial Zimbabwe: Sport, the Scottish Diaspora and White Africa." *Journal of Scottish Historical Studies* 37, no. 1 (2017): 73–99.

Poli, Raffaele. "Migrations and Trade of African Football Players: Historic, Geographical and Cultural Aspects." *Africa Spectrum* 41, no. 3 (2006): 393–414.

Poli, Raffaele, Loïc Ravenel, and Roger Besson. "Exporting Countries in World Football." *CIES Football Observatory Monthly Report* 8 (October 2015): 1–11.

Steinbrink, Malte. "The Role of Amateur Football in Circular Migration Systems in South Africa." *Africa Spectrum* 45, no. 2 (2010): 35–60.

Taylor, Matthew. "Football's Engineers? British Football Coaches, Migration and Intercultural Transfer, c. 1910–1950s." *Sport in History* 30, no. 1 (2010): 138–63.

Tiesler, Nina Clara. "Three Types of Transnational Players: Differing Women's Football Mobility Projects in Core and Developing Countries." *Revista Brasileira de Ciências do Esporte* 38, no. 2 (2016): 201–10.

Williams, Jean. *Globalising Women's Football: Migration and Professionalization, 1971–2011.* Bern: Peter Lang, 2013.

Chapter 3

Adam, Thomas. "The Intercultural Transfer of Football: The Contexts of Germany and Argentina." *Sport in Society* 20, no. 10 (2017): 1371–89.

Conn, David. *The Fall of the House of FIFA.* London: Yellow Jersey Press, 2017.

Dejonghe, Trudo, and Hans Vandeweghe. "Belgian Football." *Journal of Sports Economics* 7, no. 1 (2006): 105–13.

Eisenberg, Christiane. "Football in Germany: Beginnings, 1890–1914." *The International Journal of the History of Sport* 8, no. 2 (1991): 205–20.

Giulianotti, Richard, and Roland Robertson. *Globalization & Football.* London: SAGE, 2009.

Hare, Geoff. *Football in France: A Cultural History*. Oxford: Berg, 2003.

Jennings, Andrew. *Foul! The Secret World of FIFA: Bribes, Vote Rigging and Ticket Scandals*. London: Harpersport, 2006.

Kuper, Simon, and Stefan Szymanski. *Soccernomics: Why England Loses, Why Germany and Brazil Win, and the Why the U.S., Japan, Australia, Turkey—and Even Iraq—Are Destined to Become the Kings of the World's Most Popular Sport*. New York: Nation, 2009.

Leach, Stephanie, and Stefan Szymanski. "Making Money out of Football." *Scottish Journal of Political Economy* 62, no. 1 (2015): 25–50.

McFarland, Andrew. "Ricardo Zamora: The First Spanish Football Idol." *Soccer & Society* 7, no. 1 (2006): 1–13.

Onwumechili, Chuka. "Nigerian Football: Interests, Marginalization, and Struggle." *Critical African Studies* 6, nos. 2–3 (2014): 144–56.

Peeters, Thomas, and Stefan Szymanski. "Financial Fair Play in European Football." *Economic Policy* 29, no. 78 (2014): 343–90.

Starc, Gregor. "Bad Game, Good Game, Whose Game? Seeing a History of Soccer through Slovenian Press Coverage," *Journal of Sport History* 34, no. 3 (2007): 439–58.

Chapter 4

Bolsmann, Chris, and Dilwyn Porter. *English Gentlemen and World Soccer: Corinthians, Amateurism and the Global Game*. Abingdon: Routledge, 2018.

Darby, Paul. "'Let Us Rally around the Flag': Football, Nation-Building, and Pan-Africanism in Kwame Nkrumah's Ghana." *Journal of African History* 54, no. 2 (2013): 221–46.

Davies, Pete. *All Played Out: The Full Story of Italia '90*. London: Heinemann, 1990.

Giulianotti, Richard, and Francisco Klauser. "Security and Surveillance at Sport Mega Events." *Urban Studies* 48, no. 15 (2011): 3157–68.

Horne, John, and Wolfram Manzenreiter, eds. *Japan, Korea and the 2002 World Cup*. Abingdon: Routledge, 2002.

Hughson, John. *The 1966 World Cup in England: A Cultural History*. Manchester: Manchester University Press, 2016.

Magee, Jonathan, and Ruth Jeanes. "Football's Coming Home: A Critical Evaluation of the Homeless World Cup as an Intervention to Combat Social Exclusion." *International Review for the Sociology of Sport* 48, no. 1 (2013): 3–19.

Manzenreiter, Wolfram. "The 'Benefits' of Hosting: Japanese Experiences from the 2002 Football World Cup." *Asian Business & Management* 7 (2008): 201–24.

Manzenreiter, Wolfram, and Georg Spitaler, eds. *Governance, Citizenship and the New European Football Championships: The European Spectacle*. Abingdon: Routledge, 2012.

McDowell, Matthew. "Queen's Park FC in Copenhagen, 1898–1903: Paradoxes in Early Transnational Amateurism," *idrottsforum.org: Nordic Sport Studies Forum*, May 14, 2014. https://idrottsforum.org/mcdowell140514/.

———. "'To Cross the Skager Rack': Discourses, Images, and Tourism in Early 'European' Football—Scotland, the United Kingdom, Denmark, and Scandinavia, 1898–1914." *Soccer & Society* 18, nos. 2–3 (2017): 245–69.

Moore, Kevin. "Football and the Olympics and Paralympics." *Sport in Society* 17, no. 5 (2014): 640–55.

Whang, Soon-Hee. "Korea and Japan 2002: Public Space and Popular Celebration." In *National Identity and Global Sports Events: Culture, Politics and Spectacle in the Olympics and the Football World Cup*, edited by Alan Tomlinson and Christopher Young, 215–31. Albany, NY: State University of New York Press, 2006.

Chapter 5

Archetti, Eduardo. *Masculinities: Football, Polo, and Tango in Argentina*. Oxford: Berg, 1999.

Christopherson, Neal, Michelle Janning, and Eileen Diaz McConnell. "Two Kicks Forward, One Kick Back: A Content Analysis of Media Discourses on the 1999 Women's World Cup Soccer Championship." *Sociology of Sport Journal* 19, no. 2 (2002): 170–88.

Cox, Barbara, and Richard Pringle. "Gaining a Foothold in Football: A Genealogical Analysis of the Emergence of the Female Footballer in New Zealand." *International Review for the Sociology of Sport* 47, no. 2 (2011): 217–34.

da Costa, Leda Maria. "Beauty, Effort and Talent: A Brief History of Brazilian Women's Soccer in Press Discourse." *Soccer & Society* 15, no. 1 (2014): 81–92.

Elsey, Brenda, and Joshua Nadel. *Futbolera: A History of Women and Sports in Latin America*. Austin, TX: University of Texas Press, 2019.

———. "Marimachos: On Women's Football in Latin America." *The Football Scholars Forum*, December 6, 2014. http://footballscholars.org/uncategorized/marimachos-on-womens-football-in-latin-america/#more-1834.

Guttmann, Allen. *Women's Sport: A History*. New York: Columbia University Press, 1991.

Hong, Fan, and J.A. Mangan, eds. *Soccer, Women, Sexual Liberation: Kicking Off a New Era*. London: Routledge, 2003.

Linne, Carina Sophia. *Freigespielt: Frauenfußball im geteilten Deutschland*. Berlin: be.bra wissenschaft verlag, 2011.

Longman, Jere. *The Girls of Summer: The U.S. Women's Soccer Team and How It Changed the World*. New York: Perennial, 2001.

Magazine, Roger. *Golden and Blue Like My Heart: Masculinity, Youth, and Power among Soccer Fans in Mexico City*. Tucson, AZ: University of Arizona Press, 2007.

Markovits, Andrei, and Steven Hellerman. "Women's Soccer in the United States: Yet Another American 'Exceptionalism.'" *Soccer & Society* 4, nos. 2–3 (2003): 14–29.

Mitchell, Jason. *A Culture of Silence: The Story of Football's Battle with Homophobia*. London: Lulu, 2012.

Mond, Assaf. "Chelsea Football Club and the Fight for Professional Football in First World War London." *The London Journal* 41, no. 3 (2016): 266–80.

Osborne, Carol A., and Fiona Skillen. "The State of Play: Women in British Sport History." *Sport in History* 30, no. 2 (2010): 189–95.

Whannel, Garry. *Media Sport Stars: Masculinities and Moralities*. London: Routledge, 2002.

Williams, Jean. *A Game for Rough Girls: A History of Women's Football in Britain.* London: Routledge, 2003.

Williams, Jean, and Rob Hess. "Women, Football and History: International Perspectives." *The International Journal of the History of Sport* 32, no. 18 (2015): 2115–22.

Wood, David. "The Beautiful Game? Hegemonic Masculinity, Women and Football in Brazil and Argentina." *Bulletin of Latin American Research* 37, no. 5 (2018): 567–81.

Zhao, Aihua, Peter Horton, and Liu Liu. "Women's Football in the People's Republic of China: Retrospect and Prospect." *The International Journal of the History of Sport* 29, no. 17 (2012): 2372–87.

Zheng, Tintian. "Embodied Masculinity: Sex and Sport in a (Post) Colonial Chinese City." *The China Quarterly* 190 (2007): 432–50.

Chapter 6

Bains, Jas, and Sanjiev Johal. *Corner Flags and Corner Shops: The Asian Football Experience.* London: Phoenix, 1998.

Borges Buarque de Hollanda, Bernardo. "Echoes of the Tragedy: The Sport Memoir and the Representation of the 1950 World Cup." *The International Journal for the History of Sport* 31, no. 12 (2014): 1287–1302.

Brenner, Michael, and Gideon Reuveni, eds. *Emancipation through Muscles: Jews and Sport in Europe.* Lincoln, NE: University of Nebraska Press, 2006.

Chipande, Hikabwa D. "Challenge for the Ball: Elites, Fans and the Control of Football in Zambia's One-Party State, 1973–1991." *Journal of Southern African Studies* 44, no. 6 (2018): 991–1003.

———. "Mining for Goals: Football on the Zambian Copperbelt, 1940s to 1960s." *Radical History Review* 125 (2016): 55–73.

Da Silva, Ana Paula. "Pelé, Racial Discourse and the 1958 World Cup." *Soccer & Society* 15, no. 1 (2014): 1–12.

Dixon, Kevin, Jacqueline Lowe, and Tom Gibbons. "Show Racism the Red Card: Potential Barriers to the Effective Implementation of the Anti-racist Message." *Soccer & Society* 17, no. 1 (2016): 1–15.

Dumas, Hélène. "Football, politique et violence milicienne au Rwanda: Histoire d'un sport sous influences." *Materiaux pour l'histoire de notre temps* 106 (2012): 40–46.

Gumbrecht, Hans Ulrich. *In Praise of Athletic Beauty.* Cambridge, MA: Harvard University Press, 2006.

Herzog, Markwart, ed. *Die "Gleichschaltung" des Fußballsports im nationalsozialistischen Deutschland.* Stuttgart: Kohlhammer, 2016.

Jijon, Isabel. "The Glocalization of Time and Space: Soccer and Meaning in Chota Valley, Ecuador." *International Sociology* 28, no. 4 (2013): 373–90.

Kassimeris, Christos. *European Football in Black and White: Tackling Racism in Football.* Lanham, MD: Lexington, 2008.

Korr, Chuck, and Marvin Close. *More Than a Game: Soccer vs. Apartheid.* New York: St Martin's Press, 2011.

Leite Lopes, José. "Class, Ethnicity, and Color in the Making of Brazilian Football." *Daedalus* 129, no. 2 (2000): 239–70.

Llopis-Goig, Ramón. *Spanish Football and Social Change: Sociological Investigations*. Basingstoke: Palgrave Macmillan, 2015.

Onuora, Emy. *Pitch Black: The Story of Black British Footballers*. London: Biteback, 2015.

Vasili, Phil. *The First Black Footballer—Arthur Wharton 1865–1930: An Absence of Memory*. London: Frank Cass, 1998.

———. "Walter Daniel Tull, 1888–1918: Soldier, Footballer, Black." *Race & Class* 38, no. 2 (1998): 51–69.

Chapter 7

Bairner, Alan. "Emotional Grounds: Stories of Football, Memories, and Emotions." *Emotion, Space and Society* 12 (2014): 18–23.

Bale, John, and Patricia Vertinsky, eds. *Sites of Sport: Space, Place, Experience*. London: Routledge, 2004.

Bromberger, Christian. "Football as World-View and as Ritual." *French Cultural Studies*, 6, no. 18 (1995): 293–311.

Darby, Paul, Martin Johnes, and Gavin Mellor, eds. *Soccer and Disaster: International Perspectives*. London: Routledge, 2005.

Flowers, Benjamin. "Stadiums: Architecture and the Iconography of the Beautiful Game." *The International Journal of the History of Sport* 28, nos. 8–9 (2011): 1174–85.

Gaffney, Christopher. "Stadiums and Society in Twenty-First Century Buenos Aires." *Soccer & Society* 10, no. 2 (2009): 160–82.

Hill, Jeffrey, Kevin Moore, Jason Wood, eds. *Sport, History, and Heritage: Studies in Public Representation*. Woodbridge: Boydell Press, 2012.

Inglis, Simon. *The Football Grounds of Britain*. London: Willow Books, 1983.

———. *The Football Grounds of Europe*. London: HarperCollinsWillow, 1990.

———. *Sightlines: A Stadium Odyssey*. London: Yellow Jersey, 2000.

Palvarini, Pietro, and Simone Tosi. "Stadiums as Studios: How the Media Shape Space in the New Juventus Stadium." *First Monday* 18, no. 11 (2013). https://firstmonday.org/ojs/index.php/fm/article/view/4959/3791_2.

Peterson, Rick, and David Robinson. "Excavations and the Afterlife of a Professional Football Stadium, Peel Park, Accrington, Lancashire: Towards an Archaeology of Football." *World Archaeology* 44, no. 2 (2012): 263–79.

Poenaru, Florin. "Power at Play: Soccer Stadiums and Popular Culture in 1980s Romania." In *Socialist Escapes: Breaking away from Ideology and Everyday Routine in Eastern Europe, 1945–1989*, edited by Cathleen M. Giustino, Catherine J. Plum, and Alexander Vari, 232–51. New York and Oxford: Berghahn, 2013.

Pyta, Wolfram, and Nils Havemann, eds. *European Football in Collective Memory*. Basingstoke: Palgrave Macmillan, 2015.

Scraton, Phil. *Hillsborough: The Truth*. 6th ed. Edinburgh: Mainstream, 2016.

Van Der Meer, Hans. *European Fields: The Landscape of Lower League Football*. Göttingen: SteidlMACK, 2006.

Wood, Jason, and Neville Gabie. "The Football Ground and Visual Culture: Recapturing Place, Memory and Meaning at Ayresome Park." *The International History of the Journal of Sport* 28, nos. 8–9 (2011): 1186–1202.

Young, Christopher. "Kaiser Franz and the Communist Bowl: Cultural Memory and Munich's Olympic Stadium." *American Behavioral Scientist* 46 (2003): 1476–90.

Chapter 8

Armstrong, Gary, and Jon P. Mitchell. *Global and Local Football: Politics and Europeanization on the Fringes of the EU.* Abingdon: Routledge, 2008.

Cere, Rinella. "'Witches of Our Age': Women Ultras, Italian Football and the Media." *Sport in Society* 56, no. 3 (2002): 166–88.

Collins, Sandra. "The Imperial Sportive: Sporting Lives in the Service of Modern Japan." *The International Journal of the History of Sport* 29, no. 12 (2012): 1729–43.

Dunn, Carrie. *Female Football Fans: Community, Identity and Sexism.* London: Palgrave, 2014.

Dunning, Eric. *Sport Matters: Sociological Studies of Sport, Violence and Civilization.* London: Routledge, 1999.

Dunning, Eric, Patrick Murphy, Ivan Waddington, and Antonios A. Astrinakis, eds. *Fighting Fans: Football Hooliganism as a World Phenomenon.* Dublin: University College Dublin Press, 2002.

Dunning, Eric, Patrick Murphy, and John Williams. *Football on Trial: Spectator Violence and Development in the Football World.* London: Routledge, 1990.

Edelman, Robert. "Playing Catch-Up: Soviet Media and Soccer Hooliganism, 1965–1975." In *The Socialist Sixties: Crossing Borders in the Second World*, edited by Anne E. Gorsuch and Diane P. Koenker, 268–86. Bloomington, IN: Indiana University Press, 2013.

———. *Serious Fun: A History of Spectator Sports in the USSR.* Oxford: Oxford University Press, 1993.

Giulianotti, Richard. "Supporters, Followers, Fans, and Flâneurs: A Taxonomy of Spectator Identities in Football." *Journal of Sport & Social Issues* 26, no. 1 (2002): 25–46.

Guttmann, Allen. *Sports Spectators.* New York: Columbia University Press, 1986.

Hognestad, Hans. "Transnational Passions: A Statistical Study of Norwegian Football Supporters." *Soccer & Society* 7, no. 4 (2006): 439–62.

Spaaij, Ramón. "Football Hooliganism as a Transnational Phenomenon—Past and Present Analysis: A Critique—More Specificity and Less Generality." *The International Journal of the History of Sport* 24, no. 4 (2007): 411–31.

Stodolska, Monika, and Scott Tainsky. "Soccer Spectatorship and Identity Discourses among Latino Immigrants." *Leisure Sciences* 37, no. 2 (2015): 142–59.

Tanaka, Toko. "The Positioning and Practices of the 'Feminized Fan' in Japanese Soccer Culture through the Experience of the FIFA World Cup Korea / Japan 2002." *Inter-Asia Cultural Studies* 5, no. 1 (2004): 52–62.

Taylor, Rogan. *Football and Its Fans: Supporters and Their Relations with the Game, 1885–1985.* Leicester: Leicester University Press, 1992.

Tempany, Adrian. *And The Sun Shines Now: How Hillsborough and the Premier League Changed Britain.* London: Faber & Faber, 2016.

Tynan, Mark. "'Inciting the Roughs of the Crowd': Soccer Hooliganism in the South of Ireland during the Inter-war Period, 1919–1939." *Soccer & Society* 18, nos. 5–6 (2017): 648–62.

Chapter 9

Benoit, Macon. "The Politicization of Football: The European Game and the Approach to the Second World War." *Soccer & Society* 9, no. 4 (2008): 532–50.

Claret, Jaume, and Jaume Subirana. "1970, 1925, 2009: Whistling in the Stadium as a Form of Protest." *Journal of Iberian and Latin American Studies* 21, no. 1 (2015): 75–88.

Couto, Euclides de Freitas. "Football, Control and Resistance in the Brazilian Military Dictatorship in the 1970s." *The International Journal of the History of Sport* 31, no. 10 (2014): 1267–77.

Daniel, Petra, and Christos Kassimeris. "The Politics and Culture of FC St. Pauli: From Leftism, through Anti-establishment, to Commercialization." *Soccer & Society* 14, no. 2 (2013): 167–82.

Dietschy, Paul. "Football Imagery and Colonial Legacy: Zaire's Disastrous Campaign during the 1974 World Cup." *Soccer & Society* 13, no. 2 (2012): 222–38.

Kapuściński, Ryszard. *The Soccer War.* Translated by William Brand. New York: Vintage, 1992.

Maddox, Steve. "Gulag Football: Competitive and Recreational Sport in Stalin's System of Forced Labour." *Kritika* 19, no. 3 (2018): 509–36.

Shaw, Duncan. "The Political Instrumentalisation of Professional Football in Francoist Spain, 1939–1975." PhD diss., University of London, 1988.

Shirt, Matthew. "Playing Soccer in Brazil: Socrates, Corinthians, and Democracy." *The Wilson Quarterly* 13, no. 2 (1989): 119–23.

Walker, Harry. "State of Play: The Political Ontology of Sport in Amazonian Peru." *American Ethnologist* 40, no. 2 (2013): 382–98.

Index